TRIBUTES

NEW
YORK
CITY
BALLET

TRIBUTES

CELEBRATING FIFTY YEARS OF NEW YORK CITY BALLET

Preface by Peter Martins

Foreword by Mikhail Baryshnikov

Conceived and edited by Christopher Ramsey

William Morrow and Company, Inc.
New York

It is the policy of William Morrow and Company, Inc., and its imprints and affiliates, recognizing the importance of preserving what has been written, to print the books we publish on acid-free paper, and we exert our best efforts to that end.

Library of Congress Cataloging-in-Publication Data

Tributes : celebrating fifty years of New York City Ballet / foreword
    by Mikhail Baryshnikov ; preface by Peter Martins ; conceived
    and edited by Christopher Ramsey.
        p.   cm.
    ISBN 0-688-15751-3
        1. New York City Ballet—Anniversaries, etc.   I. Ramsey,
    Christopher. II. Title: Celebrating fifty years of New York City Ballet.
    GV1786.N4T75   1998
    792.8'09747'1—dc21   98-13671
                                                CIP

Printed in Singapore

First Edition

1   2   3   4   5   6   7   8   9   10

BOOK DESIGN BY SUSAN EVANS AND BRIAN SISCO, SISCO & EVANS, LTD.

www.williammorrow.com

Frontispiece: Edward Gorey, *Serenade*, pen and ink on paper, 6 × 3 inches, c. 1970

EDWARD GOREY
From 1957 to 1982, Gorey maintained a "perfect attendance record" at NYCB.

For the dancers of New York City Ballet

Editor's Note

This book describes New York City Ballet primarily through the experiences of important writers and artists of this century who found themselves—by design or happenstance—connected to the Company.

The book's organizing principle has been impressionistic rather than comprehensive. Detailed portraits of George Balanchine, Jerome Robbins, and Peter Martins are included, since these men shared responsibility for the Company's artistic leadership during its first fifty years. Lincoln Kirstein has also been singled out for his various roles as the Company's cofounder, visionary, and champion.

Beyond these four cornerstones, the book has drawn from the firsthand experiences of those apart from New York City Ballet in order to establish a broader portrait. Aside from Balanchine, Kirstein, the preface by Martins, and the foreword by Mikhail Baryshnikov, no Company members contributed to this book. Nor are any dance critics represented, with the exception of the late Edwin Denby, whose excerpted personal letter about the Company's formative years is included for its historical significance.

Finally, in a nod toward the objective and the comprehensive, a reference section has been added. Best efforts have been made in this section, despite spotty records from the Company's early years, to represent fifty complete years of New York City Ballet repertory, dancers, music, videography, and a strict chronology.

—C.R.

Preface

by Peter Martins

This is what ballet is about, I realized, when I danced for the first time with New York City Ballet. I had performed with many other companies, but they had not interested me. In other companies, dancers did steps; here, they did much more. Here, the steps, beautiful in themselves, led into a world of infinite images, combinations, and emotions. It was a compelling idea of dance, a metaphor for all of life. It was rigorous, intellectually and physically; it was ultimately a process that had at its heart a question: What next?

When I first joined this company, what I loved doing most was watching the ballets. If I danced in the first ballet, I would stay backstage to watch the rest of the ballets from the wings. If I danced last, I came to the theater early to watch the beginning of the program. I watched from every angle; I watched every class.

I am still watching. I can rehearse a ballet by George Balanchine that I have seen two hundred times, and suddenly my focus shifts from dancer to ballet; I see something new. So that's how he did it, I marvel. Sometimes the steps themselves are very simple. In *Mozartiana*, for several measures, the ballerina just walks. In *Serenade* the dancers move their feet into first position. Ordinary steps, but in their combinations, in their relation to the music, they always connect to our emotions, they always surprise. That is what I look for, what I aim for in my own choreography. That is what New York City Ballet's audience looks for: this mystery.

This book celebrates fifty years of watching New York City Ballet. Dance is ephemeral, but it leaves permanent memories. We have collected some of these memories, of dances and dancers, of music, of sets and costumes, of debuts and farewells. Each page reflects a moment in the company's history: an observer's recollections, a poet's response to a ballerina, a designer's drawing for a set, a photographer's flash of stopped time. Together they reveal how profoundly City Ballet has resonated and continues to resonate in the culture of New York and America and the world.

At its core New York City Ballet has always been a choreographer's company, and it continues to be. When people think of New York City Ballet, they think of Balanchine, of course, and they think of Jerome Robbins, but there were always other choreographers as well. That is the source of our strength, our continuity, and our constant renewal. This is a place where choreographers come to make new ballets. The dancers are equipped not only with superb technique, they are also tuned in to a choreographer's mind; they have the tools, mental and physical, to offer a choreographer.

Our dancers, in turn, require new choreography. It stretches them, it keeps them engaged; it keeps them fresh. It enables them to discover things about themselves. The same goes for the audience. They want new ballets, they want to be a part of the evolution of dancing. It is a faith that we, dancers and audience, share: a faith in the future of dance.

At the same time, New York City Ballet is the place where the tradition of classical ballet remains strong, perhaps stronger than anywhere else in the world. Balanchine believed in this idiom, in the classical vocabulary, and his belief still informs us. When choreographers come to work here, I insist—or try to—that they use this vocabulary. It is what our dancers know. We have women for whom it is second nature to dance on pointe; we have men who can jump and turn.

This language is very difficult to speak, but it is very beautiful. I am always looking for people who understand this. I keep looking; I keep opening the door. It would be the antithesis of Balanchine's belief to close the door on the new, to exclude the rest of the world only to polish Balanchine. Dance exists in the present. With each performance, with each performer, a ballet changes. Balanchine first made *Apollo* in 1925; over half a century he refined it, eliminating passages, paring sets, streamlining it into its final, distilled form.

Dancers also generate change; they push ballet's evolution. In the fifteen years since George Balanchine died, the level of skill has risen dramatically. Ballets exist only in the moments of their performance, but, paradoxically, ballet is one of the most enduring arts. That is because it is predicated on teaching. A dancer takes class every day, learning, simultaneously, to dance and to teach. Generations are short, traditions are cherished. Dancers of my generation are teaching today's company members. I was among Balanchine's best dancers, but I would be hard-pressed to keep up with the Company's dancers today. Balanchine's ballets are danced by dancers who can do a higher arabesque, who can turn faster and jump higher than the original dancers could. His ballets can't avoid looking different, even though the dancers are performing the same steps.

It follows, too, that choreographers have different instruments to work with now. As dancers explore new possibilities for movement, they inspire new choreographic ideas. The basic vocabulary remains intact, but it has grown. Balanchine said, "There is nothing new; there are only new combinations." So every year, on his birthday, January 22, I have a program I call "New Combinations." It is a remembrance, a birthday present, a gift of new ballets.

I was very lucky when I came to New York City Ballet. Here was the greatest choreographer of his time, maybe the greatest choreographer ever, and he had the interest and the inclination to give me music. "Here, dear, make a ballet with this for next week." So I did, and a week later I made another ballet, and then another. Some lasted, some were thrown out. The important thing was that I made ballets. That is what this company ultimately is for: to provide the inspiration and the opportunity to make dances.

New York City Ballet has already grown generations of dancers. While some of our principals danced for Balanchine, most company members never knew him. But they know his beliefs, they know his teaching, they know his ballets. They understand that ballet is ongoing and vital. There are people born in 1984, after Balanchine's death, who will soon be fifteen or sixteen years old and will come to the School of American Ballet to learn how to dance his ballets. What could be a greater tribute?

Serenade was the first ballet Balanchine made for his new American company more than fifty years ago. We still present it, and fifty years from now we will be performing it still. When it begins, the dancers stand with their feet parallel to each other, like ordinary, earth-bound people. Then they turn their feet out into first position. Suddenly they can do anything. They can soar. I can see my daughter, who is only three, looking at *Serenade* and thinking, "I want to dance that."

That moment of transformation— from a man or a woman into a dancer, from movement into metaphor— defines this company. That moment is what every lover of ballet watches for, what every dancer feels capable of: the first step, the first stretch, the moment that leads into new combinations, into infinite possibilities, into the future.

Foreword

by Mikhail Baryshnikov

Balanchine always talked about his ballets as if they were something only for the moment, for *now*—his familiar word. He never built a shrine to his work, or even to the profession of choreography. I remember when I was a dancer at New York City Ballet, he asked me several times if I wanted to choreograph. No, I told him, I was there to work on his ballets, not to make ballets of my own. "Dear," he said, "it's not so hard. Simpler than you think. Nothing much, really. Just go and do, and don't think so much about it." That's easy for you to say, I thought. But no, he said, "Just, if you like some piece of music, go and do. Just make something interesting."

That was his criterion: interesting. He really, seriously, thought of dance as entertainment. In his mind he was the ballet-master-in-chief-of-entertainment. More than anything, he hated whatever was boring . . . in music, in dance, and in films, too. He looked for interesting tastes in food, interesting smell in perfume, interesting hairdo on a young woman, interesting way to twist the human body. He was a man who was interested, period. That's the way New York City Ballet was constituted, as he was. His ballets and his dancers

were supposed to be interesting, and this was all he cared about. He claimed he had no thought for the future of his ballets. He was fond of the phrase *"Après moi, le déluge."*

I wonder about this. It seems to me, actually, that he built New York City Ballet in very deliberate relation both to the future and to the past—that he *knew* he was creating what we now call neoclassical ballet, the modernist extension of Marius Petipa's work in Russia, and that he meant to give this to the people who came after him. I remember asking him which choreographers, besides Petipa, he had admired when he was young, and the only confession I was able to wring out of him was that he was impressed by Bronislava Nijinska's early ballets. This was fitting. He and Nijinska, together with her brother, Vaslav Nijinsky, by whom she was so much influenced, formed a kind of troika, the first three neoclassical choreographers. All three, when they came to the West, could have done very well as traditional classical choreographers. They could have staged Petipa's ballets. They were perfect ballet masters, all of them. They could have survived easily— more easily than they did—setting *Giselle* and *Raymonda* and *The Sleeping*

Beauty in England, Germany, France, or Italy. But they chose a much harder, more daring path: a quest for new forms, new musical collaborations, new ways of moving, based on the old way, Petipa. For different reasons Nijinsky and Nijinska fell away, and because they did, Balanchine has lost his context. He seems unique. But he was part of something larger, the birth of neo-classical ballet.

Balanchine's school, the system of dance he inculcated, was also a continuation of Petipa's practice. As many people have said, the Russian Imperial Ballet was a marriage of the French, Italian, and Scandinavian schools. The Scandinavian precision was provided by the old Swedish teacher Christian Johansson, with his cold, academic eye. The French lyricism came from Petipa and his predecessors at the Imperial Ballet, Didelot, Perrot, and Saint-Léon. Then came the Italian contribution— strength, attack—through the influx of Italian virtuoso ballerinas and above all through Enrico Cecchetti, who arrived at the Imperial Ballet School in 1892. Petipa clearly knew that his dancers needed more sparkle and fire, so he brought in Cecchetti. He *built* his school,

PAUL KOLNIK

George Balanchine and Mikhail Baryshnikov rehearsing

Prodigal Son, photograph, 1979

COSTAS

George Balanchine and
Mikhail Baryshnikov rehearsing
Orpheus, photograph, 1979

combining the elements he wanted.
Then, after him, a series of great teachers,
from Pavel Gerdt to Alexander Pushkin,
passed down the tradition he created.

Balanchine did the same as Petipa. When
he founded the School of American
Ballet in New York, he brought in his
Russians, Pierre Vladimiroff, Felia
Doubrovska, and Anatole Oboukhoff.
Later he added others, such as Alexandra
Danilova, Antonina Tumkovsky, and
Helene Dudin. So the Russian school was
the backbone. But he also engaged
Muriel Stuart, with her modern dance
training, and in the 1960s he brought in

Stanley Williams of the Royal Danish
Ballet. Balanchine had worked at the
Danish company in the early 1930s,
before he came to America, and he must
have admired it very much. With its styl-
istic range from classical dance to
character dance to mime, and the
common practice of having young ballet
students participate in professional
performances, it would have reminded
him of the Imperial Ballet. But especially, being a traditionalist, he would
have admired the discipline, the *method*
of Danish ballet, and he gave this to his
own dancers in the person of Stanley
Williams. So, like Petipa, he combined

elements in order to build his school.
And, like any well thought-out school, it
became integrated and flexible, changing
so as to accommodate the extraordinary
gallop of his imagination. Balanchine
may have constructed this style for
"now," but clearly he had the future in
mind. In any case, it was strong enough
to bear fruit in the future. As in Russia
after Petipa, the great dancers produced
by Balanchine's unique methods have
carried on as teachers after him.

There is also the matter of the help that Balanchine gave to other companies. Time and again, for little or no compensation, he allowed other troupes to present his ballets, asking only that the person staging the piece be paid for his or her time. Of course, his liberality on this score was related to his idea of his ballets, his belief that the piece was all there in the choreography, so that if the dancer would just listen to the music and do the steps, the ballet would be there. Still, he was exceedingly generous, and this was probably part of his building for the future. In many small companies, those Balanchine ballets became mainstays of the repertory— the reason many people in Pittsburgh and Philadelphia and Cincinnati went to the ballet.

It was not just other companies that he helped. He took an interest in other artists, inviting Martha Graham and Antony Tudor and Frederick Ashton to take part in his enterprise. Balanchine was so productive that he did not need collaborators, yet he knew enough to make Jerome Robbins a ballet master of the company, with the result that this other extraordinary career unfolded alongside his own. He nourished dance beyond himself, as he nourished music. He sent out waves of vitality into American art.

Looking over the history and prehistory of New York City Ballet, one can see it as a series of glittering moments. There is Balanchine's creation of *La Chatte* and *Apollo* and *Prodigal Son* for Diaghilev. Then, in 1930, we have Lincoln Kirstein in his very first essay on dance, writing prophetically that with these works Balanchine is leading ballet to "a revivified, purer, clearer classicism." Three years later, Kirstein finally meets Balanchine—and makes him the offer that could not be refused: basically, "You make the ballets, I'll do the rest." Then we have Balanchine's arrival in America and the opening of the School of American Ballet. Then Ballet Caravan, with its lineup of American talent: Lew Christensen, Eugene Loring, Elliott Carter, Aaron Copland. Then the South American tour of 1941, which gave us *Concerto Barocco* and *Ballet Imperial*, and Ballet Society, with *The Four Temperaments*. Soon after, the founding of New York City Ballet, with Maria Tallchief, as the Firebird, flashing in red feathers across the stage—an annunciation. And then, all that came after, for the next fifty years.

But every one of those moments was prepared for, years before, and each was a preparation for the next. Though he asked for what he wanted in the moment, Balanchine knew how to wait. I heard a story once that Melissa Hayden told. One day when she was a new dancer at New York City Ballet, Balanchine was trying to teach her a certain kind of turn. He wanted it done in a special way. She attempted it again and again and couldn't quite get it. "Just keep trying, dear," he said to her. "You will do." "How long do I have?" she asked. "Oh, ten years," he said. He was a patient man.

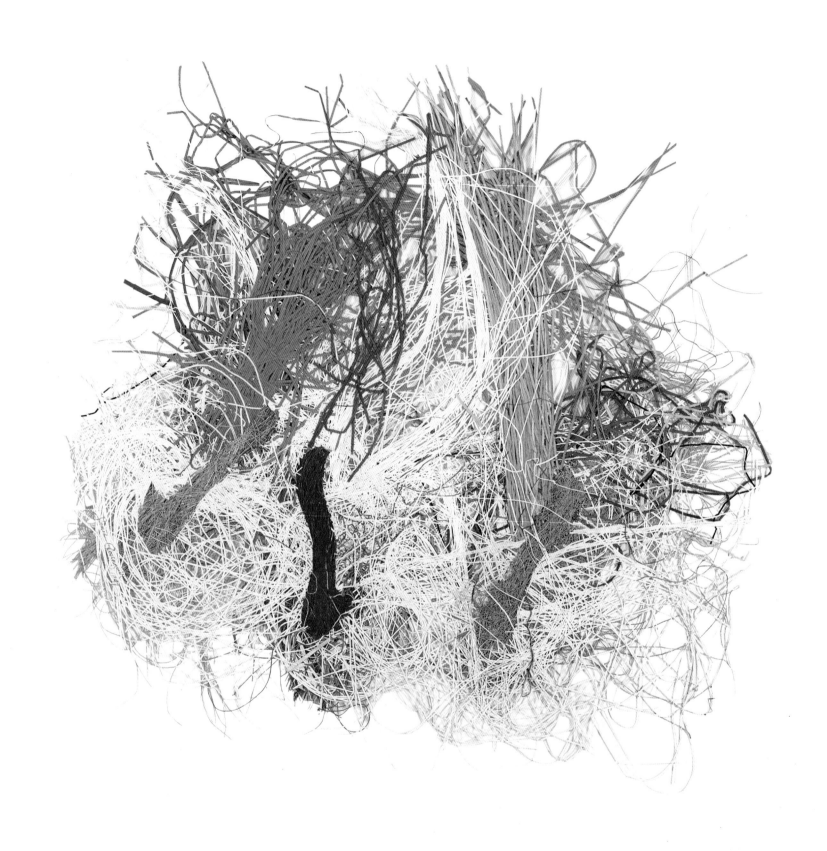

Lincoln Kirstein

by Susan Sontag

Born in 1907, the "107th year of the nineteenth century," as he once dubbed it, Lincoln Kirstein devoted his life to promoting and exemplifying standards that were both confidently old-fashioned and recklessly visionary. His widest claim to fame is that, through his initiative and unflagging attentions, both a great art and the cultural life of a great city were transformed. Lincoln Kirstein made classical ballet an American art, by giving America its first ballet school and giving an American home to one of the supreme artists of the twentieth century. And that artist, George Balanchine, made New York the dance capital of the world: the best dances being made anywhere, performed by consummately trained great dancers, created the most knowledgeable audience anywhere, one better prepared than audiences in any other metropolis to welcome and evaluate dance in all its varieties, "modern" as well as ballet.

His actual titles were general director of New York City Ballet and president of the School of American Ballet. But Kirstein's association with dance was only one aspect of his genius. Like Diaghilev, who is often (if not too accurately) invoked when assessing Kirstein's role and importance, he started off as someone with interesting, fiercely partisan tastes in all the arts and literature, a connoisseur and proselytizer of indefatigable appetite, charm, social energies—who narrowed his focus to dance. Great tastemakers need a capacious institution to bend to their will, a vehicle. Diaghilev started, precociously, by founding a magazine (*The World of Art*), well before the Ballets Russes was thought of; so did Kirstein in the late 1920s, while still an undergraduate at Harvard, found a magazine, a splendid magazine, *Hound & Horn*, to write for and to discover other talents, new and forgotten. He might have had a career not unlike other exceptionally prescient aesthetes of his generation, such as A. Everett "Chick" Austin and Julien

Levy, who used museums and an art gallery to celebrate and sponsor their disparate enthusiasms: a museum or a gallery is an anthology institution, as is a magazine or a publishing house. But Kirstein had the means, the daring, and the tenacity to put all his avidity, all his piety, into an institution exhibiting one genius. One genius only. And unlike a publishing house or a gallery or a museum or a magazine, institutions that are invaluable in the soliciting and disseminating of work but are not indispensable to its creation, a dance company is a living organism that inspires and makes possible the work that it then exhibits to the public. It was Kirstein's vision, his stamina, his fidelity, his integrity, that brought into being and guaranteed the survival of the greatest dance company of our time, without which most of the dances made by the genius he imported, who turned out to be the greatest choreographer of all time, would not have been made.

These roles, of tastemaker and supreme enabler of another's genius, are service roles . . . and Kirstein was devoted to the idea of service. The magnificent *Movement and Metaphor* and many other books (and articles) about the history and ideology of dance made him an important *author*. What made him something larger, an important, thrilling *writer*, was the quality of his prose. (I exclude the early novel and volume of poems—interesting mainly because they are by L. K. The novel, *Flesh Is Heir*, relates how he happened to be present in Venice at Diaghilev's funeral in 1929; *Rhymes of a PFC*, about his military service during World War II, tells how he loved being in the army.) What's more, when his work with the great institution he founded and kept alive for decades was virtually over (*"Après moi, le Board,"* as he quotes Balanchine as saying), his work with English sentences was not. There is more than fifty years of writing, going back to *Hound & Horn*, and he got better all the time, more subtle, more sonorous, more intense. I am thinking of the articles that appeared in the 1980s in *The New York Review of Books* and, in particular, of four stupendous pieces of autobiographical writing—triumphs of elliptical prose and anguished, ecstatic sensibility—published in the literary quarterly *Raritan*. In 1991 a generous sampling of Kirstein's writing on all subjects (including photography, painting, film, and literature as well as dance) was published under the title *By With To & From/A Lincoln Kirstein Reader*, and in 1994 *Mosaic, a Memoir* appeared, which incorporated some but not all of the material in *Raritan*. And there is much, much more, still to be collected or brought back into print.

A votary of systems of ideal order, Kirstein more than once expressed his love of ballet as a commitment to certain spiritual values—to an exalted abnegation of self. But as the attraction to the impersonal is sometimes the good taste of a truly strong personality, so the militant attraction to ideally regimented communities is, usually, the hallmark of a truly eccentric temperament. The collective enterprise to which Kirstein devoted his life does illustrate the ideals he said it did—perfect discipline, service, devotion. His own life, like any individual life when examined closely, yields a double meaning. Kirstein's life and accomplishments supply model lessons about the necessity of eccentricity—about being eccentric (including being "difficult" personally) as a spiritual value and a precondition of real seriousness.

We were fortunate to have had this noble and complicated man among us.

HENRI CARTIER-BRESSON

Lincoln Kirstein, photograph, 1960

On Learning

It must appear that I had little contact with "life," or rather that *Hound & Horn* at its start was a rich boy's dilettante toy more than a genuine literary assemblage or an aspirant to academic experiment. My father felt I should not enter college without some knowledge of "life" as he had lived it in his youth. He was a poor boy who lived by his wits; his father had been a lens grinder from Jena who had emigrated to Rochester, New York, after the troubles of 1848. Father and son had a large sense of craft; lens grinding is something of a jeweler's trade. I wanted to be a painter, preferably a portrait painter (like Sargent or Holbein), but I found myself in a stained-glass factory that turned out windows for the National Cathedral in Washington and the Cathedral of St. John the Divine in New York. I designed some roundels with figures of jazz-band players. They were conceived after the renderings of Viollet-le-Duc, but I had been given *Mont St. Michel and Chartres* by my sister, who as a graduate student at Radcliffe had finished a dissertation on Henry Adams; I felt comfortable combining the thirteenth and twentieth centuries. More important, I became involved with the craftsmen and manual laborers responsible for making stained-glass windows. Situations arose that led to the unpleasant eventuality of a strike. Although I was an unpaid apprentice, nevertheless I could not help taking sides, identifying with a man who had befriended me and who was the leader of the labor action. I had assumed that beauty was imagined, invented, or created in "beautiful" surroundings or under "beautiful" conditions. We know the Hans Christian Andersen story of the flower pot and the flower, the furnace that fires the clay, as well as the dunghill that breeds the blossom. I had some sleepless nights trying to decide how, or what, to risk in the dispute over wages and conditions. I found, of course, I had nothing to gain or lose and it made absolutely no difference how I acted about what I felt. Anything I suffered or agonized over was sheer luxury. And yet the atmosphere in the shop was ugly, my presence embarrassing (to me), the issues obscure. However, I did get inklings of human extremity, degrees of despair. These, then, I found, as well as words well arranged, also contributed to "literature." So, in a way, my education started before I was a freshman, and a certain confidence in being able to talk with and feel for more than one class of person was useful.

— Lincoln Kirstein

On Dance

The essence of ballet is order. What one sees in Balanchine's ballets are structures of naked order, executed by celebrants who have no other aim than to show an aspect of order in their own persons, testifying to an impersonal purity and a personal interest.

There has undoubtedly occurred what must be called an unfocused but active revival of religious interest in the West, seeking unfamiliar access to an absolute. It is not too much to consider a well-performed ballet a rite, executed and followed with intense devotion, that shares in some sort of moral figuration. The response of the audience to good dancing is a release of body and breath, a thanksgiving that is selfless, generous, complete, and leaves the spectator corroborated in the hope that, despite the world and its horrors, here somehow is a paradigm of perfection.

The consideration of last things, millennial factors, the approach of another century, wars and the rumor of war, surrounds us. We have a sense that the times we lie in are extremely frail, that frailty is the single cohering net that connects. Nothing is more frail or transient than a ballet. Every action is evanescent, and after its enactment it is gone for good, or until a next time,

MARTHA SWOPE
George Balanchine in rehearsal
at the Saratoga Performing Arts
Center for the premiere of
Coppélia on July 17, 1974. Saratoga
PAC has been summer residence to
NYCB for thirty years.

when the same conditions obtain. Human bodies are frail. The design that dancers thread is also frail, and to a degree entirely imaginary. It can be learned, but never completely documented.

The whole operation of a ballet company is a microcosm of a civil condition. The frailty of its operation is that of any artistic or cultural institution in a civilization that prefers to spend its bounty on armament and consumer goods. However, a ballet company, existing in the interstices of the community, almost vaunts its hardy frailty. In an infinitesimal way, each good performance clears a small area of menace and for the moment reminds us of the possible, which, if it is not perfection, approaches it.

In this process of asserting the importance of the classic dance, Balanchine acts as a public servant of order. He is a maker and teacher. The twentieth century has specialized in the metrics of time and space. Nobody before has ever danced as fast as Balanchine's dancers; no one has ever had such markedly separate structures of steps to dance. No dancers before have been obliged to analyze with their feet the kinds of musical composition that Balanchine has set for them. Only a dancer dancing can say for him what he says to them.

1983

—Lincoln Kirstein

George Balanchine

by Bernard Taper

In the programs, he was listed along with Jerome Robbins and John Taras simply as ballet master. The listing was alphabetical, so if you were an utter innocent you could believe, scanning the program, that someone named George Balanchine came first in that particular list because his name happened to begin with a "*B*," and that being a "ballet master," whatever that might mean, was all that he did. Yes, and Joseph Stalin was only the Communist Party's secretary. Balanchine once said to me when we talked about his title, "What's wrong with 'ballet master'? God doesn't have to call himself God, does he?"

L'état, c'est moi. New York City Ballet, from the time of its founding in 1948, was his stage, his company, his empire, his world, his life. Like Lao-tzu, he believed in the absolute necessity of what is of no use. To that proposition Balanchine dedicated his peculiar genius. In the world of fantasy that is ballet, he was the supreme realist, the most practical of fantasists: "My muse must come to me on union time." He met his deadlines, worked with astonishing speed, took his often frugal budgets seriously, could not be derailed by unexpected obstacles. An artist of the highest standards, he was also a master of the art of getting the job done.

To meet his company's needs he choreographed for it in the thirty-five years of his regime 114 ballets in nearly every conceivable mode, mood, and genre. It was my good fortune to be present in the company's studios during the making of 29 of these ballets. Watching Balanchine work was always a revelation—a continuing demonstration of the paradisiacal promise that chaos could be mastered, a world made orderly, and that order and beauty could be one. Martha Graham has expressed very well what it was like to watch Balanchine choreograph, after observing him working on *Episodes* one evening in 1959. "It's like watching light pass through a prism," she said. "The music passes through him, and in the same natural yet marvelous way that a prism refracts light, he refracts music into dance."

His facility was like that of Mozart, or Matisse. Once when we were talking about the way he worked, Balanchine said, "With me, it has to come easy or it doesn't come at all. I could never make a ballet by wrinkling my brow and concentrating." The term "easy," of course, was relative, for a choreographer who made ballets the way Balanchine did—physically showing each dancer every step—had to be athlete as well as artist.

As we know, masterworks galore resulted from Balanchine's efforts, but he always treated transcendence as happy accident. "If you set out deliberately to make a masterpiece," he once said, "how will you ever get it finished?" And anyway, he would also claim, he wasn't in the business of making masterpieces. All his life, he would say, he had been a man of the theater, and the business of such a person was providing entertainment. "Yes," he would repeat, relishing each Russian-flavored syllable, "en-ter-tain-ment."

Dance is the most ephemeral of the arts. One of the amazing achievements of Balanchine's extraordinary life is that he, with the help of his prophet Lincoln Kirstein and a handful of devoted adherents, found a way to institutionalize the manufacture of these miraculous ephemera, these somehow meaningful soap bubbles. And that meant establishing not just a company but also a school to supply the world-class dancers it would be his delight to challenge, so that they, in turn, could challenge him. It also meant training an audience that would learn how to look at what was being put before its eyes and accept the experiments that failed as well as the ones that worked. Thus Balanchine managed to achieve what Diaghilev never could—security and continuity.

John Martin, the former dance critic of the *New York Times*, once wrote, "Nowhere else in the world is there a ballet company that is similarly the creation of a single mind." Like a chief executive officer, Balanchine had the ultimate power to say yes or no on any question. Indeed, as I think about all the infrastructure Balanchine had to put in place and maintain just so he could make his dances, I find myself wondering whether there has ever been anyone in the history of any of the arts who had to take on quite so much. Names come to mind—Molière as author, actor, director of his company; Brecht and his Berliner Ensemble; Wagner at Bayreuth; Ingmar Bergman as scriptwriter, director, and assembler of his repertory film company—but none of these people operated under the imperatives that Balanchine did or with the scope of his powers and concerns.

Some of this has to do with ballet's being fundamentally an illiterate art—that is, an art without a generally accepted notation system. "I'm not one of those people who can create in the abstract, in some nice quiet room at home," Balanchine

TANAQUIL LE CLERCQ
George Balanchine,
photograph, 1952

WALKER EVANS

George Balanchine, photograph, c. 1945

once said to me. "If I didn't have a studio to go to, with dancers waiting for me to give them something to do, I would forget I was a choreographer." In order to make his ballets, he *had* to make his company, and in order to make his company he *had* to make his school. It's as if in order for Verdi to be able to write *La Traviata* he would have had to establish and prudently manage La Scala as well as to offer daily vocal lessons for the company's singers.

From the start Balanchine ran New York City Ballet as if it were a family, and he continued to do so even after it grew to more than ninety dancers. When he returned from a trip to Europe, like a good father he brought back presents,

often perfume for the ballerinas— L'Origan for Karin von Aroldingen, Via Lanvin for Patricia Neary, Caline for Colleen Neary, Narcisse Noir for Carol Sumner. They were convinced that he knew exactly which perfume was right for each of them. And he would say that for him this was a practical kind of gift; he was able to tell as soon as he entered the State Theater's elevator which of his ballerinas had already arrived. He liked being able to keep track.

The relationship between Balanchine and his dancers was intimate, intricate, subtle, and pervasive. From morning, when they took class from him, till evening, when they saw him standing in the wings, watching, he was a constant presence. And when he wasn't physically

present, he was seldom absent from their awareness. When they looked at themselves in the mirror, it was through his eyes they tried to look. Dancers used to joke that after he was gone, if that day ever came, they would put a life-size placard of him in the wings to remind them that wherever he might be, he probably still had his eye on them. It didn't matter how great a success they might have with critics or audiences if they suspected they had not come up to Balanchine's standards. Only he, they believed, really perceived what they were doing in performance, and only his judgment mattered. It was said, in the school as well as in the company, that Balanchine could tell from seeing just one demi-plié everything he needed to know about a dancer's future.

In her book *Winter Season,* Toni Bentley, a corps de ballet member, wrote, "A lover once said to me, 'If I could have even half the power over you that this Balanchine has . . .'

"Most women," she continued, "have two important men in their lives—their father and their lover. We have three. Mr. Balanchine is our leader, our president, our mother, our father, our friend, our guide, our mentor, our destiny."

Balanchine could be merciless in his expectations and his judgments, and he seldom praised even the most fabulous of his dancers. Yet he valued them for what they were and, even more, for what they might be. He loved dancers as a breed, even with all his awareness of the breed's faults and inadequacies. Sometimes, frustrated by the limitations of the human organism, he would expostulate, in mock despair, "Even a cat has a better body!" But then he would take comfort in not having to choreograph for centipedes—all those legs to have to make steps for! He often said he had been put on earth to make dancers work as they should, to make them extend themselves to the limit. "A dancer is like a musical instrument," he told an interviewer. "It must be played with a full-bodied tone—and pitilessly."

Sometimes he compared dancers to horses who, he said, were lazy by nature and would never race if you didn't put a rider on them. He was that rider. But he was also perfectly well aware that his standard of work, his idea of laziness, was not that of the ordinary human being; he knew very well how hard dancers worked compared with most other mortals. He was always quick to defend dancers against slights by outsiders. To hear people utter the commonplace remark that dancers have no brains annoyed him exceedingly. "That's not true!" he would say indignantly. Sniffing his dry sniff, he would name one after another of his dancers and talk about how intelligent they were. All his life it was his dancers with whom he identified, not with the famous, rich, or fashionable. In 1934, at the very first gala given to celebrate the establishment of the American Ballet Company, his first company in America, he gave up the place set for himself among dignitaries and celebrities and went to one of the tables set for the lowly dancers. In 1952 in Barcelona, during New York City Ballet's second tour of Europe, he raised a fuss when he learned that dancers would not be allowed to sit in the box seats. "My dancers will sit where they want," he declared. "They are good enough to sit anywhere." Jean Rosenthal, the designer who lit the ballets in the early years of New York City Ballet, told me

this story. She said that in ten years of working with Balanchine this was the only time she ever saw him really angry.

When Jerome Robbins joined New York City Ballet shortly after it was established, he was appalled, he has told me, by the company's apparent lack of discipline. "I had to hush the dancers. Balanchine, though, seemed able to concentrate and work serenely in the midst of any hubbub. I asked him why he wasn't more strict. He said that when he had been in a ballet company as a young man, there had always been a harsh taskmaster over him and the others, like a jail warden. He had hated that, and he didn't want to be one himself now that he was in authority."

To a surprising extent Balanchine ruled without rules. He was a dictator but not a disciplinarian. His commands generally were put in the form of suggestions. "I think maybe it's better if you do like this—" The only discipline he valued was the self-discipline that came from the desire to achieve. Most performing arts organizations enunciate codes of company regulations, specifying required conduct and penalties for such infractions as missing rehearsal, being later than the established check-in time for performance, not wearing the proper costume, etc. Balanchine did not put much stock in such codes. "If someone doesn't come early enough to the theater and warm up properly," he said when the subject was once raised, "she won't dance well. And I'll know it. And after a while, she'll want to go somewhere else."

Unlike the directors of other major companies, he did not sign his dancers to exclusive year-long contracts. He was liberal with leaves of absence. If an opportunity arose for a lucrative engagement elsewhere, he readily granted

ERNST HAAS

George Balanchine rehearsing *Noah and the Flood*, photograph, 1962

permission, even if it sometimes meant having to recast a scheduled ballet. He knew he was not paying the principals what many of them could get at other companies or in special appearances. When they worked with him, he wanted their participation to be wholehearted, not merely the fulfillment of a legal agreement. Part of his motivation in regard to granting requested leaves, some suspected, may also have been that he never wanted to admit that he needed anybody, not even the greatest in the world—not Farrell, not Nureyev, not Makarova, not Baryshnikov, not Tallchief, not anyone.

What he was after from his dancers could not be obtained by fiat, he knew. He asked the impossible, and the impossible could not be commanded. Those who wanted to try to achieve it were those he wanted to have stay. The others, no matter how talented, were free to leave, as were those who had other ambitions—whether of money or stardom or a more time-honored repertory or a less rarefied ambience—that could not be satisfied at New York City Ballet.

"It's like the pope represents Christ. I represent Terpsichore, goddess of the dance," he once told a reporter, and he probably meant it, though one could never be certain how seriously he intended such utterances to be taken. Dancers enlisting in his company were expected to take on faith that he knew what was best for them and for the art of ballet. In short, all he asked of them was their souls—freely given. Some found this the most diabolical of demands, and intolerable to sustain. Others found it the way to their artistic salvation.

He never tried to hold on to anyone who was not totally committed. A talented ballerina told Balanchine she was thinking of leaving the company. "Go in peace!" was his reply. She went in tears to Lincoln Kirstein, hurt that Balanchine hadn't tried to persuade her to stay. How could he be so cruel and unfeeling?

Within New York City Ballet, there was only one form of punishment that mattered. That was for Balanchine to lose interest in a dancer, withdraw his attention from him or her—in effect, leave the dancer in limbo. Once he had made a judgment, he could be implacable. A dancer whom he had stopped casting wanted to know why. He told her she was simply not interesting to look at. What should she do to become more interesting, she asked. His reply was "Suffer!"

Early in his career, Peter Martins suffered the experience of being relegated to Balanchine's limbo. In Denmark, he had already attained principal status at age twenty. In New York City Ballet, which he joined at twenty-three, his first year went badly. Baffled by Balanchine's company class, he avoided it, then found himself no longer being scheduled for parts he had counted on. So miserable was he that he came very close to accepting an offer from American Ballet Theater.

But when the time came to sign the contract, he backed out, recognizing, as he later wrote, that "I couldn't risk the loss of working with Balanchine." He set about convincing Balanchine by words and deeds that he was committed to what Balanchine had to offer, which meant in his case ceasing to hold back out of fear of looking imperfect or foolish, meant letting himself go to meet Balanchine's challenges and demands, whatever they may be. In the 1972 Stravinsky Festival, Balanchine for the first time choreographed on Martins, using him in two new masterpieces, *Violin Concerto* and *Duo Concertant*.

These ballets were a breakthrough for Martins. Reviewing *Duo Concertant* in *Ballet Review,* Paul Gellens wrote of him: "Balanchine has understood that there is another part of [him] that is not Apollo, not that large, glamor-boy, space-filling dancer. He has given him steps and movements that are very small, and he has made Martins articulate in a way we have never seen before. Balanchine has made him a role that lets him be fast and delicate, and he is brilliant."

A frequent allegation has been that Balanchine's dancers were expected to suppress their personalities. Most of those who danced for Balanchine deny this. Their experience, they say, is that he encouraged and cherished true differences in personality, but discouraged stage mannerisms that were not true to their natures. His message was that a dancer expresses personality most truly not by gestures or acting or facial expressions but by the way the dancer dances. And by the time of the Stravinsky Festival, Martins had gotten that message.

Balanchine once said to me, "I always hear people talking about my importance as a choreographer. I think my real importance has been as a teacher." At the time he said that, I had difficulty accepting it or grasping what he meant. Gradually I think I came to understand what he was getting at, and to see the large sense in which he was using the word *teacher.* Of course he taught in his company classes in a way no other artistic director did. There he was tremendous—fierce, demanding, funny, obsessive, inhumanly patient, with gnomic utterances and apt, far-fetched metaphors for every occasion. That teaching was quintessential. For he had to develop his dancers to new levels of proficiency in order for them to be able to execute choreography that he was not even able to conceive until they had attained those levels. Beyond the classroom studio, he also taught them various lessons in ballets he made. His choreography was often his most potent teaching instrument. One lesson was the kind he gave Merrill Ashley in *Ballade*: to not think of herself as limited, or typed purely as a super technician. Many years previously he had done something similar for Maria Tallchief, then famed as America's most brilliant bravura dancer. To bring out her latent lyricism, he choreographed *Scotch Symphony* and his version of *Swan Lake* for her. For Mimi Paul he once did the exact opposite. He made for her a pas de deux full of jumps—the *Valse Fantaisie* section of *Glinkiana*—because she was convinced she was not a jumper. In her early years Suzanne Farrell had difficulty with bourrées. So in each act of *Don Quixote* he set her a different problem in bourrée. Many choreographers routinely choreograph to a dancer's strengths. "Show me what you can do here!" they might say. "Good, let's keep that." But I know of no other who so thoughtfully choreographed to a dancer's weaknesses.

In a real sense, the audience became part of this pedagogical process and provided the supportive environment that enabled it to flourish. The audience had to learn to be patient, to appreciate what was happening when they saw dancers from whom they expected one kind of perfection or achievement striving to achieve something quite different—and to take positive pleasure in such explorations and adventures. So Balanchine throughout all those years taught his audience as well. It became, indeed, one of the world's great audiences.

If one accepts Balanchine's description of himself as a teacher, his lifelong aversion to stars becomes more understandable. A star doesn't learn; a star shines. A star doesn't want a part, but a vehicle. Makarova's complaint that Balanchine preferred someone he could mold rather than a dancer of her consummate talents was true, but she couldn't understand why. The explanation does not lie in his having the nature of a Svengali, as some have claimed. There was something of that in him, certainly, but he was motivated at least as much by curiosity: what could this person become? Developing promising young dancers to their limits and beyond was his satisfaction and stimulation. It was this that constantly renewed him.

MARTHA SWOPE

Balanchine, Diana Adams, and Jacques d'Amboise rehearsing
Movements for Piano and Orchestra, photograph, 1963

In the foreword to my book, *Balanchine: A Biography,* I have told what it was like to work with Balanchine as a biographer—how patient and gracious he was in answering my myriad questions while never once trying to suggest what I should say or how I should evaluate or present the facts of his life. "It's *your* biography, not mine," he said. I was not expected to submit the manuscript to him for approval, and it went to press without his seeing it. In truth, I did not expect him to read the book after it

appeared, but apparently he did, for when he learned that I was intending to revise it for a subsequent edition, he had one suggestion to offer. "In your book," he said, "you've written too much about me, and not enough about my dancers." And, you know, he was right.

Jerome Robbins

by Anka Muhlstein and Louis Begley

Genius, like religious faith, is very difficult to discuss or write about, because each is a gift that inherently transcends our understanding. So is choreography, an art we cannot experience fully except during the fleeting moment of performance, when its achievement, the amalgam of movement and music, decor, costumes and light, is before our eyes. Then the logic and beauty of a masterpiece overwhelm us. And we can *recognize* genius. A little bell rang in Gertrude Stein's head to tell her Picasso was one when she met him. The rest of us distinguish genius from mere great talent according to another, less peremptory signal: the power of those who have it to revolutionize our perceptions, to fit us, as Proust would have it, with a new pair of glasses. We put them on and get used to the new prescription; they slide to the tip of our nose; *presto* the world changes. Sometimes, our acceptance of its new aspect turns out to be so complete that we wonder how we managed, until that magic moment, not to see how things really are.

Jerome Robbins has accomplished just such a miracle. In a series of masterpieces of choreography spanning five decades—from *Fancy Free* through *Afternoon of a Faun, The Concert, Dances at a Gathering,* and *In the Night, Watermill, Glass Pieces, I'm Old Fashioned,* and *Ives, Songs* to *West Side Story Suite,* all but the first composed for New York City Ballet—he has revealed a fresh and totally original understanding of the lineaments of American experience, as well as the exquisite possibilities of translating that unique subject into the idiom of classical ballet. In *The Goldberg Variations* and *Brandenburg,* he fashioned a modern lexicon for the art of classical ballet, an achievement akin to Picasso's meditations on his great masters, Velázquez and Poussin and Ingres and Delacroix.

Not even artistic genius is independent of history and context; context creates or denies opportunities. Robbins was fortunate to work in the ballet within a context, New York City Ballet, the existence of which was the fabulous creation of two other geniuses: George Balanchine and Lincoln Kirstein, that hothouse and nursery of the company.

Jerome Robbins has also revolutionized that magnificent American invention, the Broadway musical comedy. There had been dancing in musicals before Robbins. It took the form of set pieces executed by gifted hoofers. Never again, not when he conceived, directed, or choreographed a show. Starting his vast Broadway oeuvre with *On the Town* (based on his first ballet, *Fancy Free,* after the premiere of which he burst into fame), in play after play, including the fabulous *The King and I, West Side Story,* and *Fiddler on the Roof,* Robbins has integrated dancing into the theater, making it pulsate within shows like a big heart. And what dancing! An exuberant outpouring of fun, longing, and compassion that draws on scrupulous research and observation, a knowledge of movement that's in Robbins's bones and lets him meld boogie with the steps of classical ballet and Hasidic feasting, all of it propelled by an astonishing and eclectic gift for music.

To put American content in a radically new focus, to free it of "Ol' Man River" and *Oklahoma!* sentimentality, to convey his vision when he wasn't working for the stage in the idiom of the classical ballet, may have been in part Jerome Robbins's conscious or instinctive reaction to the work of his mentor, partner, and friend, George Balanchine, and its Russian emphasis. It could not have been accomplished without the qualities that mark Robbins's genius: limitless

STEVEN CARAS

Antique Epigraphs, 1984

empathy for the American scene, an irrepressible and unpredictable sense of humor, nurtured, one is tempted to say, in equal measure by Mark Twain, Damon Runyon, and Mack Sennett, the ability to see and retain everything around him, as though filmed by a battery of cameras pointing in every direction, and above all the humility and simplicity of attitude that is given only to very great men. When Jerome Robbins, apparently idle, stands at the top of the steps of the Metropolitan Museum and watches the crowd, it is a safe bet that he is in fact accumulating data for use in his work.

One may doubt that anyone who has looked closely at *Fancy Free* and *On the Town* will ever think of sailors on leave looking for girls except as an extension of Jerome Robbins's three gobs dancing their hearts out against the backdrop of stools and tables of a bar, or forget how it captured the sadness and devil-may-care gallantry of this country at war. *Afternoon of a Faun,* which he fashioned into a delicate, tentative reaching out of one dancer to another as they work in the studio, broken when absorption with their own bodies prevails over interest in the other, has locked inside it the loneliness and grace of kids from the School of American Ballet one may watch at rehearsal, in the corridors on a break from class, at intermissions.

In Robbins's world everything is possible and yet uncertain and perhaps foredoomed. Kids aren't the same everywhere; Robbins's faun and Robbins's nymph are kids trying to make it in New York.

Only Ed Koren has drawn a bead on the denizens of the Upper West Side as accurately as Jerome Robbins in *The Concert.* The mismatched couple, the intellectual lady who won't brook the least distraction, the fall guy straight out of a cafeteria on Broadway—our fellow citizens are caught like butterflies in Robbins's net. In *Dances at a Gathering* and *In the Night,* which form a Chopin continuum, Robbins does far more than examine the technical

MARTHA SWOPE

Jerome Robbins rehearsing Edward Villella in *Watermill*,

photograph, 1972

possibilities of partnering and patterns of group movement. The subject is social interchange, diffuse and often distant in the earlier ballet, more intense and personal in the second, which followed one year later, marked by loneliness, diffidence, and passion that doesn't dare to trust in itself, "whose hand is ever at his lips/Bidding adieu . . ." Set to music by a Japanese composer, grave, inspired by No plays, *Watermill* is nevertheless quintessentially American. This prodigious recollection of time past by a hierophantic figure almost immobile under an August sky, on a beach fringed with tall reeds and caught between the ocean and Mecox Bay, is defined by the tension Robbins has created. On one side, Utopian serenity and sensuality; on the other a catalog of barely contained violence; a species of violence that, in spite of the exoticism of the assailant's appearance, is bitterly American, like our serial killers. In *I'm Old Fashioned*, Robbins accomplished an impossible and glorious marriage: the best of American movie dance, Fred Astaire's sinuous and rhythmically bewitching romp with Rita Hayworth to the music of Jerome Kern, matched with the best of American ballet, New York City Ballet's take on the Astaire-Hayworth theme danced to a variation on Kern by Morton Gould. *Glass Pieces* is a paean to the American city of walkers—whose apotheosis is New York—and the perpetual movement of its nomads, rushing optimistically and purposefully to a destination that may never be reached. By contrast, *Ives, Songs* is a celebration of an America that is no more: pleasures and disappointments of small-town family life, children pretending to be soldiers and real soldier

boys marching off to the Great War that was to make the world safe for democracy, young love, recollections of innocence and guilt. Robbins's most recent addition to the genre shines among his works in the native grain. It is *West Side Story Suite*, a rethought version of the dances he had created for the musical, with the Sharks and the Jets as fresh, beautifully observed, and convincing as they were forty years ago.

Every supreme artist must master the form he works in and then struggle to bend or break it. That is what Jerome Robbins's *The Goldberg Variations* and *Brandenburg* are most spectacularly about, although of necessity the same effort goes on in each of his works. *Goldberg* decomposes every step and device of the classical ballet repertory and then so recombines their elements that the structure of dance is presented and explicated. The experience of the whole of that ballet is rather like watching very attentively Merrill Ashley dance a sustained solo movement. One realizes that she executes it, even when the textual content is most passionate, with a certain detachment, so that its structural necessity is revealed. A similar decomposition and fusion occur in *Brandenburg*, which was created more than twenty-five years after *Goldberg* but has the exuberance of a masterpiece by a young man. Robbins's contribution to classical ballet as an art form is immense. Because he infused it so thoroughly with the American vernacular of jazz, boogie, and ballroom dancing, it may be that he is even more responsible than George Balanchine for the way New York City Ballet looks today, for the ways in which it differs from the ballets of Petipa or Bournonville.

No, we had no doubt that Jerome Robbins was a genius before he became our friend Jerry. But although we were used to seeing him here and there in New York, we didn't actually meet him until 1982. On the West Side, on the stage of the New York State Theater, he was an elegant silhouette in black taking a bow; on the East Side, he was an amazingly determined and straight-backed figure on a bicycle, pedaling calmly toward the Seventy-ninth Street entrance of the park. We realized that he was our neighbor because we would run into him so often late at night, when we were coming home and he was out walking his dogs, Nick, large and dark, leading the way, followed by wiggly little Annie, whose dark-rimmed eyes made one think she might have been, in a previous incarnation, a silent movie star. We never spoke to him until one summer evening he entered our lives as a guest, brought to our house by the late duo pianists Arthur Gold and Robert Fizdale. It so happens that in our part of Long Island—at the beach, as Jerry Robbins puts it—we are also his neighbors. As a matter of principle and practice, Arthur and Bobby couldn't tolerate the anomaly of any of their friends not all knowing each of the others. They had been Jerry's friends forever; we were relatively recent acquisitions. Yet, there it was: we had never been introduced. The solution Arthur and Bobby found was to invite him to a birthday dinner one of us was giving for the other at our house in Long Island. It was their present, they declared, and it turned out to be the best one we ever received.

MARTHA SWOPE

Dances at a Gathering, opening night bow,

photograph, 1969

That evening Jerry was, at first, a silent presence. Small talk is completely foreign to him, and we were not going to chatter about ballet in the presence of the greatest living choreographer. Therefore, the conversation followed the course that was preordained when the Gold-Fizdale team was around: we started out discussing food, and then briskly moved on to books. All at once, Jerry jumped in. He was reading Proust, for the first time, and had just finished *Swann's Way.* He wondered whether Proust had a passion for the ballet. We were surprised by the question. There is a glorious, nostalgic scene in *Remembrance of Things Past* that takes place at a performance by the Ballets Russes, but we thought it was the only

important mention of ballet in Proust's work. A free-for-all argument began, with the senior Proustians at table, Arthur and Bobby and us, all concluding that no, Proust had not been particularly interested in dance. Very quickly, Jerry persisted. It can't be a coincidence, he explained, that Proust chose the unusual name Swann for a central personage and made him fall in love tragically with Odette, whose character shifts so quickly from white to black: obviously, he had *Swan Lake* in mind. From then on, Proust was present at every meal we shared. Jerry is the most personal reader we have known, in the sense that he never remains on the outside of the story a novel tells. In the case of Proust, Jerry's relation to Swann's jealousy, to the Narrator's possessiveness, and to the

havoc it wreaks, became so intense he couldn't bear to go on reading. He did return to Proust eventually, and as soon as he had finished *Remembrance of Things Past,* began rereading it. When we saw *In Memory of . . . ,* we wondered how much the story of Albertine had contributed to that ballet's exploration of lovers' drifting apart, death, and despair.

We were struck by the way Jerry reads; and we are continually struck with equal force by his searching, almost restless curiosity about things and people. It isn't just a dancer's love of motion or an ingrained impatience. Jerry takes nothing at face value; he is always questioning. It is a fact that he doesn't like to sit too long at table, especially in the noise of a gala dinner. We remember how one evening, at the State Theater, he leapt to the edge of the floor as soon as the band began to play and studied his dancers, those elegant, hair-in-chignon, toes-on-point ballerinas, transformed for that evening into boys and girls out for a night on the town, kicking up a storm, dancing their own way. He was, of course, amused. But his interest in one girl was truly intense. Jerry had known her and used her in his ballets for years, but just then he was seeing her indelibly in a new way. He came back to the table very excited: I didn't know she had that in her, he informed us, it was as if she had pushed another button. That button could open for her the door to the great Chita Rivera role in *West Side Story Suite*.

One winter, we met Jerry in Paris. He was staging three ballets at the Opéra. New dancers, new stage. A lot of work. He invited us to a rehearsal. We were to meet him at the *cantine*. He showed up looking relaxed, fit and tanned as usual, a dark navy blue cap on his head. This was no American in Paris. Our friend Jerry, who had never uttered a word of French in our presence, was speaking it with authority, and with a perfect accent. He ordered a *boudin avec pommes purées* and proceeded to explain the difference between Paris Opéra's dancers and his own New York City Ballet "jewels." The Americans, he told us, dance in relation to one another, the French always want to let in the public. And that was contrary to the spirit of *In the Night*, the ballet he was working on with them. As we waited for the elevator that would take us to the rehearsal room tucked away in the Opéra's top rotunda, Jerry's dancers

appeared as if from nowhere and surrounded him. The *étoiles* kissed him on the cheek, the younger girls and boys hovered at the edge, hoping to touch the Master's parka. There was a sense of shared joy and anticipation. It was then that Isabelle Guérin unexpectedly told us, point-blank, "I hate rehearsing, except with Jerry." We asked her why. "Because he is so serious," she replied.

We settled down on a bench and watched. In their workout clothes, traditionally motley and casual, as though the dancers were in search of an antidote for the artifice of tulle, satin, and velvet, interrupted every few minutes by Jerry's assistant, Jean-Pierre Frohlich, or Jerry himself, they went about the work of dissecting a pas de deux, putting together the mysterious bits and pieces that go into making a ballet that on the stage, when the lights go on, will seem so inevitable and limpid.

Laboriously counted and repeated, time and time again, under Jerry's implacably attentive gaze, the steps slowly blended. Patient, encouraging, tireless, he led his dancers to the result he wanted to attain. He used few words. The work was in the showing. Patiently, he translated his own gestures into the fluid movements the girls then took up. His hands and feet compelled imitation. Never allowing himself to appear frustrated, he dealt with his dancers very gently. Time passed. They went on repeating what he had taught them until, at last, they met his expectations. He lost his temper only once: at the pianist, who was going through the Chopin pieces as though he were alone in an empty room. Stop, cried Jerry, stop, you must look, you must always look at the dancers.

Jerome Robbins, 1980

Peter Martins

by Deborah Weisgall

Peter Martins was a perfect dancer, almost. He was tall and blond, with bright blue eyes, full lips—he looked like Apollo, which was the first Balanchine ballet he ever danced. He was strong and musical. He could dazzle with his jumps. Partnering, he assumed a gallant reticence. But he was not a performer. Onstage, he was not transformed. What he did was breathtaking, but he had no need of a performer's magic: the trick of shedding an ordinary self. He took little pleasure in displaying his perfection—his looks, his body, his intelligence, his mastery of technique—and in re-creating himself onstage. He was not ingratiating; he did not need applause. Dancing, he often seemed bored.

He often was bored, he admitted to me. He stood in the wings in costume: Apollo's white tights and the vaguely Greek length of white gauze draped over one shoulder and wrapped at the waist. In 1967, he substituted for Jacques d'Amboise, who had been injured, in a performance of *Apollo* at the Edinburgh Festival. At that time, Martins, born and trained in Denmark, had just been named the youngest principal dancer in the history of the Danish Royal Ballet, but he was already restless. A few months later, he came to New York to dance the Cavalier in *The Nutcracker* at the State Theater. Then, in 1970, Balanchine asked Martins to join his company.

By 1980, it was becoming evident that he was going to be Balanchine's successor. Martins had begun choreographing, and Balanchine had put some of his ballets in the repertory. From backstage, I watched a matinee during a run at the Kennedy Center in Washington, D.C. One of his own ballets, *Eight Easy Pieces*, set like *Apollo* to music by Stravinsky, was going before *Apollo* on the program. Martins, in costume, studied his ballet. He was chafing under the constraints of his apprenticeship, profoundly aware of the gifts Balanchine was giving him, but at the same time frustrated with setting ballets to music Balanchine chose, using dancers Balanchine picked.

The three young dancers came offstage panting, drained from the ballet's nonstop, complicated steps. They looked at Martins to see how they had done, and he thanked them, with some diffidence, not yet accustomed to conferring approval.

"One minute," the stage manager whispered over the sound system.

Martins turned to me. "You've never seen *Apollo*?" he asked. He shook his head and smiled. "Watch."

The blue spots went up. Backstage the Muses in their short tunics stretched and adjusted their pointe shoes. The orchestra began: Stravinsky's dissonant, electric chords. Martins picked up Apollo's lute. His arm wheeled. He was breathtaking. His detachment had vanished. He soared in huge, skewed, effortless leaps. He wound through the intricacies of partnering the three Muses at once, dominating them, becoming trapped in the maze of their arms. He took Suzanne Farrell on his back, surrendering to her or carrying her away. It was heartbreaking, watching this dance of the ambivalence of love, of possession, of the possibilities of movement.

"I do not come alive in front of an audience," Martins had told me. That afternoon, he was not showing me how he could dance. He was showing me the dance. He was showing me *Apollo*.

Soon after the performance began, Balanchine, almost transparent in the darkness, white hair like mist in moonlight, materialized like a magician in the wings opposite from where I stood. His appearance shocked. He stayed absolutely still, watching his dancer and his dance, and then he vanished.

George Balanchine with Peter Martins rehearsing

Sonate di Scarlatti, photograph, 1979

Balanchine died in 1983. Peter Martins and Jerome Robbins became co–ballet masters in chief. Martins stopped dancing that winter. He ended his career at the New York State Theater as he began, in *The Nutcracker*, the Cavalier to Suzanne Farrell's Sugar Plum Fairy. Their hands trembled as she tried to find a balance in a pas de deux they had done hundreds of times. Martins flew through the *tours en manège*, the circle of jumping turns, in his solo. Afterward, he took his bows with Farrell in front of the curtain. The audience stood and stamped and cheered; they tossed flowers. Martins had to come out again and again. Each time, he dragged Farrell with him, holding her waist, presenting her to the audience. Finally she ducked out from under his arm and shoved him forward and fled back behind the curtain, forcing him to take his applause alone.

From the beginning, Peter Martins had a difficult time as head of the Company. Although he shared his title with Jerome Robbins, Martins was involved with the day-to-day details, artistic and administrative. Balanchine had given birth to New York City Ballet, and many people, both in and out of the Company, felt that it should die along with Balanchine. City Ballet, they argued, expressed a personal esthetic that was impossible to preserve. Martins understood that everything he did, from the dancers he hired to the ballets he made, would be judged in terms of Balanchine, but he already judged himself in those terms.

For Balanchine, Martins never danced *The Prodigal Son*. Growing up without his own father (his parents divorced when he was very young), he chose substitutes and remained loyal to them:

Balanchine, Lincoln Kirstein, his teacher, Stanley Williams, who taught Martins in Denmark and whom Balanchine brought to the School of American Ballet. Yet he was taken to task, by dancers and critics, for betraying Balanchine's legacy, for bringing along the wrong dancers, for encouraging the wrong choreographers. He never responded publicly to such criticism.

Martins undertook his job with the same kind of self-effacing assurance with which he danced. "You check your ego at the door when you come in here," he said. He knew what he would have to do even before he took over the Company: "It cannot become a museum. Ballet has to evolve." Yet it seemed that everyone knew better than he what shape that evolution should take.

Martins did not intend to lead a company dedicated to the preservation of an existing repertory of works by Balanchine and Jerome Robbins; that would be deadly. He understood that dancers needed new works to thrive. Although Jerome Robbins stepped down from his position as co–ballet master in chief in 1991, he has continued to choreograph for the Company. As did Balanchine, Martins gives Robbins first choice of dancers for his new ballets.

Balanchine built a school and a ballet company from an idea; he translated an old, aristocratic language of movement into a new century and a new, democratic continent. Martins has the elements of that language in his bones and believes passionately in Balanchine's ballets and in Balanchine's idea of classical ballet as a potent and renewable art. From the beginning, he ran the Company according to Balanchine's precedents and Balanchine's methods;

he adhered to Balanchine's ways of tying the past to the future. He is not Balanchine, but he studied how Balanchine did things—how he watched his dancers to learn their strengths and pushed them to overcome their limitations. Martins understood this painful process from his own experience; he understood how bending to Balanchine's will could turn out to be the way to uncover one's bedrock identity.

As chairman of the faculty of the School of American Ballet, Martins ensures continuity of instruction. The new teachers he hires have all danced under Balanchine; they possess that fast technique, that understanding of how to link steps without seeming to pause to prepare for jumps or turns. Martins, too, teaches in the school and often teaches Company class; he directs rehearsals of Balanchine's ballets.

One January afternoon, I watched as Martins conducted a run-through of Balanchine's *Swan Lake*. Martins considered a dancer new in the role of the evil von Rothbart. Martins stopped the rehearsal. In silence, he lifted his forearm to mask his face; then his elbows shot back like the wings of a bird of prey. He took a step, hip thrust forward, aiming his body into a threatening, possessive swoop. The dancer watched, transfixed. Martins was never the sorcerer—for Balanchine he always danced the Prince—but he knows how enchantment should look.

Balanchine, the sorcerer, encoded enchantment in his ballets, and Martins has taught those ballets to a new generation. The dancers dance those same steps, but under Martins, the Company is a very different place from what it was in 1983. Less than half of the current principals danced for Balanchine; every

ALAIN VAËS

Study for Rothbart—Swan Lake,
watercolor, 27½ × 19½ inches, 1998

other member in the Company has danced only for Martins. He is less autocratic than Balanchine and gives more dancers a chance onstage. He changes casts more frequently and relies less on favorites; one ballet during a season can have two or three separate casts.

Martins does not possess his dancers as Balanchine did. He does not hold them in thrall, but he requires and receives commitment of a different kind. Many dancers explain: "We used to dance for Balanchine, now we dance for ourselves." Times have changed; under Martins,

City Ballet has become quite domestic. Dancers used to hide their affections from Balanchine; they feared his disapproval. Now they get married and have babies and bring their babies to the theater, and they keep dancing.

City Ballet dancers are more athletic now; they are stronger, and they are not always so thin. The amplitude of their leaps makes the big State Theater stage look small. They are extremely adaptable, too; Martins brings many choreographers in to work with the Company. Sometimes these choreographers, like William Forsythe, are

exploring the idiom of classical ballet for the first time; sometimes, like Christopher Wheeldon or Miriam Mahdaviani or Christopher d'Amboise, they come from the ranks of Company dancers. No single choreographer can replace Balanchine, but it is important to remember that Balanchine and Robbins were never the Company's only choreographers. Again, Martins continues what Balanchine began: he gives his dancers new ballets and lets the magic take care of itself.

Balanchine's drama was love, the action of romance: consummation or a broken heart. Martins's drama is the ever after. Even his first ballet, *Calcium Light Night*, is a pas de deux for a man and a woman who explore connection, who battle over identity. In *Calcium*, Martins also grappled with the language of Balanchine's ballet; with Balanchine's insistence that ballet is about women and the man's role is to present the ballerina. Dancing, Martins had by his very presence subverted that notion, and from the first steps of *Calcium Night Light*, when the man walks onstage with his toes curled under, experimenting with dancing on pointe, Martins pushed his dancers past gallantry. In content and in style, Martins's ballets begin where Balanchine's end.

Martins's dancers already know each other. They know each other's bodies; each knows what the other is capable of doing. His pas de deux are encounters between two people testing their power against each other. *The Waltz Project* is a series of duels in three-quarter time. The pas de deux from *Ecstatic Orange* begins with the dancers facing away from each other, echoing steps as they

stalk each other around the stage, connected despite themselves. When they touch, it is with dangerous intimacy. If the stronger man can lift the woman, she can tangle him up and slither out of his grip; he can't keep her where he wants her. Or he lowers her to the ground into an aching back bend, props her on her knees, and lets her go, but she doesn't collapse; she doesn't need his support.

Sometimes a pas de deux is pure combat, as in the last movement of *Barber Violin Concerto*, where the woman buzzes around the man, taunting him, enraging him, forcing him to engage. But his size and strength cannot restrain her. He cannot dominate her; she cannot leave him alone. A push is a gesture that recurs again and again in Martins's choreography. In *Beethoven Romance*, one of Martins's most courtly ballets, what begins as a push—a hand on a waist—turns into a lift. Or a push has a boomerang effect, and the dancers come together again, a push melted into a caress.

His ballets have been called cold by friends and critics alike, but then, so was his dancing, so was he. The chill is only on the surface; Martins disguises passion with intricacy. When Martins's dancers hurt each other, they do so out of experience; each has discovered where the other is vulnerable.

In January 1996, Martins made *Reliquary* as an homage to Balanchine. The curtain rises on a row of women arranged diagonally across the stage in a mirror image of the beginning of Balanchine's *Symphony in Three Movements*. The dancers wear black and white tights and leotards against a blue scrim. At the end, they sink to one knee in a *révérence*, the bow that traditionally marks the end of a ballet class. While it declares Martins's abiding loyalty to a vocabulary and to a metaphor, *Reliquary* is also a key to how the company had changed. Martins's inventions are complex and elegant, a kind of mannerism, an inevitable extension of Balanchine's classicism. This is how the dancers move now: even more quickly than they did under Balanchine, with even greater agility.

The central pas de deux unfolds as a collision of equal energies, nothing like a Balanchinian seduction. It also reveals a change in Martins. It is not so combative; the dancers no longer fight their underlying collusion. Instead, they dance their faith in each other.

Peter Martins watches almost every performance. Before each ballet he talks to the dancers; afterward he thanks them. He wears jeans and sneakers. He is impossible to miss; his blond hair attracts light even in the backstage shadows. Watching, he looks almost like one of the dancers, but his brow is heavier, hooding his eyes, and his hair is graying at his temples. He is thinner than when he was dancing.

He has transformed New York City Ballet into an institution, overseeing not only the dancing but also administration and finances. He has built a framework for continuity. His fathers have died: Balanchine in 1983, Kirstein in 1996, Stanley Williams in 1997. The Company is his now. He has been ballet master in chief for fifteen years. They have not been easy years. He has continued the story, realized the ever after. New York City Ballet has remained loyal to Balanchine, and it has evolved, too. Peter Martins has kept faith.

Sitting in his office before the beginning of a new season, Martins talked to me about a new ballet he was thinking of making. It was to have its premiere on Balanchine's birthday, at the end of January. He had found the music he wanted to set. His voice deepened, and he leaned forward in his chair. He started to show me the steps with his hands, but he couldn't stay still. He stood and spun in a turn in the small space, and he opened his arms wide, possessed by the dance.

He worked fast, and he never changed a step. He finished *Stabat Mater* in

PAUL KOLNIK
Peter Martins, *Apollo*, photograph, 1982

February 1998. It is dedicated to Stanley Williams. Three couples dance, as partners and ensemble; they are tender, supportive; they never go offstage, but stay to watch each other. There is a set: a classical ruin, like an eighteenth-century folly. Martins takes motifs from Balanchine—a man dancing with three women, for instance, as in *Apollo* and *Serenade*—the way Balanchine borrowed from Petipa, to transform them and make them his own, to bring them into another time. His inventions unfold

so quickly that it seems as if the dancers have moved beyond steps into a new language, a means of expression they have evolved from long experience of each other. It is a result of Martins's own long experience, as dancer, observer, choreographer. Each combination carries images that linger, layered and translucent. In *Stabat Mater*, Martins has found his language: faithful to classicism, brilliant, eloquent, and new.

On Weightlessness

Watching New York City Ballet perform *Monumentum Pro Gesualdo* and *Movements for Piano and Orchestra*, Balanchine dances set to the Stravinsky music that seems to have been written by the winds of modernism gusting through the chimes of the celestial, I'm reminded of how often the ballet arranges the unlikely but happy marriage of opposites: the cultivation of muscle to give the illusion of weightlessness, the maniacal training of the body to create the impression of bodilessness. Balanchine's supremely graceful and fluid choreography reconciles the apparent and deceptive contradictions of grace and toughness; of the flesh and the spirit; of the most obsessive attention to time, moments counted out in eighth notes, all arranged to convey the illusion that time has ceased to exist, vanquished along with gravity—its slower, duller partner.

The great surrealist Joseph Cornell fell in love with Allegra Kent in 1954, after reading reviews of her appearance with New York City Ballet in Balanchine's *Ivesiana*—a dance that Kent performed while carried aloft by four male dancers, who kept her perpetually airborne, so that her feet never touched the ground. It's easy enough to imagine how this notion (a woman lighter than air!) so appealed to this solitary genius—with his legendary reservations regarding the earthier aspects of life. How that image must have enchanted a man whose work drew so heavily on the romanticization of the ethereal ballerina, on the notion of suspension, of preservation—of art as a permanent rescue from the ravages of age and time, and from the physical laws that govern the mundane, earthbound world.

In his *Via Parmigianino*, a shadow box dedicated to Kent, Cornell has created the visual equivalent of the airborne, weightless sylph. The Renaissance portrait of the young woman—at once haunted and serene—evades our gaze and stares dreamily down the long tunnel of centuries separating her life from ours. The colors are those of fog and mist, coolness and airy indecision.

Of course, Cornell's *amour fou* was romantic ballet, those shimmering swans in tutus, skimming on their trembling toes over the glossy stage. The stars of his waking dream life were the ballerinas of earlier centuries, lonely in their lifetimes, lonelier now that they're dead. He dreamed of them touring the grand hotels, exhausted, unpacking their jewel cases, then falling asleep and dreaming, perhaps about Joseph Cornell. Who knows what he would have made of today's dancers—otherworldly combinations of rippling grace and weightless fanciful machinery—themselves the embodied, bodiless equivalent of Stravinsky's music?

And what about the moment when the male dancers lift Heléne Alexopoulos, and for an instant she seems to hover in the air beyond their hands? That weightless midair suspension would have affected Cornell just as it affects the rest of us: for an instant, our hearts stop. Balanchine, Cornell, and Stravinsky remind us that there is something stronger than what we accept as the rules: the natural, inexorable laws of gravity, weight, the body. The weightlessness of the dancer repeats the promise of great art: you can levitate off the face of the earth—and art will be there to catch you.

1998

Via Parmigianino (for Allegra)

box construction,
12³/₈ × 8³/₈ × 3³/₈ inches, 1956

FRANCINE PROSE

As a child growing up in Brooklyn, Prose attended New York City Ballet, which she credits with informing her views on both art and gravity.

JOSEPH CORNELL

Cornell watched Allegra Kent dance for nearly two years before giving her this box in 1956.

Poet to Ballerina

My verses cannot comment

on your immortal moment,

or tell you what you mean;

only Balanchine

has the razor edge,

and knows that art of language.

1961

ROBERT LOWELL

Lowell composed this poem
during a visit to NYCB while on
a Ford Foundation fellowship
to write poetry about the
opera.

HENRI CARTIER-BRESSON

Disliking stylized "salon" photography, Cartier-Bresson's only shots
of NYCB were unposed, like this one
of Balanchine teaching class.

George Balanchine

photograph, 1959

Gathering at the Dances

The one tragedy of my parents' splendid marriage was that while my mother's great love was painting, my father was color-blind; and while my father's great love was music, my mother was tone deaf. Ballet was the place where their pleasure met. My mother took me to the museums that my father did not have time to visit, and my father took me to hear the operas that bored my mother, but to the ballet we went all together, and so I grew up with the notion that the ballet was where love prospers and comes into its own.

New York City Ballet has been something of a cousin, inevitable and unchosen, loved and constant, so much a part of my life that I have never imagined a world without it. I was two when I came to my first *Nutcracker*. In the poor black-and-white of early memory, I can still see the scene in which the snow began to fall and the tall ballerinas rushed out from among the pine trees. By the time I was six, two girls from my class were actually in the production; I would peer at the angels as they filed out, thrilled to find these schoolmates, fascinated that they had been given permission to live in that world of dance. In a family ritual as deep-seated as Christmas stockings and favorite carols, we have all gone to *The Nutcracker* every year since. This year, I saw my thirty-third performance.

As I grew up, I often heard my parents discussing ballet performances. I would ask to be taken along on their Tuesday night subscription, but they told me that I would be bored, that things would go on past my bedtime, that it wasn't all like *The Nutcracker*. Finally, when I was eleven, they took me to a program that included *Symphony in C*, late in the summer, on my grounds that if I was old enough for sleep-away camp, I was old enough for the ballet. I can remember how my parents tried to explain, in that serious tone of voice that meant I was growing up, something of form and balance, of what succeeded and what did not. Later I understood the connoisseurship, but that night I knew simply that the ballet was now part of my list of things that were a treat, along with travel and chocolate and being read aloud to and sledding.

ANDREW SOLOMON
Solomon first attended NYCB in 1965 when he was two.

Ten years after my first *Nutcracker*, I began to appreciate the breadth of Balanchine's accomplishment and to recognize differences between his work and that of other choreographers. I was a clumsy child and watched the dancers' human grace so masterly attenuated with wonder. I did not resent it, as I did the skill of athletes, but I was fascinated by it. I could not conceive how anyone had learned to move like that. Soon the dances—and the dancers—became individualized and eroticized. I watched them with longing, with flashes of recognition, with the pleasure of five senses.

In adolescence, I came fashionably to believe that what was vital was what was hard and a little bit raw. I disparaged the ballet for being insufficiently intellectual and honest, was dismayed that it did nothing to respond to the world's social and economic crises, and decided that it was not a living art. I announced that about once every two months, and in between I went to performances because my family had invited me. Eventually, I came back around and saw that though beauty may be the ornament of other interpretive systems, it is the armature of this one, the single basis for it, and for this reason alone ballet among the arts has survived uncompromised its flirtations with modernism and postmodernism. I came to revere the way that, even stripped back and made minimal, ballet did not grate as so much architecture, music, literature, and modern dance had begun to do.

I fell in love with New York City Ballet again in my twenties. I would go to bathe in it the way Turks go to steam chambers and monks to prayer, to be purified and uplifted and massaged by it. I felt as though my body were stretched by what I saw and knew my own limbs differently after a performance; and found ecstatic the whirling patterns and lovely shapes. I began to realize how much of the mind goes into great dancing, and I began to find that ballets presented technical questions and logical conundrums, that beauty was not the whole picture. Until then, I had narrativized every performance: the couples dancing were in love, or falling out of love, or enraged, or ambivalent, and the solitary dancers were proud or lonely, magnificent or sad. Now I realized that you need human figures for movement, but that sometimes movement can stand on its own. I became a formalist.

With time, this formalism, beauty, and passion took up triplet thrones, and my experience of ballet became fluid and multidetermined. It is a private secret, a luxury beyond the pale, to know more each year about this world of sublime artistry. In our postmiracle age of space probes, still nothing seems more astonishing to me than the fact that the human bodies of dancers can achieve such symmetries and that the human minds of choreographers find such ways to order them.

1998

GEORGES ROUAULT
Commissioned by Diaghilev's
Ballets Russes, this backdrop
premiered at the Théâtre
Sarah-Bernhardt in Paris and was
re-created by Esteban Francés
from Rouault's sketches in 1950
for NYCB, where it continues
to be used.

Prodigal Son, scene 1 set design

pastel, ink, tempera,
and watercolor on paper,
21 × 29³/₈ inches, 1929

From *And Promenade Home*

... Robbins's most easily recognized trait is, praise heaven,
his humor. In its grossest aspects, it takes the form of straight
gags—very good ones, but bald and outrageous. In its more
sophisticated manifestations, he introduces surprising and
impertinent conclusions into his pattern, deliberately leading
one on to expect a certain resolution and then insolently
offering another, untraditional and slightly rude, though always
logical because he is never foolish. He jokes with rhythms,
with space, with relations of bodies, with light, with silence,
with sound. These are all elements of style.

The grosser emotional fixtures of theme and content are plainly
manifest—fixtures such as, in the case of Robbins, a preoccupation with childhood and games, with the bewilderment
of growing up, with the anguish of choice. The unexpected,
the joke, in this field seems to turn back on the choreographer
and sit hard; each love story splits into three or more people;
each romance spells destruction or transience; all repeats
over and over. There is no resolution. In short, life turns out
not to be a joke.

1956

AGNES DE MILLE
On seeing Jerome Robbins's ballet
Fancy Free, de Mille declared it to
be the finest "theatrical" premiere
she had ever seen.

RICHARD AVEDON
This portrait of Jerome Robbins
appeared in *The New Yorker* for
the first time in 1995.

Jerome Robbins, New York City

photograph, 1947

The Ballet

In a cage of light, the splendid creatures
With faces amenable to anything,
Doing whatever you like—fountains
Of work or cascades of pretty failure.
With flanks as clean as bone they signal one another,
On the far side of a trench of music—
Such breasts and hair, such bold genitals

Until you would think we were the caged ones
Where our bodies shift and mumble
In the dark-tunneled house,
Waiting for feeding time and after that, sleep;
We watch the loping things from the zoo of ourselves.

Yet it is not only their perfection detains
Us in the paunchy dark, it is pity too.
That they must signal that way, like eloquent mutes?
Yes, and a longer affliction of splendor:
That it cannot reproduce its kind.

1997

WILLIAM MEREDITH
Meredith wrote his first ballet
poem for NYCB's 1962 souvenir
book.

WALTER OWEN
Owen is known for his studio
dance photographs, without which
there would be no photographic
record of NYCB's earliest works.
Here, Nora Kaye and Michael
Maule.

The Cage

photograph, 1951

Building a Theater for Dance

Lincoln Kirstein and I were friends at Harvard. He was always interested in the arts and had many wonderful ideas, but spoke of one with particular passion—to build a theater for ballet in the United States that would house the premier dance company in the world. Lincoln's vision proved a great inspiration.

In the 1930s, in Paris, we went to a theater and first saw dances by George Balanchine. Immediately, Lincoln felt that Balanchine was the only artist in the world who could realize his dream of a theater for ballet. I believe he was right. Ballets by Balanchine were light-years ahead of those by Fokine and Massine and other choreographers of the day. That was perfectly clear, even to an amateur like me. Balanchine balanced the Classicism of his training at the Imperial School in St. Petersburg with his vision of ballet in the twentieth century.

The New York State Theater was designed with Classicism in mind. When I began to plan the ballet theater in the 1950s, I felt I was being pretty reactionary. I found my inspiration mainly in eighteenth-century rococo theaters in Bavaria, and felt the ballet theater should resemble a state theater from that time. The reason was simple: in those festival spaces one gets the unmistakable feeling that there is no place but the theater. Though I was reaching back to an earlier century, I also had to deal with contemporary problems, like having the maximum number of seats in the auditorium. Decent rococo theaters seat four to five hundred. We had to seat three thousand.

Lincoln's original idea was to build a theater for dance in Central Park at Fifth Avenue and Fifty-ninth Street. He wanted the most exciting and prestigious address in town. Unfortunately, that idea didn't go over very well with the politicians—there was no chance of getting city money, city land, or city permission for that. Fortunately, Governor Nelson Rockefeller persuaded Lincoln to join the future complex going up on the Upper West Side, known as the Lincoln Center for the Performing Arts. I then wanted the building to be situated opposite the concert hall on a diagonal site, where the Julliard School is now. My reasoning was this: my original idea was for a rounded building, and the facade was a half circle, which fit better to a diagonal street than to the orthogonal street system of New York. But that was not to be, and my idea was knocked down by the committee that included the architects of the other buildings, and was headed by Wallace Harrison, who designed the Metropolitan Opera House. You put four architects in a room and you get four different opinions. But, of course, the half-round building that I designed didn't look well in a campus setting with rectangular buildings around. So I changed it to its present shape. That gave unity to the square.

Once the siting was agreed upon, we needed to use materials that would reflect the Classicism I was striving for. Poured concrete was big at the time, but I didn't want to go that way. I suggested to the other architects the use of travertine, that being the noblest and oldest Roman stone. We didn't want our buildings to clash. I proposed keeping a uniform spacing for the columns of twenty feet. That seemed monumental and would give the look of a classic, masonry building. Avery Fisher Hall is built of the same module. Their column system is entirely different looking from mine, but at least the rhythm of the columns is the same throughout the plaza. That gave unity to the square.

All buildings have the same aim, which is to give you an elevation of spirit. In building the New York State Theater, I didn't see any sense in redesigning the spoon and doing "moderne" just for the sake of "moderne." I wanted to do one for eternity.

1998

New York State Theater

ink on paper, 1958

A Building as a Ballerina

Many years ago, a mother asked Balanchine if her daughter, as yet an unknown quantity, could ever be a great dancer. *"Ah, madame,"* answered the ballet master, *"la danse—c'est une question morale."* Architecture, monuments, are also moral questions. Do we still have the right to hunger for splendor when actual physical want is so prevalent? Is public luxury politically ethical? If not, to what shrewd limits must we restrict ourselves? How do we gauge the strictures of necessity? Does man live by bread alone? Must we rely for our criteria of excellence only upon the masterpieces of the past? Have we no chance or desire today to risk our own capacities for mastery? Difficult questions. In the New York State Theater at Lincoln Center we are given one answer. Enlightened patronage, implemented by the willing taxability of an educated electorate, has dared risk one single absolute affirmative. A city, a state, spoke. This courage is rewarded by a monument. Citizens, rejoice. *Plaudite, omnes.*

1964

LINCOLN KIRSTEIN
One of Kirstein's dreams was to bring about a classical theater designed as a permanent home for NYCB.

ROBERT INDIANA
In the early 1960s, Indiana lived and worked in a loft that was later demolished to make way for the New York State Theater.

New York State Theater

poster, offset,
46 × 30 inches, 1964

Order and Exactness

When I was nine years old, I took my first ballet class. I remember it chiefly as a great relief. There was one hour of order and certainty. One hour of exact places to put fingers and feet. There was the music, and if you were lucky there was grace.

When I was eleven, I studied for a summer at the School of American Ballet. Balanchine watched our class. I have an indelible memory of this quiet genius watching our feet.

When I was sixteen, I danced in a local production of *Guys and Dolls.* I said a line and I got a laugh. That began acting. Acting was not a relief. There was no certainty, no exactness, no music. And I resented speaking. For years I said a lot with my body and then ruined it when I opened my mouth. For years I had a confidence, a security, and, perhaps, a grace that ballet had given me. For years it all evaporated when I spoke.

I tell my young daughters, Emily and Lily, who may or may not be drawn to the ballet, that I don't know what I can give them to make up for ballet—what combination of music, gym, sports, art, and performance training would give to them what ballet had given to me.

I go to New York City Ballet now and watch these magical creatures onstage. It is a relief to be there. It is order and exactness. There is music and there is grace beyond comprehension. No one interrupts this grace by speaking. I am jealous and I am very grateful.

1998

DIANNE WIEST
Wiest studied ballet in 1959 at the School of American Ballet studios on Broadway and 82nd Street.

ALFRED EISENSTAEDT
This photograph is one of the few extant images of the School of American Ballet's original Madison Avenue studios.

School of American Ballet

photograph, c. 1935

Late to the Ballet

I came to ballet very late, and even then I had to be lured into going.

As late as 1981, when I was forty-five years old, I had never seen a ballet, although ever since 1973, when I finished my biography of Robert Moses, my publisher and editor, Robert Gottlieb, for many years a member of City Ballet's board of directors, had been trying to get me to go, saying that he knew me and knew I would like the ballet. But in 1981, while we were working on my book on Lyndon Johnson, his efforts intensified, and when, despite his urging, I still did not purchase a season subscription, or even a ticket for a single performance, he said he would arrange for me to subscribe for the upcoming season. If I did indeed enjoy going, he said, I would have to take care of my subscription in future years myself, but he would go to the trouble this first time—just to get me there.

To so gracious an offer, what could I do but assent, and some weeks later, there I was, at a ballet at last.

The ballet was *Divertimento No. 15*, and all I saw in the first instant after the curtain rose were arms, curved arms, bare and still and almost indescribably elegant against an unadorned backdrop I remember as a deep and beautiful blue. And then, as I took in the still tableau of dancers, the tableau broke and moved. I certainly didn't appreciate any of the subtleties of the dancers' steps, much less know the steps' names. All I saw was beautiful movement. Then there were patterns—four dancers entering on either side from between heavy black curtains and the two lines of dancers crisscrossing,

and then the soloists weaving among them, in a stageful of grace—more grace than I had ever imagined. When they disappeared back into the black, I knew that something new and wonderful had come into my life.

Now I have been attending the ballet—on my own nickel—for sixteen years, missing only those subscription performances that occur when I am away. The ballet has never lost its wonder for me, and I try to make sure it never will—by not learning too much about it.

In my writing, I'm constantly required to analyze—to dissect political power, or the interplay of power and personality, or historical trends so that I can try to explain them—and anyway I am cursed with a mind that has to try to learn as much as possible about anything in which I become interested. I have tried to make ballet the exception to this. In other words, I deliberately try to learn very little about it. I'm helped in this by the fact that some of my favorite ballets—*Jewels*, for example—have no plot or story, so one possible area for analysis is eliminated right off the bat. But my willed ignorance goes beyond that. The movements of the dancers are so beautiful; I don't want to know the movements' names. The dancers' technical skill is magical to me; if there are flaws in their technique, I don't want to know it. The steps embody the music—often so perfectly that you feel you are watching notes dance. I love music; ballet, to me, makes music more than itself. I don't want to know *why* the music becomes more than itself. There is a mystery in ballet for me; I don't want to unravel that mystery. And I don't

want it unraveled for me. I have friends who are experts on ballet; I try not to discuss ballet with them. There is wonder in ballet for me; expertise could only dilute it, and I don't want it diluted. I want there to be something in life that I enjoy just for the beauty of it—and what better way could I do this than to respond, simply and without intellectualizing it, to an art that is so very close to pure beauty.

When the curtain rises on a ballet, I frequently take off my eyeglasses. Therefore, I can still see what's happening, of course, but the colors and the movements become a little hazy. The lines of the corps and the soloists swirling among the lines become more like pure patterns to me—captivating patterns. I am lost more than ever in that world onstage—that wonderful world.

1998

ROBERT A. CARO
New York historian Caro always associated the New York State Theater with power broker Robert Moses— until he saw his first ballet.

PAUL KOLNIK
A specialist in dance photography, Kolnik's work captures signature moments from the Company's repertory. Here, Peter Martins and Suzanne Farrell.

Diamonds from *Jewels*

photograph, 1977

Ode to Tanaquil Le Clercq

Smiling through my own memories of painful excitement your wide eyes
stare
                and narrow like a lost forest of childhood stolen from gypsies
two eyes that are the sunset of
                                    two knees
                                            two wrists
                                                    two minds
and the extended philosophical column, when they conducted the dialogues
            in distant Athens, rests on your two ribbon-wrapped hearts, white
    credibly agile
                flashing
                    scimitars of a city-state

where in the innocence of my watching had those ribbons become entangled
        dragging me upward into lilac-colored ozone where I gasped
            and you continued to smile as you dropped the bloody scarf of my life
                        from way up there, my neck hurt

        you were always changing into something else
        and always will be
        always plumage, perfection's broken heart, wings

        and wide eyes in which everything you do
        repeats yourself simultaneously and simply
                        as a window "gives" on something

it seems sometimes as if you were only breathing
    and everything happened around you
because when you disappeared in the wings nothing was there
        but the motion of some extraordinary happening I hadn't understood
the superb arc of a question, of a decision about death

    because you are beautiful you are hunted
            and with the courage of a vase
                you refuse to become a deer or tree
            and the world holds its breath
                to see if you are there, and safe

            are you?

1960

FRANK O'HARA

O'Hara was a Row L regular in the late 1950s and early 1960s, during the Company's tenure at City Center.

IRVING PENN

Penn photographed (*from left to right*) designer Corrado Cagli, composer Vittorio Rieti, Tanaquil Le Clercq, and Balanchine for *Vogue*.

The Triumph of Bacchus and Ariadne

photograph, 1948

New York City Ballet and Russia

When New York City Ballet first came to Moscow and Leningrad in 1962, it was barely known outside the narrow confines of local ballet circles. Even within those circles, its reputation depended mostly on rumors. Few Soviet dancers had seen its performances firsthand. But all this changed overnight on October 9, 1962, when the heavy—though not iron—curtain rose at Moscow's Bolshoi Theater, revealing, in one historically charged instant, the beautiful formation of Balanchine girls ready to bloom in the intricate patterns of *Serenade*.

Balanchine was extremely nervous. The Soviet audience was bewildered. I can attest to these facts, since I saw most of New York City Ballet's performances in St. Petersburg (then Leningrad), where Balanchine's troupe went after Moscow. The fallout from the Cuban missile crisis hadn't yet dissipated, but people in the Kirov foyer in intermission weren't fighting about politics; they were at one another's throats over *Agon*. Older dance lovers called it *Agony*, and mocked "those formalists who solve algebra equations with their feet." But for us young musicians and artists, *Agon* meant a breath of fresh air. The ever-familiar stage was suddenly transformed, as if a gigantic wet sponge had obliterated the traditional dusty scenery. And here is what happened: all our ideas about what ballet was and could be in the second half of the twentieth century— what it could express and how it could relate to contemporary music—changed dramatically.

New York City Ballet's momentous appearance (and a subsequent tour in 1972) shaped the creative outlook of a whole generation of the Russian artistic elite—not only dancers and choreographers, but also composers, musicians, painters, and filmmakers, who felt, from this moment on, that new horizons in art were attainable, fascinating destinations instead of mirages in the desert.

An especially deep impression on the Petersburg intelligentsia was left by Balanchine himself, by his nothing-less-than-miraculous materialization in the flesh. Here he was, elegant, smartly dressed, courteous in an old-fashioned (read: prerevolutionary) way, yet decidedly modern in his outlook and aesthetics, and quite determined *not* to play the part of a prodigal son. The great paradox, the great surprise of this visit, was that New York City Ballet had brought, all the way from America to 1960s Leningrad—a city that had long ago lost its status of capital, along with the accompanying perquisites— the image of old St. Petersburg, with all of *its* potent political and cultural reverberations.

Denigrated and suppressed at home by Soviet authorities, this glorious and nostalgic Petersburgian image had been preserved intact in the United States, thanks largely to the creative efforts of such artistic giants as the writer Vladimir Nabokov, the composer Igor Stravinsky, the choreographer Balanchine. In the latter's ballets, St. Petersburg themes with their pervasive imperial and court associations were used persistently— especially (and to a striking effect) in works choreographed to the music of Tschaikovsky, Glinka, and Glazounov. As Nathan Milstein told me once,

Balanchine was "a monarchist and a democrat: one does not preclude the other at all." This paradoxical combination ensured the success of Balanchine's "imperial" ballets with American audiences. Thus, the balletic idea of prerevolutionary St. Petersburg, with all its brilliance, its artistic vitality, and its romantic fervor, was first tried out on the liberal denizens of New York's Upper West Side, first rooted in their consciousness—so as to be brought back later to Russia and implanted anew on the inhospitable granite embankments of the Neva River.

And so began a long, arduous, and complicated process, which has had its highs and lows, but which has continued through the present day, enriching, I believe, the cultures of both Russia and America.

*Translated from the Russian by Elizabeth Kendall.
1998*

SOLOMON VOLKOV

A happenstance meeting on Broadway between Balanchine and Volkov turned into a conversation about Tschaikovsky's art and, finally, into a book on the subject.

ROUBEN TER-ARUTUNIAN

Rouben Ter-Arutunian created
more stage sets for NYCB than any
other designer. This design for
Ballet Imperial was used for the
Company's earliest performances
of the work.

Ballet Imperial, set design

watercolor,
14³/₄ × 20 inches, 1964

Little Ode to Suzanne Farrell

No ode is big
            or fast enough to have
the very all of you inside it, so
            I will have to be like you
and climb inside myself and fly
            into the outline that the pattern
of my moving self has left behind

the outline of the possible you impossibly beautiful in everyone

        like a little girl suddenly seeing the angles in
        a light blue protractor and therefore being them

Where was I and who?

You for whom
we get dressed up
and go uptown and up
the elevator shaft as
        the curtain goes up and when
                you glide in on your diagonal
we fall into the elevation of the dream
        that has a hummingbird and Saint Teresa of Avila in it

                and you

who hover in the air like a disembodied heart
shocked into eternity for the split second the music
turns to face you and you find your face up there
in the dark where we are and a smile on it

There is space here and air and breath, clarity
        of perfect tears that beauty makes us cry so automatically

                as you wrap the world around
                your finger, then wrap yourself around the world

1998

RON PADGETT

Padgett first came to NYCB
while an undergraduate
at Columbia University in the
early 1960s.

FRED FEHL

Fehl captured one of Balanchine's
few appearances onstage as
an NYCB dancer. Here he partners
Suzanne Farrell in *Don Quixote*.

Don Quixote

photograph, 1965

If I Were President

If I were president, I would devote at least one speech to a very large section of our population which is not usually thought of or addressed as a separate unit by people in the government—I refer to the intellectuals and artists of the United States and to people who are interested in the intellectual and artistic life of our country, in other words in the spiritual and not just the material values of our existence.

There are a great many of us: writers, painters, sculptors, actors, composers, instrumentalists, and dancers. And there are uncounted millions of those for whom their interest in our creative efforts is as important and sometimes more important than all the other ordinary details of their lives. That is why we would like the president to show an interest in and speak to us about that other half of our life—the nonmaterialistic part of life, which we represent. Actually this very large group of citizens of whom I am speaking has never made any very great demands. None of us is especially interested in money or power, but all of us want to be recognized and given the possibility to create and to enjoy art. Certain forms of art have received wonderful support from the public itself, from private citizens and groups of interested people, who have created libraries and museums and supported symphony orchestras, and we owe them a great debt of gratitude. But writers and artists have never been accorded full recognition by a government body or official—and the person who first gives us this recognition will earn our wholehearted gratitude and support.

I firmly believe that woman is appointed by destiny to inspire and bring beauty to our existence. Woman herself is the reason for life to be beautiful, and men should be busy serving her.

That is why I feel that if the woman will take into her hands the task of restoring the true purpose and values of life, then the man, who in our civilization is caught like a squirrel in the wheel of fortune, will find the strength to escape out of it and bring all his highest qualities to this purpose.

This brings us to the important problem of our children who are our future. Their taste for art should be developed from early childhood. They should learn to love the beautiful and impractical as well as the useful and practical. One should give them fairy tales, music, dance, theater. This is real magic for children, and it is strong enough to overcome many dangers that threaten them, mainly because their minds are unoccupied and their imaginations unfed. Developing these qualities in our children is the first step to promoting peace in the world—by giving them true standards of what is most important in human life. Inner nobility will safeguard them from the cynicism of utilitarianism. Some twenty thousand young children saw special performances given for them by New York City Ballet. It was absolutely extraordinary to see how avidly they devoured those performances. The children must be reached before they are corrupted by life.

In conclusion I would like to say a few words about my special field of art—the ballet. American people have a special affinity to movement in general and to ballet in particular. They are superb dancers, and their interest in this art deserves to be encouraged and channeled in the right way.

In ballet, woman is all-important. She is the queen of the performance, and the men surround her like courtiers. This is perhaps why I have thought so much about the woman's role and enormous possibilities in real life as well as on the stage.

1961

GEORGE BALANCHINE
Balanchine was the first official visitor to the Kennedy White House, which coincided with NYCB performances in Washington, D.C., during the time of the inauguration in 1961.

AL HIRSCHFELD
Hirschfeld observed Balanchine in rehearsal for this series, which originally appeared in *The New York Times*.

George Balanchine

pen and ink on paper,
21 x 27 inches, 1974

On Stravinsky and Balanchine

I was the only witness to Igor Stravinsky and George Balanchine's working together in the creation of two masterpieces, *Agon* and *The Flood*. That said, let me disqualify myself in part. One would have to *be* Russian, as well as speak the language, in order to understand the exchanges, at the creative level, of these two twentieth-century colossi. I satisfy neither requirement. At the time of *Orpheus* (1948), they conversed in Russian almost exclusively, rarely slipping into English, and then only out of consideration for the frustration of onlookers such as myself. By the time of *Agon* (1954–1957), both artists had become fully effective in English, notwithstanding Balanchine's tendency to omit verbs and the ends of sentences, and Stravinsky's heavily accented but maddeningly macaronic vocabulary. By the time of *The Flood* (1962), the English of both was resourceful, fluent, original, and not quite correct. But of course verbal language was not their principal means of communication. Stravinsky could articulate musical thoughts at the piano, and Balanchine choreographic ones through movement and gesture.

Balanchine persuaded Stravinsky to expand the *Orpheus* pas de deux, which not even Diaghilev would have tried to do. So, too, Balanchine convinced the composer to repeat the prelude to *The Flood* near the end, thereby changing its theology as well as its dramatic shape. How different was the relationship in 1937, when Stravinsky obliged Balanchine to jettison part of his choreography for *Jeu de cartes,* but by all accounts the composer treated his young collaborator imperiously then, having

only that one proof of his genius, *Apollo*. But *Jeu de cartes*, which has no slow music, no adagio pas de deux, and therefore no love interest, did not, I think, inspire Balanchine.

Balustrade (1941) was the rebirth of Stravinsky's appreciation of the young "ballet master," as he wished to be called. Stravinsky also praised Balanchine's choreography for *Danses Concertantes* (1944), but was less than enthusiastic about Eugene Berman's set and costumes, even after the artist had simplified them to the composer's specifications. It does not matter that both ballets were concert pieces, like all of Balanchine's later Stravinsky repertory. The change in the relationship came with *Orpheus*, in which, before a note had been composed, the two artists together plotted the scenario and dance numbers. By coincidence, Stravinsky's full realization of Balanchine's musical gifts came during the *Orpheus* rehearsals. On April 20, 1948, eight days before the premiere, Stravinsky and I heard and saw him conduct Tschaikovsky for Ballet Theater, in tempi, feeling, phrasing, flow, refinement, it was the performance of a lifetime, utterly unlike anything even Stravinsky had ever experienced. Balanchine could have, but fortunately did not, become a "great maestro," being content to remain what he so perfectly was.

The *Agon* collaboration was much closer. By this time, Balanchine had become the composer's cocreator, an equal partner from conception to execution. He arrived at the Stravinsky home in Hollywood on June 6, 1954. Something called twelve-tone music was in the air at the time, and *Agon* is about

twelve dancers and twelve tones. Balanchine himself recalled that "we constructed every possibility of dividing twelve," meaning dance solos, duos, trios, quartets. The year before, Balanchine was in Brentwood, California, dining with Mrs. Arnold Schoenberg, her mother, daughter, and myself, seeking the widow's permission to base a ballet on one of her husband's twelve-tone works. Since he did not know any of them, I proposed the *Accompaniment to a Cinematographic Scene* Opus 34, partly because it is short, employs a small orchestra, and has a classical structure. The next day, in the Stravinsky home— the composer himself was in the hospital recovering from surgery—I explained the score's pitch organization and scheme of proportional tempi, and we listened to a tape of the piece several times. Balanchine immediately grasped the dramatic structure of the music but wondered why a twelve-tone composition began and ended in triadic harmony. We listened again the next day, and the next, and the result was the inception of Balanchine's ballet *Opus 34*. I was the catalyst in another Balanchine "twelve-tone" opus a few years later, in that he learned the Anton Webern music used in *Episodes* from my 1957 recordings. Later still, he followed my suggestion to base a ballet on the Brahms-Schoenberg Quartet, which he heard for the first time in my recording. And finally, he choreographed Stravinsky's *Monumentum* and *Movements* at my instigation.

Ballet critics refer to a "conference in the summer of 1954, when work on *Agon* began," and to a "chart that Stravinsky made afterward listing the order of dances ... and the number of dancers, with stick figures for males and females." In truth, the chart dates *from* those conferences, not after them. The succession of dances and their titles were Balanchine's, written down by Stravinsky during the discussions. Stravinsky also drew the stick figures—triangular tutus for the females—as they worked, not afterward, when he would have taken more pains with them. In fact, he composed the *pas de quatre* immediately after Balanchine had gone, using a fanfare he had written in December 1953. The chart also reveals that not all of the dances were decided upon in those first meetings; the *Sarabande* and *Gailliard*, for instance, were not entered until these pieces were completed three months later.

1998

ROBERT CRAFT

Craft has been a guest conductor
at NYCB.

IGOR STRAVINSKY

Agon was the product of an
intense collaboration between
Balanchine and Stravinsky, out of
which grew a deep friendship and
other works.

I   At the → Four boys standing
    start   back to the audience

1) Quartet
   Variation
   1' *(minute)* 30" *(seconds)*

2) Double Quartet
   Variation
   1'30"

Quartet and Double Quartet   Coda
                          1' in imitation

II   A–Introduction 0'40" percussion
     for
     Pas de Trois No. 1

     Variation (he)
     sarabande
     1'15"

     Variation (they)
     gailliard
     1'00"

     Coda for 3   1'30"

     B–Introduction 0'40" percussion
     for
     Pas de Trois No. 2

     Variation (they)
     0'50"

     Variation (she)
     0'45"

     Coda for 3   1'30"

     These 3 introductions are
     in the same music but in variation.

     C–Introduction 0'40" percussion
     for
     Pas de Deux

     Adagio

     Variation (he)

     Variation (she)

     Coda (both)

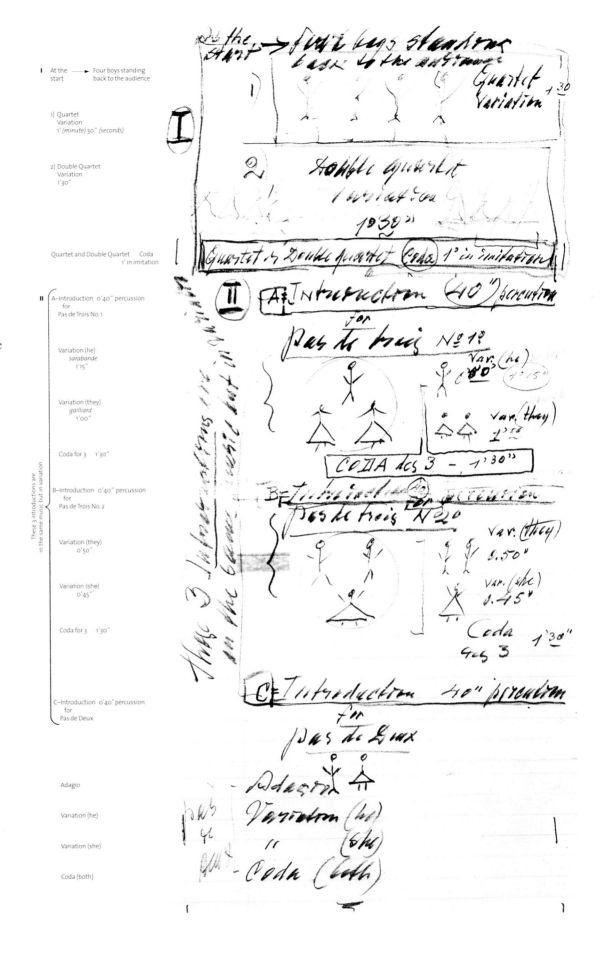

Agon

pencil and colored pencil on paper,
23¼ × 7 inches, 1964

Ballet's Present Eden—Example of *The Nutcracker*

Every artistic medium has its peculiar nature, which allows it to express some things better than any rival medium and prohibits it from expressing other things altogether. The medium of ballet is the human body moving in rhythmical balance within a limited area of space. What it can express is whatever is immediately intelligible in terms of variety of motion—fast-or-slow, to-and-fro, round-and-round, up-and-down; and variety of spatial relations—absent-or-present, face-to-face, back-to-back, side-by-side, above-below, at-the-center, on-the-outside, far-or-near, approaching or receding, etc.

Ballet time, that is, is a continuous present; every experience which depends on historical time lies outside its capacities. It cannot express memory, the recollection of that which is absent, for either the recollected body is onstage and immediate or it is off and nonexistent. Memory distinguishes between the object and its invoked image; ballet deals only in the object. No character in a ballet can grow or change in the way that a character in a novel changes; he can only undergo instantaneous transformations from one kind of being to another. Ballet can show A protecting and comforting B, but it cannot tell us whether A is the mother, the aunt, or the fairy god-mother of B. These observations, it should be said, refer to the forming principles of ballet; as with the other media, tension and excitement come from pushing against the form. A choreographer may take this risk again and again, but he will watch closely,

being careful to make himself clear. And he will return in good time to safe ground.

In its dazzling display of physical energy, on the other hand, the ballet expresses, as no other medium can, the joy of being alive. Death is omnipresent as the force of gravity over which the dancers triumph; everything at rest is either a thing, or it is asleep, enchanted, or dead. If it moves, it comes to life, and its kind of life—man, bird, or animated toy—is a minor matter, to be indicated by slight details of costume, compared to the fact of life itself which dancing expresses. The more energy implied by an emotion, the more dance-able it is. Thus defiance can be danced but despair is impossible, and joy is the most danceable of all. Since suffering, as human beings understand it, depends on memory and anticipation, which are alien to the medium, it may be said that nobody suffers in ballet: if they did, their movement would become unbalanced and ugly.

When ballet portrays funeral rites for the death of a hero, the glory and the pleasure in the rite itself are what it conveys. In other words, all real ballets take place in Eden, in that world of pure being without becoming and the suffering implied by becoming, a world where things, beasts, and men are equally alive, a world without history and without seriousness. The ballet character who becomes serious must either come to rest and die or he must exit. One could turn *Pickwick Papers* into a ballet up to the point where Mr. Pickwick enters the Fleet Prison (The Fallen World), but neither the

Fleet, nor Mr. Pickwick after he has been in it and tasted of the fruit of the knowledge of good and evil, are ballet subjects. It is not an accident that so many of the most successful ballets are based on fairy tales.

E. T. A. Hoffmann, who wrote the original story (in 1816) on which *The Nutcracker* is based, was haunted by nostalgic visions of a childhood Eden with its magical wonder. At the same time he was haunted by terrors and visions of evil. Black magic was as real to him as white. His Drosselmeyer is a much more complex and sinister character than Drosselmeyer in the ballet; the horrid things that happen to Princess Perribou and to Nutcracker, or to Drosselmeyer Jr., have quite rightly

W. H. AUDEN

Auden's Pulitzer Prize–winning poem *The Age of Anxiety* was the inspiration for the Jerome Robbins ballet.

HORACE ARMISTEAD

Armistead designed the original sets for Balanchine's production of *The Nutcracker*.

Sketches for Balanchine's *The Nutcracker*

grease pencil, ink, and oil, 24 × 18 inches, c. 1954

NUTCRACKER   Sc 2

SCALE ½" = 1'-0"

Jan 13 HArmistead

been kept off the stage, and the ballet battle is not the sadistic thing it is in the story.

Dumas turned Hoffmann's often fierce German tale into *Casse-Noisette*, a story for French children. Since children's stories also take place in a present Eden, he thus tended to preserve the incidents that Petipa and Ivanov could use for their scenario. What comes down to us now in dance are most of the ceremonial scenes like the Christmas party and the festivities in Confectionland. All the history of Nutcracker and Clara is telescoped into one ballet and a transformation scene; the long romantic journeys of the story are represented by the lovers in a snowstorm. Certain charming scenes had to be left out, not only on account of length, but also because they are too literary. For example, the sausage feast in which the King rushes from a Privy Council meeting to see how things are going in the kitchen:

"Gentlemen!" he cried, rising from the throne, "will you excuse me? I will return in a minute."

Then, hardly able to prevent himself from running to the door, he rushed to the kitchen, where, after embracing the Queen many times, he began to stir the contents of the cauldron with his sceptre. Afterwards he put it in his mouth, and, in a calmer state of mind, returned to his Privy Council, where, though still a little absentminded, he succeeded in taking up the question of foreign policy whether he had left it.

Some of this, e.g., "hardly able to prevent himself from running," is mimeable though not danceable, but not even mime can take up foreign policy; that

requires words, as do Hoffmann's philosophic reflections on the difference between the ideal and the real. In ballet only the ideal remains.

In order of composition, *The Nutcracker* is the last of three full-length ballets which Tschaikovsky wrote. There is beautiful ballet music in the operas of classical composers like Gluck and Mozart, there are mid-nineteenth century ballet scores of great charm like those of Adam and Delibes, but Tschaikovsky was the first to raise ballet music to its present status as a serious orchestral form equal to that of the symphony. Before Tschaikovsky the choreographer and the composer had little to do with each other: the former told the latter what kind of dances he wanted and how many bars long they should be, and the composer went off and wrote them without bothering to find out what actions were to accompany his music. Tschaikovsky wrote to Petipa's orders, but he also wrote to sense, and in his ballet scores the music is always apposite to the scenario. The very difficulties which Tschaikovsky found in training his musical imagination to the traditional sonata and symphony forms may well have been an advantage when he came to write ballet music, which makes such different formal demands. Today, many of us find his compositions in this form his best music, the closest in spirit (though completely original) to the work of Mozart, who was his confessed idol.

Outside Russia, where it has become popular, the ballet has hardly been seen, and only the orchestra suite Tschaikovsky made out of some of the music is well known. After seeing the

Vic-Wells 1934 revival, Cyril Beaumont complained in his *Complete Book of Ballets* that the first scene was suitable only to a juvenile audience and that the character dances in the last scene were ridiculous, but praised highly the solo numbers.

Apart from the fact that it requires a number of professionally trained children, which most ballet companies do not possess, *The Nutcracker* is not suitable for a company built, like the majority, around a few star soloists and with a corps de ballet capable of little more than calisthenics. George Balanchine has always set his face against such a structure. The ideal he has worked for is a company in which every member is technically capable of dancing a solo *rôle*: in his choreography, instead of the conventional corps de ballet acting in unison, every one has his unique part to play. Balanchine sees *The Nutcracker* as a festival of joy, a sort of Christmas pantomime, and only those who have lost their sense of joy and for whom, consequently, ballet is a meaningless art will find it juvenile.

1954

ERIC CARLE
These fairies were inspired by another of Balanchine's fantastic full-length story ballets, *A Midsummer Night's Dream*.

Fairies

acrylic and tissue paper on canvas board, 18 × 14 inches, 1998

I'LL GIVE THEE FAIRIES TO ATTEND ON THEE

Arthur Mitchell

Slim dragon-fly
    too rapid for the eye
        to cage,
contagious gem of virtuosity
make visible, mentality.
Your jewels of mobility
reveal
    and veil
        a peacock-tail.

1956

MARIANNE MOORE
An avid fan of New York City Ballet, Moore corresponded regularly with Lincoln Kirstein regarding her views on the Company.

WILLIAM VASILLOV
Vasillov, a colleague and contemporary of George Platt Lynes, was known for capturing the clean lines and supple ease of dancers' bodies.

Arthur Mitchell

photograph, 1960

Untitled

For a long time I thought of dance as a kind of exotic spectacle, dependent for its interest on "costume" and "story," often beautiful or moving, sometimes tedious, in any case a remote performance that bore no structural relation to what I did, which was write. "To write" was to make something, an act exactly as tactile and specific as weaving fabric or blowing glass, with exactly as tangible a result: an object, whether it was a novel or a poem or a piece or for that matter a piece of music, that showed the hand of its maker. The relationship between writing and composing music and making art had always seemed clear: writers and composers and artists all made things, and we spoke of the process of making things in remarkably similar terms. A novel has, for the writer who is making it, not "chapters," never an "outline," but "movements," and "structure," and "color." I wrote one novel that was for me all blues, and greens, shallow water seen from the air. I wanted to make another all white, all between the words, a novel carried entirely by what was not said. I tried to make a third an oil slick, its surface iridescent, the colors shifting, thrown away, an evanescent shimmer. The awareness that these objects I was making would fall short of their intentions was itself part of the process: the whole point, if you were making a novel or a painting or a piece of music, was to set for oneself the most difficult possible task, the finally impossible exercise: *make time past and time present exist simultaneously*, in my case, or *make a novel so fast that it reads unbroken, uninterrupted*, or *make a sentence so strong that it will carry the whole thing, one sentence, the novel. Make the reader hear what cannot be heard. Make the reader see what is not there to see. Make a novel without language.*

Make a novel a dance, I might as well have been saying, but I did not yet know this, nor would I know it now, had I never seen New York City Ballet. I remember, the first time I did see it, leaning forward transfixed, excited in a way I had never expected. I remember thinking again and again of a line from a poem by Gerard Manley Hopkins, a poem I rarely remembered and a line that had no application except in its rhythm, in the sharp clarity of its verb and the cool irony of its second clause: *"Honour is flashed off exploit, so we say."* This was not spectacle, this was not costume, this was not "story." This was different. This was dance as a thing made, an object that showed the hand of its maker. This was a kind of dance that did everything I had wanted to do myself. It had the speed, it had the clarity, it had set for itself the most difficult possible task, the impossible exercise. You could see the exercise. You could see the technique, you could see how it worked, you could see the blind devotion to making it work. Balanchine, I later read, called himself a cook, a gardener, a tailor, a craftsman. *So we say.*

1998

JOAN DIDION
When Didion emigrated from California to New York in the early 1980s, Lincoln Kirstein initiated her into New York cultural life by leading her backstage during *Serenade*.

ELLSWORTH KELLY
Color, form, movement, dedicated to George Balanchine.

Untitled

ink on paper,
28½ x 22½ inches, 1962

To New York City Ballet

Marabout de mon coeur aux seins de mandarine . . .

—Emile Roumer

Oh dancers of New York, arranged by Balanchine,
You are more beautiful than groves of evergreen!
You have aesthetic distance, like the blue-white sea
Outside the porthole—Agon, or Symphony in C!
And how the image lasts, with houselights going on,
Of the prince standing gazing at a disappearing swan!
Is it Odette? Was it Odile? The two are so the same,
But every smile or gesture seems to give away the game.
There's only one who brings this honest beating of the heart:
George Balanchine! Of all the kings of choreographic art,
Great Balanchine, who lifts us, with his dancers, in the air
As if there were no stage at all, to tell his stories there.

1998

KENNETH KOCH
During the late 1950s and early 1960s, Kenneth Koch and his friends came often to City Center to watch NYCB.

FRANCESCO CLEMENTE
Clemente first collaborated with NYCB when he contributed a painting for the American Music Festival in 1988.

Untitled

pastel on paper,
10½ × 9½ inches, 1998

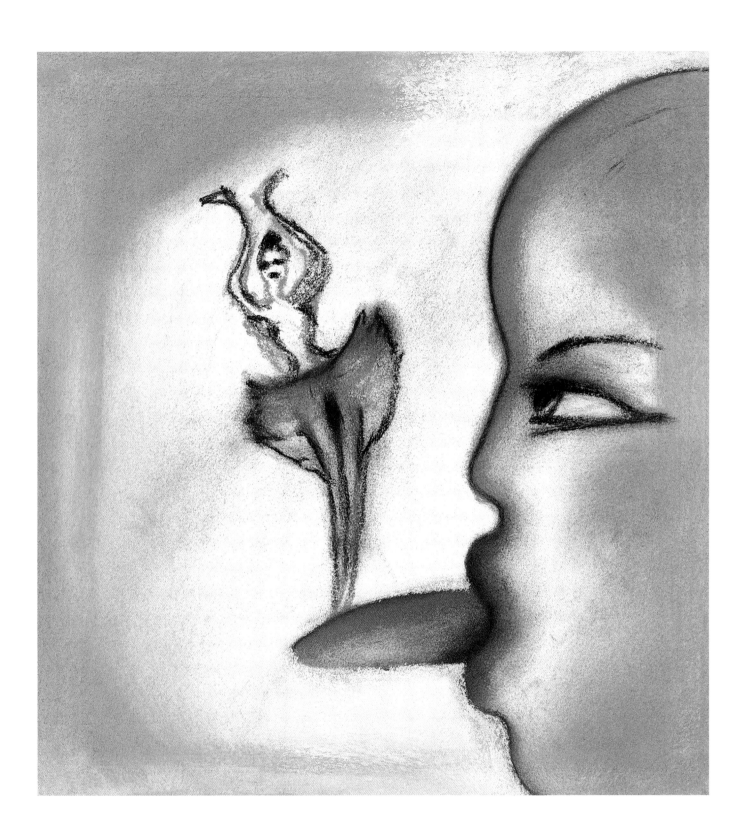

An Engineer and an Artist

In preparation for their chosen careers, some people go to graduate school; I went to New York City Ballet. It was Balanchine who taught me the rudiments of composition—how to structure an experience that unfolds over time—which I call upon daily in my life as a writer. And it was Karinska, the Company's costume designer, who demonstrated for me the exact science involved in showing a woman's body to its best advantage— the ingenuity and the sleight-of-hand that are the tricks of the dressmaker's trade. I think of her often now, in my capacity as a fashion editor, and studying each new season's clothes as they come down the runway, I admire her achievements all the more.

Born in 1886, in Ukraine, Karinska emigrated to Paris and London and, finally, to New York. Her wide-ranging career included commissions for the stage in Europe in the thirties, for Broadway and Hollywood in the forties (she won an Oscar for *Joan of Arc*), for the Metropolitan Opera and the Ice Capades. For a brief period in the forties, she opened her own couture house on Fifty-sixth Street. But it was in her work for Balanchine and New York City Ballet that her talents found a home, and over the course of some forty-five years, she lavished her imagination on more than nine thousand costumes for the Company.

Since the start of this century, when Paul Poiret liberated women's torsos from their Victorian corsets (only to restrain their legs in hobble skirts),

freedom of movement has been one of fashion's rallying cries, inspiring countless innovations. And yet, to my mind, some of the most eloquent solutions to the problem of adorning the body without hindering it have come not from the so-called laboratory of haute couture but from Karinska, an engineer and an artist. The foundation in every case was the waist, she proclaimed; she built up and down from there. In order to accommodate the expansion and contraction of a dancer's rib cage, she devised bodices with as many as sixteen panels, some on the bias. At Balanchine's instigation, she overhauled the shape of the tutu, suspending it from a yoke that emphasized the narrowness of the hips, shortening it to expose the line of the thighs.

Lately, when I see New York City Ballet's *Nutcracker,* I come away thinking that it would be hard to find a better training ground for fashion designers than the ballet's second act— a tropical Candyland in which every citizen has been outfitted by Karinska. The precision of the cut and the intricacies of the construction are perhaps most evident at close range, but during the finale every member of the audience is in a position to appreciate Karinska's sublime skill as a colorist. She worked only in natural fibers, primarily silk, because she loved their luminosity, the way they take the light, and their ambiguity, the way they take the dye unevenly. In the blizzard that closes *The Nutcracker*'s first act, the Snowflakes' skirts are rendered in layers of white tulle interspersed with beige, pink, and blue—

in keeping with Karinska's conviction that a single color makes for dead flatness on the stage.

Like haute couture, her costumes exude a sense of luxury in the smallest details—many of them so subtle as to be imperceptible: the Marzipan Shepherdesses' wired tutus are edged with a gold thread, invisible from a distance, that glimmers when the dancers turn. Some flourishes were intended to be secret. The women in the Spanish variation wear lockets with a picture of Balanchine inside. I read somewhere that once, for a production of *La Traviata*, Karinska went so far as to cover the hoops of the underskirts in lace. "They ask me why, when the lace doesn't show," she said. "It is for the soul, I say."

1998

HOLLY BRUBACH

Best known for her writing on fashion, Brubach has been fascinated by the relationship between costumes and couture since her earliest days observing NYCB.

KARINSKA

Karinska, NYCB's first costume mistress, revolutionized the tutu by using only material made of "living fibers": this made them durable, comfortable, and beautiful.

Costume for *Brahms-Schoenberg Quartet*

satin bodice and tulle skirt, 1966

From *A Letter on New York City's Ballet*

. . . American ballet is like a straight and narrow path compared to the pretty primrose fields the French tumble in so happily. The NYC style is the most particularized and the clearest defined of all the American ones; the most Puritan in its uprightness. For me an immediate attraction of the NYC's style is the handsomeness of the dancing, and another is the absence of glamour, of glamorization. To have left glamour out is only a negative virtue, but there is a freshness in it to start with.

Handsome the NYC way of dancing certainly is. Limpid, easy, large, open, bounding; calm in temper and steady in pulse; virtuoso in precision, in stamina, in rapidity. So honest, so fresh and modest the company looks in action. The company's stance, the bearing of the dancer's whole body in action, is the most straightforward, the clearest I ever saw; it is the company's physical approach to the grand style— not to the noble carriage but to the grand one. Simple and clear the look of shoulder and hip, the head, the elbow, and the instep; unnervous the bodies deploy in the step, hold its shape in the air, return to balance with no strain, and redeploy without effort. Never was there so little mannerism in a company, or extravagance. . . .

It is an attention turned outside rather than inside. It is turned not to sentiment and charm, but to perspicuity and action. It suggests a reality that is not personal, that outlives the dancer and the public, like a kind of faith. The company is not trying for an emotional suggestion; it seems to be trying for that much harder thing, a simple statement. A painter who is a very bright critic told me that at the opening of *Symphony in C,* during the rush and surge of the finale, tears came to her eyes because it was all so entirely objective.

1952

EDWIN DENBY

Denby wrote about the nascent world of dance in postwar America for the *New York Herald Tribune;* this is an excerpt from an early personal letter.

CAROLYN GEORGE

This photograph was taken in London during the Company's last tour under Balanchine.

Symphony in C

photograph, 1978

ERTÉ

Jerome Robbins first saw this
design when visiting the Paris
Opera Ballet; he brought
the set back with him, and it
continues to be used in NYCB's
production of *In G Major*.

In G Major, set design

gouache on paper,
21 × 29⅜ inches, 1975

Afternoons of a Fan

Nothing makes more sense to me than a night at the ballet. I have no contradictory opinions about it. I refuse to get into any critical conversation about which dancer is on the way up and who is on their way out. I will not stop to analyze the choreography of Balanchine vs. Robbins or Martins. To me, it is a privilege to see all their work performed by the company they created it for.

I have been a regular at New York City Ballet since I was eight and my big sister, Sandra, who was in college at the time, first took me to see *Stars and Stripes* at City Center. Who knew that something as good for you as ballet could be so much fun? Previous to that trip, ballet reminded me of my own two flat feet and my ballet teacher, Mr. Thomas, telling my mother that my prospects for going up on pointe were about as likely as my being cast as the Sugar Plum Fairy on Mars. My talent was strictly port de bras.

As a high school student my feminine ideals became Suzanne Farrell and Patricia McBride. They weren't slurpy girls who denied their intelligence in favor of femininity. Their grace, unlike those of teen idols in magazines, was neither surface nor empty. They were muses: strong and competent. They could be alone on a stage and command attention. And on top of that they always wore the most perfect dot earrings.

During my professional life as a playwright the ballet came to mean even more to me. There's the tremendous attraction that no one talks. The construction of character and desire is completely in movement. Romantic yearning, which requires an aria in opera or at the very least an entire scene in a play, can be literally elevated to a greater height in a ballet. Any playwright in search of a structure can find it in a Balanchine ballet. I could watch for hours just the exit of *Vienna Waltzes*. How do they get off the stage when we don't even notice? In a world where not much is perfect, the moment those waltzers vanish is. The ballet is the ultimate stage for unspoken truths.

On the nights when I'm either sentimental enough or desperate enough to count my blessings one of them is that my hometown happens to be the hometown of New York City Ballet. I know no tour jeté will shatter the earth or bring the stock market down, but it will consistently remind me to strive for that ultimate synthesis of art and discipline. In the ballet the respect for craft is as basic as first position. The genius of the tradition is a never-ending exploration of artistic possibilities based on those fundamental basics.

Watching Kyra Nichols recently dancing *In Memoriam* I applauded wildly for the piece and a life well spent. Contemplating seeing Jock Soto in *West Side Story Suite* later that season I will once again fantasize about our wedding day. Noticing that Yvonne Borree has just become a principal I know it was because I spotted her all along.

One cold winter night I saw by chance Peter Martins put a scarf around his wife, Darci Kistler. Looking at them I saw the history of the company and my coming of age during all those afternoons and evenings of a fan. In seeing Peter onstage after the debut of his *Sleeping Beauty* I saw the hand of Balanchine guiding him with the incomparable Suzanne Farrell and the magnetic Heather Watts. Watching Darci saluting center stage in *Stars and Stripes* I see the ghosts of Patricia McBride, Merrill Ashley, and all the great signature dancers who had saluted in that same spot.

New York City Ballet is my extended imaginary family. James Stewart had Harvey the rabbit, and I have Damian, Albert, and Wendy. Actually, on some days I even pretend Wendy Whelan and I are the W. W. Siamese twins separated at birth. She dances perfectly and I write. She pirouettes while I store her body fat. It's a perfectly symbiotic relationship.

Some girls want to have breakfast at Tiffany's. I just want a glass of champagne during the interval between *Glass Pieces* and *Scotch Symphony* on the State Theater Promenade.

1998

WENDY WASSERSTEIN

During her college and graduate school years, Wasserstein was a Fourth-Ring regular at NYCB.

ANNIE LEIBOVITZ

Leibovitz took this photograph of Darci Kistler and Peter Martins shortly after they were married.

Untitled

photograph, 1992

Letter to Lincoln Kirstein

Dear Fellow-Pioneer—

Let nothing stop you—your book is marvelous—I am disturbed by parts of it—that is good, because I see now much that I did not want to see.

I will write to you about it—unless you say "spare me"—*not* tonight—because I need to exercise care and thought.

When I saw the Ballet the second evening I spent most of it planning a dance, ironic in nature, for myself.

I thought of Apollo—and how when Lifar became too petulant to take seriously—

There is no ecstasy there. What is mistaken for passion is simply the nervous hysteria of inbreeding—in the organization—in the ideas—except "St. Francis."

Lincoln—we must stand—you and I—separately and perhaps together— I am not right yet—that is clear—direct—I have not yet the realism that lies behind the eyes—not in the outer lines of things—

And you are not clear yet, either—But greater than all else is a deep inner primal power—in the body of the *danse* here.

You see I believe in you—and I believe in the bodies of my dancers and of your dancers—

Best wishes for the tour—I hope you see Carlos—I hope you will not be shocked by his so great youth—

With love
Martha

ca. 1940

MARTHA GRAHAM
Graham worked with George
Balanchine on the two-part ballet
Episodes, the only collaboration
between the two choreographers.

LUCIAN FREUD
After a friendship-ending argument with Lincoln Kirstein, Freud
left this portrait unfinished.

Lincoln Kirstein

oil on canvas,
19¾ × 15½ inches, 1950

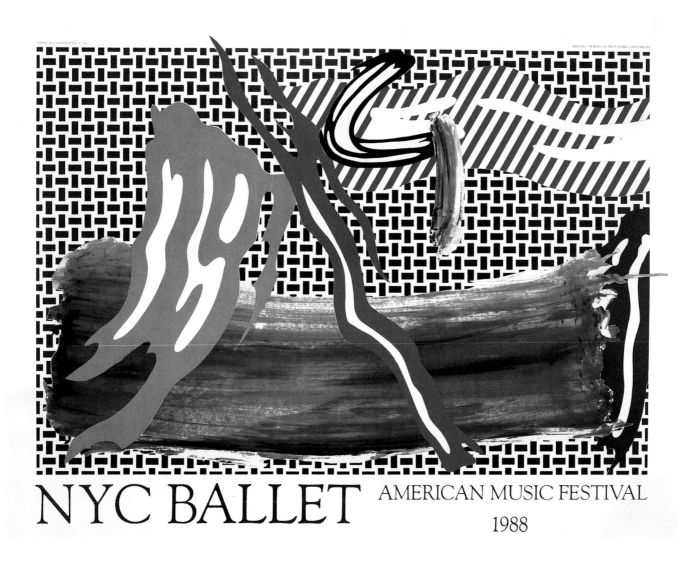

NYC BALLET AMERICAN MUSIC FESTIVAL
1988

ROY LICHTENSTEIN

A frequent member of NYCB's
audience, Lichtenstein created
this piece especially for the
American Music Festival.

American Music Festival

above: poster, offset lithograph
(from four-color process) on
smooth, white wove paper,
20⅝ × 30¾ inches, 1988

right: poster, silk screen on paper,
24 × 36 inches, 1988

KEITH HARING

This Haring poster was projected
onstage during the overture for
the closing-night program of the
American Music Festival.

The Pas de Deux of Athletes and Artistry

For many, the most prominent marriage of the performing arts and sports had probably occurred when Mike Reid, the six-foot-three, 255-pound defensive tackle for the Cincinnati Bengals in the 1970s, appeared with symphony orchestras. He was extraordinary. Not only could he play the piano, he could lift it, too.

But then in 1988 along came Herschel Walker, the mighty running back of the Dallas Cowboys, who slipped into tights and performed for one night only with the Fort Worth Ballet.

Walker, it turned out, was no Nijinsky. Nijinsky, after all, could perform the entrechat, changing position of his feet while in midair, ten times. But then Walker was no Nijinsky. Walker, after all, had knocked ten tacklers into midair while shifting his feet.

Walker, however, was closer to Edward Villella, whom I saw perform and interviewed some thirty years ago, when he was the premier danseur of New York City Ballet. For Villella was also an accomplished athlete. It was less than widely known that Villella had been a welterweight boxing champion at the New York State Maritime College, and also played football and baseball.

I went to see him at Lincoln Center to talk about the connection between sports and ballet. Earlier I had watched him dance, and for anyone with two eyes and even a soupçon of sensitivity, you had to be impressed with his athleticism (I particularly was taken by his *Tarantella*). In fact, one had to be respectful of the athleticism of all the dancers onstage.

I was about twenty-eight at the time, and regarding the ballet, I was, I confess abashedly, but a dewy-eyed naïf. I had never before seen a ballet, and I was thunderstruck. Such grace, such precision—such power!

I had been well aware of comparisons of sports and the performing arts, particularly with a dextrous double play, or a sweeping drive to the basket, or a swivel-hipped touchdown run. They are sometimes described as balletic.

Villella, I learned, had got his start in ballet through a strange set of circumstances. When he was ten years old, he was struck in the head by a baseball thrown in a sandlot game and was knocked unconscious. To keep an eye on him, his mother began dragging him along with his sister to ballet lessons.

He remembered getting his first pair of spike shoes. "It was thrilling," he said. "I can also remember getting my first ballet slippers. It was traumatic."

Ballet, to the boy, was not supposed to be "masculine." But he soon found that, in fact, it was highly athletic. "Ten minutes on stage," he told me, "is as grueling as playing a doubleheader."

Villella's vigorous dance interpretations took not only great skill, but substantial muscle, too. The differences, however, between dancer and athlete are distinct.

"The athlete is not concerned with line and form," he said. "He just wants to get the job done any way he can. In dancing, you must be theatrical, sensitive, tasteful, and have dramatic expressions."

But similarities are striking, too, Villella said. He marveled at the physical ability of Gale Sayers, then the great running back for the Chicago Bears. "He's incredible. Even when he seems off balance, Sayers still has total control of his body muscles. Just like in ballet. The best make the unnatural look natural. If Sayers had started young in the ballet, he might have been one of the best dancers ever."

Sometime after that, I saw Sayers and his wife and told them what Villella had said.

Mrs. Sayers laughed. Sayers smiled, though a bit sheepisly.

I asked what was so funny. Was it the image of Gale cavorting in tights?

"No," said Mrs. Sayers. "It's just that Gale can't dance."

1998

IRA BERKOW

New York Times sports columnist Berkow was introduced to NYCB when he interviewed Villella in 1968.

BERT STERN

A legendary Madison Avenue photographer, Stern brought an artist's touch to photographing NYCB dancers, including this moment from *Bugaku*.

Edward Villella and Allegra Kent

photograph, 1963

Untitled

To make even the body propose profundity.
Whatever beauty it has, as flesh, simple
meat, there is a sense that prolongs what
for the most part might be considered
ephemeral. That is, a performance, stops.
Unlike the demon Guttenberg produced.

But the dance, and what I have seen at the
Center especially, proposes that performance
is an artifact, as well as anybody's printed
word or hacked up metal.

What they have called "Twelve Tone Night" is
alone enough dance for most of us. (What do
we deserve?) The Pas de Deux in *Agon* is *more*
dance than we deserve. And it is an artifact
of constant vitality, even hidden and quiet
in my mind.

1961

AMIRI BARAKA
This poem was discovered in
a carton in the fifth-floor attic
"motor room" of the New York
State Theater.

MARTHA SWOPE
During the creation of *Agon*,
Swope took a series of informal
rehearsal shots that led to her
becoming NYCB's company
photographer in 1957.

Agon

photograph, 1957

How New York City Ballet Killed Broadway

Conversation overhead after theater at Orso:

Just hear me out. When I saw my first show, *Annie Get Your Gun*, at a matinee in 1946—it was my eighth birthday—I did not know for many years that I was also seeing my first ballet. Waiter? I'm drying up. The double's for Ricky—thank you—the water is for me. Is this your only water? Let me taste—fine. Not Golden Age NY tap water but—to this day I can still remember at that show being alarmed by two things—one, Ethel Merman, who was alarming enough, and, two, a wild dance to a song you couldn't get away with today called "I'm an Indian Too." The sunny funny Irving Berlin song in no way prepared me for anything like the sight of a wild Native American—another phrase unknown at that time—half naked, covered in war paint, leaping, wielding a tomahawk in a weird Indian initiation ritual that terrified the bejesus out of Merman and me. The whole stage swirled with a bedlam of savages, charging, moving in a way that I had never before seen. I didn't know it, but I was seeing my first ballet. It was choreographed by Helen Tamiris.

All those childhood years of going to musicals for birthdays, for Christmas, I never knew how much ballet I was seeing. I didn't know when I saw Ray Bolger in *Where's Charley?*, leading me in the audience in a spectacular bird dance singalong to "Once in Love with Amy" and then a Brazilian dance number where Bolger traveled to "Pernambuco (Where the Nuts Come From)"—that I was seeing my first Balanchine. I didn't know when I saw *Call Me Madam* in 1950 that I was seeing my first Jerome Robbins. I didn't know when I saw *Carousel*, I was seeing my first Agnes de Mille. I didn't know when I saw *Kiss Me Kate* or *Golden Apple* or *My Fair Lady* that I was seeing Hanya Holm. Or I was seeing Eugene Loring when I saw *Silk Stockings*. If I started sooner, I could have seen Antony Tudor in the 1945 Lerner and Loewe *Day Before Spring*, Frederick Ashton in *Four Saints in Three Acts* in 1934—okay, that doesn't count as a Broadway musical, but Leonide Massine does, and he did something called *Helen Goes to Troy* in 1944, and in 1939 you could have seen Jerome Robbins dance in the chorus of *Stars in Your Eyes* along with Nora Kaye, Alicia Alonso, Maria Karnilova, and Tamara Toumanova all giving support to Jimmy Durante and Ethel Merman. In 1944 I could have seen *On the Town*.

This is my point. Why were the musicals so great? For one reason alone. There were no ballet companies. How much of the greatness of the American musical comedy came out of that fact? Geniuses had to go somewhere to make dance. They went to Broadway. Then along comes 1948. That black year. This is not theory. This is fact. I blame Lincoln Kirstein for everything, the thing called a musical we saw tonight. Lincoln Kirstein thinks he's doing the world this big favor by founding New York City Ballet. He hires Balanchine, who never does another show. It's corporate raiding. By 1964, the plundering was through. Jerome Robbins did his last Broadway show, *Fiddler on the Roof.* The age of the great choreographer was over. It lasted from 1932, with a show called *Americana*, which had a hit song, "Brother Can You Spare a Dime?," but most historically, it featured the first serious ballet choreographed for Broadway, by the modern dancer Charles Weidman with the Doris Humphrey group. The music was by Bernard Herrmann of Hitchcock *Psycho* fame—need I say more about the state of the musical? The Golden Age lasted from 1932 to 1964. Fosse and Kidd and Bennett moved in with a new kind of show dancing—but it wasn't ballet. And shows became more technical with tracks taking precedence on the stage floor. You cannot dance serious dance on a raked floor lined with railroad tracks that allow high-tech scenery to swoop into place. I go to NYCB. I see Robbins's *I'm Old Fashioned, Glass Pieces*, they break my heart. All I think is they would have been great numbers in Broadway shows. I hate New York City Ballet. It gave too many choreographers the idea to do dances for their own companies. Ballet ghettoes. That's all they created. This water is horrible—do you remember tap? I don't mean tap dancing, Ricky. I mean, the Golden Age of New York tap water. Don't get me started on that. At the moment, I'm thinking the Golden Age of Musicals. Imagine—Vera Zorina in *I Married an Angel*.

1998

JOHN GUARE

Guare collaborated with Jerome Robbins in 1968 and then again in 1986 on a Leonard Bernstein–Stephen Sondheim musical that remains unfinished.

SAUL STEINBERG

Jerome Robbins commissioned
Steinberg to create this show
curtain for his original Ballets: USA
production of *The Concert*.

The Concert, Overture backdrop

painted muslin,
40 × 60 feet, 1956

Tour Poster

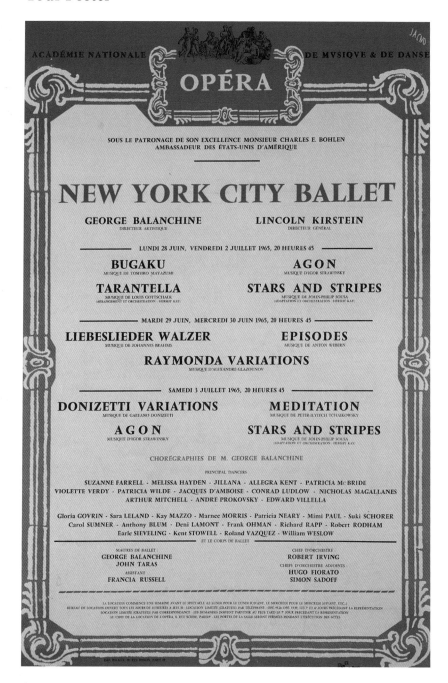

Azoulay took this photograph
of *(from left)* Arthur Mitchell,
Patricia McBride, George
Balanchine, Suzanne Farrell,
and Edward Villella atop the Paris
Opera House.

PARIS OPÉRA

**This poster publicized NYCB's
1965 appearance in Paris.**

Overlooking Paris

photograph, 1965

ESTEBAN FRANCÉS

Despite a sometimes stormy
working relationship, the collaboration between Balanchine
and Francés produced ballets
such as *Don Quixote* and
La Sonnambula.

Night Shadow, set design

gouache and cutouts,
7 4/5 × 17 inches, 1945

From *A Sculptor's World*

We breathe in, we breathe out, inward turning, alone, or outgoing, working
with others, for an experience that is cumulative through collaboration.
Theater is the latter kind. My interest is the stage where it is possible to realize
in a hypothetical way those projections of the imagination into environmen-
tal space which are denied us in actuality.

The theater of the dance in particular adds the movement of bodies, in relation
to form and space, together with music. There is joy in seeing sculpture
come to life on the stage in its own world of timeless time. Then the very air
becomes charged with meaning and emotion, and form plays its integral
part in the re-enactment of a ritual. Theater is a ceremonial; the performance
is a rite. Sculpture in daily life should or could be like this. In the meantime,
the theater gives me its poetic, exalted equivalent....

Never was I more personally involved in creation than with this piece which
is the story of the artist. I interpreted *Orpheus* as the story of the artist blinded
by his vision (the mask). Even inanimate objects move at his touch—
as do the rocks, at the pluck of his lyre. To find his bride or to seek his dream
or to fulfill his mission, he is drawn by the spirit of darkness to the nether-
world. He descends in gloom as glowing rocks, like astral bodies, levitate; and
as he enters Hades, from behind a wildly floating silk curtain the spirits of
the dead emerge. Here, too, entranced by his art, all obey him; and even Pluto's
rock turns to reveal Eurydice in his embrace (she has been married to Death,
as in the Japanese myth of Izanagi-No-Mikoto and Izanami-No-Mikoto).

With his music Orpheus, who is blinded to all material facts by the mask of
his art, leads Eurydice earthward. But, alas, he is now beset by doubts of material
possession. He tears off his mask and sees Eurydice as she really is, a creature
of death. Without the protection of his artistic powers, he is even weaker
than ordinary mortals, and he is torn apart by the Furies. But his art is not
dead; his singing head has grown heroic as his spirit returns; and as a symbol
of this resurrection, a flowering branch ascends to heaven.

1968

ISAMU NOGUCHI
Noguchi was introduced to the
theater in 1926 when he made
papier-mâché masks for the
Japanese dancer Ito Michio for
a No drama by W. B. Yeats.

JERRY L. THOMPSON
Light and shadow in Thompson's
photographs reveal a hidden
presence in otherwise still objects.

Lyre for *Orpheus*

photograph, 1998

In 1947, when Kirstein and I agreed that Ballet Society should commission a new ballet from Stravinsky, the composer consented to the project. He asked for suggestions, and I told him that I would like to do a new, modern *Orpheus*. It seemed to me that the Orpheus myth, with its powerful portrayal of the poet-musician's destiny and of his love, was particularly appropriate for ballet, and particularly a ballet with music by Stravinsky.

—George Balanchine

Tallchief in *Orpheus*

You were all of twenty-three, married
to Balanchine. The nights he spent,
absorbed, at work on "Orpheus"
you felt alone, and stayed at home,
stitching an Indian patterned skirt.
But when you danced Eurydice's

last pas de deux, you wrapped your arms
and legs around your poet husband,
"Orpheus," willing him to look
into your eyes. As Balanchine
wrote: "tormented because she cannot
be seen by the man she loves."

Attempting to seduce, you dance
the dance till finally he tears
away his mask, and you collapse
to earth and die. During rehearsal
Stravinsky asked, "How long to die?"
In the score he scratched five long counts.

The time of the ballet, "the time
of sand and snakes," "of Greek earth legends"
wrote Balanchine. And Kirstein saw
(describing their Gluck's "Orpheus")
"the eternal domestic tragedy
between an artist and his wife."

Your husband, armed with song, lays siege,
enchants the gods to claim you back,
vowing he will not look. But you
persuade him. Therefore Orpheus
throws off his mask, and loses you.
His mask becomes a lyre.

Mother, when I was young, I watched
you from the wings and saw the sweat
dripping from arms and neck, your gasp
for breath. I thought it was your last.
But no. You'd towel off, and then
step back into the spotlight, smiling.

1998

ELISE PASCHEN

Paschen is the daughter of Henry Paschen and Maria Tallchief, the dancer for whom Balanchine created *Orpheus*.

GEORGE PLATT LYNES

Lynes chronicled the early years of NYCB and its various earlier incarnations as American Ballet, Ballet Caravan, and Ballet Society. Here, Maria Tallchief.

Eurydice

photograph, 1948

The Firebird

She explodes in my memory like fire-works, scarlet, luminously fluttering across the stage of the old City Center of Music and Drama. I remember her sensual, flashing terror as Prince Igor pursued her, his dark Tartar face intent on capture. Bold hunter and sensual prey, they leapt together, they even seemed to breathe together. Then suddenly she soared, flying across the darkened space into the entanglement of his arms. My heart flew right along with her. "This is what love must be like," I thought. I was sure that the feel-ings they conjured up in the audience originated in their own hearts. I was convinced that they couldn't wait to get backstage and into each other's arms.

I was ten, and as a special, long-antici-pated treat, my mother had driven us in our secondhand Dodge Wayfarer from the suburbs into New York City. She had just learned to drive. The tickets, to see Maria Tallchief and Francisco Moncion in Igor Stravinsky's *Firebird* with George Balanchine's choreography and Marc Chagall's sets, had been ordered weeks in advance. For me the city sparkled—we had lived there until I was eight; it sparkled with what I then, at age ten, thought of as the lost promise of my youth. Was I right about Tallchief and Moncion? Of course not. I mis-took the illusion of love for the thing itself, the first of many times I made this mistake. I blame it all on New York City Ballet.

In reality, the man who owned Tallchief's heart was George Balanchine, not the man she danced with, but the man who invented the dance. Of course the Firebird doesn't love Prince Igor anyway, even in the ancient Russian legends from which the story originally came. The glorious creature is pursued and captured so that she can help Prince Igor release his chosen bride. She doesn't give him her heart; she gives him a magic feather. And did the great Tallchief, the daughter of an Oklahoma Osage Indian who became George Balanchine's first prima ballerina at nineteen years old, really love *him*? There onstage, Tallchief and Moncion created a dazzling image of a man and a woman that became my ideal—a love of pursuit and capture, a love that began with fear and proceeded with tremen-dous beauty and drama, a love forever in flight from the reality of the suburbs, the secondhand Dodge, my miserable fourth-grade life.

That was my first time at New York City Ballet, and I have gone dozens of times since then. The way the combina-tion of music and visual delight enters the heart through the sense *is* a lot like love. I fall for it again every time I go. More recently, I have been backstage, too, and seen how the greatest dancers, who are so much larger than life when they dance, are in reality small-boned people whose feet hurt. It is a small place, in the wings and behind the set where the dancers are young and intent, stretching, rubbing resin on their shoes, binding their feet.

All their energy is directed at the stage, where the illusion of love is created. And I wonder whether the connection between onstage and backstage plays itself out in our real lives.

There are three stations of the ballet— the stage, the audience, and the wings. As a child I thought what happened onstage was real—true love was that enchanted dance. Later, when I was one of a group of devoted amateurs who met at the ballet and spent intermissions in discussions of individual dances, I was sure that I was experiencing the real New York City Ballet. Now, four decades after my first *Firebird*, I'm fascinated by the mechanics of the dream. The dancers seem most real to me backstage as they stretch and listen for their cues. Who can even tell me now which of these is reality? Maybe I was right the first time.

1998

SUSAN CHEEVER

Cheever took her daughter to
the ballet for the first time
in the winter of 1998 for the
all-Balanchine program.

MARC CHAGALL

For nearly twenty years,
Chagall's name was not credited
for this backdrop on NYCB
programs because many of his
contemporaries considered
the ballet "unworthy" of the
artist's name.

Firebird, backdrop

painted muslin,
40 × 60 feet, 1945

Episodes

Dance in spring 1959 was split into two main factions: modern dance, personified by Martha Graham, and neoclassic ballet, by George Balanchine. When it was announced that the two giants would collaborate on new work, it came as a startling surprise. No less so since the man who engineered the collaboration was Lincoln Kirstein, whose militant and well-known diatribes against modern dance firmed up the firing line between the two camps. The new work was to premiere at City Center and was titled *Episodes*.

Sallie Wilson and three other Balanchine dancers were in Martha's section. I was cast in Mr. Balanchine's. (It was as if we were being traded around like hockey players.) Despite what the public and the press were told at the time, there was no further collaboration. The Anton Webern orchestral score was the only other unifying element in the two giants' widely differing approaches.

Martha's elaborately costumed Part I was about Mary, Queen of Scots, at the moment of her beheading; Balanchine's Part II, performed in practice clothes, was a less specific visualization of the music. Neither choreographer kept tabs on what the other was doing. The only known communication between them was when Martha ran out of music and asked Mr. B for some of his, a request that he graciously granted by ceding Six Pieces, Op. 6. Each half of *Episodes* turned out to be as self-subsistent as two towels—His and Hers.

Compared with Martha's rehearsals, Balanchine's approach represented a complete switch. The speed and craft with which he worked were astounding; the rehearsal time was used economically, none of it taken up by explanations of concepts, poetic imagery, or motivation.

During the course of rehearsals, Mr. B evidently decided that my section of Part II was to be a long solo. At the end of the last rehearsal, the solo's subject still remained a mystery to me. I asked Mr. B if there was any particular way that it was to be performed. "Umm," he answered, nose fidgeting and sniffing out a proper image. "Is like a fly in glass of milk, yes?"

The image was perfect. The convoluted dance, resembling the buzzing circles of something subhuman caught within a deadly vortex of its own making, seemed to be an epigram about self-ordained patterns and death.

In fact, it seemed that Mr. B was examining some of the unappetizing sides of human nature—inability to communicate, neuroticism—paring them down to the raw bones, each episode an increasingly darker view. I was especially moved by several terse consecutive duets danced by Diana Adams and Jacques d'Amboise against David Hays's portal-like set piece. Scathingly, their episode summed up the pitiful way people fail to make human contact. Grotesque it often was, but never was it fumbling or slapstick.

During the performance, while waiting an endless wait in the wings for my turn to buzz, my nervousness built into terror. It was, I felt, imperative for

modern dancers to be well represented—to match up with the best in ballet. My feeling was that ballet could learn a thing or two from us. In those days, rumor had it that if dancers were not capable of ballet, then they settled for modern. What hogwash.

With minor reservations, *Episodes* was favorably received. There were eight more performances during the season. Mr. B often watched from the wings and bowed politely when our paths crossed.

One evening he said, "You there… how you like to learn other ballets? *Apollo, Four Temperaments,* Cullberg's *Medea?*"

After seeing me rehearse them, Mr. B invited me to join his company. It was a flabbergasting honor, but one I could not accept. "Guesting" was one thing—but to become a regular member, a ballet dancer? I could never think of myself that way. I felt strongly that I had to keep heading in my own direction.

The Balanchine Part II was performed independently of Martha's Part I during City Ballet's next City Center season. I continued to perform for two more seasons with them, and when I stopped, my solo was deleted, despite my offer to teach it to another dancer.

Unrecorded at the time, except for indecipherable notes of mine, the glass-of-milk dance evaporated up into bug heaven, until revived in 1986, when I taught my part to New York City Ballet dancer Peter Frame.

1998

PAUL TAYLOR

Taylor was a guest performer
with NYCB in 1959.

DAVID HAYS

When Balanchine approached
Hays about designing *Episodes*,
the choreographer had neither a
score to play nor dances to show
and only a weekend before the
deadline. "Just do what you do,
David," said Balanchine.

Episodes, set design

watercolor, 5³/₄ × 12 inches, 1959

ROBERT RAUSCHENBERG
Created for Merce Cunningham,
Summerspace was adapted espe-
cially for NYCB in 1966.

Summerspace, backdrop and costume

painted muslin and leotard,
40 × 60 feet, 1966

An Unexpected Collaboration

I recall being present at the first set of performances of *Agon* in the late 1950s. I've seen and heard the work many times since, but never in a concert performance. As with so many other recent compositions, it isn't the mainline musical institutions of New York that present them, they are only to be found in the pit at the New York State Theater, to the accompaniment of— or rather accompanying—the stage of New York City Ballet. For a musician, this is a remarkable fact, one that reveals a unique characteristic of the ballet: musical sophistication, the taking of the new in music without polemic or condescension, simply for its own worth. If you want to hear those marvelous last works of Igor Stravinsky, say, New York City Ballet is the only place in New York where you can find them. And the same goes for many a more recent score.

This seriousness about music— the belief that the score generates the ballet, instead of serving merely as sonic wallpaper—is witnessed by one of the most extraordinary moments in my relationship with New York City Ballet. It came on a day in 1995 when Peter Martins and I were discussing our ongoing three-work collaboration. As we talked in his office, I mentioned that I had composed (almost twenty years before, in 1975) an orchestra piece called *A Reliquary for Igor Stravinsky* that incorporated and enshrined the last fragments of orchestra music that

Stravinsky had been composing shortly before his death. They had been given to me by Mrs. Stravinsky, and I had composed music around them, embedding these few short bits in a work of homage to one of the great composers of history, one to whom I have always felt especially close. Peter happened to have a recording of the piece on hand and played it immediately. His reaction was electric—I recall that he said, "This belongs in our house!"—and you can imagine my amazement that a work I had intended as a memorial, a tribute, and a rather solemn one at that, should suddenly find an entirely new life on the stage of New York City Ballet.

I was also delighted when Peter decided that just as I had paid homage to Stravinsky in my music, he would follow suit and do the same for George Balanchine with his choreography. In the event, I was very impressed by the subtlety with which Peter translated the musical into the gestural. I think a fine work resulted, and I am gratified by the happy response it has received.

I believe that for both of us, this unexpected side-collaboration has a meaning larger than its mere serendipity. So much of the core, the fabric, of New York City Ballet has come from the friendship of Balanchine and Stravinsky; their presence remains such a lively and determining one, decade after decade, that for us suddenly to fall into the intimate connection with them that the *Reliquary* affords seems almost a fated thing.

Balanchine's fine musicianship and his involvement with music of real and independent worth created the atmosphere in which my *Reliquary* could join City Ballet's repertoire; and to Stravinsky more than any other composer City Ballet owes its unique roster of dances. The more-than-shadows of those two great figures lie behind us, and for us to carry on in the same tradition is both an honor and deep satisfaction.

1998

CHARLES WUORINEN
A prolific composer, Wuorinen has been a frequent contributor of new music to NYCB's repertory in the 1990s.

JON JAMES
This is one of a series of James's abstract paintings inspired by contemporary works in NYCB's repertory.

Reliquary, 1

acrylic on canvas,
54 × 72 inches, 1996

Paper Dancer

It never came up until I met Peter Martins in his office later that day. It must have crossed my mind—that as a participatory journalist (ranging from football with the Detroit Lions to playing percussion—mostly the triangle—with the New York Philharmonic) I might inquire about a small role in a ballet. There were roles in the repertoire, after all, in which a performer has very little to do—the prince in *Swan Lake*, for example, who comes onstage and sits down to watch the dancing. I thought perhaps I could pull that off—a sweep of the robe as I settled myself onto the throne.

I watched Peter Boal, one of the Company's principal dancers, teach a class of thirteen-year-olds, all in burgundy outfits. "Hold your arms as if you were carrying a beach ball," "Move up and down as if in an elevator shaft," "Imagine yourself as a rosebud, slowly forming, and then full grown"—this last one illustrated with a graceful sweep of his arm. I followed him to the Company class. I sat by the piano. I marveled at the variety of warm-up outfits: bandannas, Mickey Mouse sweatshirts, a jacket advertising diesel oil. Watching the ballerinas exercise, I was reminded of what Henny Youngman (the comedian had died the day before), on seeing them *en pointe,* had commented: "Why don't they get taller girls?"

That afternoon there was a moment of high drama: During the performance of *The Four Seasons,* which I was watching from the wings, a ballerina hopped off the stage and collapsed, practically at my feet, with a sprained ankle. Piteous cries. Tears. One of the dancers standing over her had a streak of blood on his shin. The thought must have crossed my mind: Did I want to have anything to do with an activity so dangerous?

After the performance I took a tour of the premises, a labyrinth of corridors and stairs—the costume room, the dressing rooms, the clinic, and, far below street level, the vast storage area for stage sets. Finally, in a corner office, we looked in on Peter Martins. He rose from a sofa to shake hands—he was tall, tawny-haired, instantly recognizable, particularly for his strong jaw, which though not of Lenoesque proportions must be a caricaturist's delight. Two of his friends were in the room. One of them, aware of my participatory stints, said, "Peter, why don't you put George into one of your ballets?"

My heart jumped.

Martins's reaction was startling. "No, no, no, no, no!" he said. "Absolutely not!"

I was taken aback.

"No, no, no, no," he repeated. "The ballet is for the young, the very young."

"Not even for the young at heart?" I asked in mock desperation.

"No, no, no, no," he repeated once more, with such force that I thought he felt there must have been a *conspiracy* at hand.

"I can do an *entrechat-un,*" I said feebly.

Then, as if to compensate for his vehemence, in somewhat more moderate tones Martins began talking about a dancer, an early idol of his, who was still performing in her *eighties*: Alicia Alonso. He had seen her dance at the Met a year or so before. "She was almost entirely blind," he said. "They placed her in the middle of the stage so that when the curtain parted, there she was. She did some sort of routine, and when the curtain swung to, an arm reached out to steady her."

I could see that he wanted to get back to his friends. I thought to myself, Well, there is always Alvin Ailey, and I thanked him for his hospitality.

Two nights afterward I went as an invited guest to the Company party celebrating the close of the winter season. The midtown loft was packed. In the throng I recognized a few of the ballerinas, many of them now with their hair loose. A small band was playing. On impulse I asked one of the ballerinas, "May I have the pleasure of a dance?" I held out my hand. She took it, and as we walked to the dance floor, I said to myself, Now I can tell my grandchildren that one day I danced with a member of the New York City Ballet corps de ballet! I turned my feet slightly out as if I'd just stepped away from the barre.

1998

GEORGE PLIMPTON

Plimpton spent a typical twelve-hour day with principal dancer Peter Boal to write this piece.

PAUL CADMUS

Cadmus was first introduced to
NYCB by his brother-in-law,
Lincoln Kirstein.

Reflection

egg tempera on pressed wood
panel, 16¾ × 19⅛ inches, 1944

The Joy of Dance

I've been going to the City Ballet for at least a quarter of a century. What fun it has been (and is) to look at the corps and pick out those dancers I believe are going to move on up in the Company as principal dancer—and usually I have been right.

For instance, there was a young woman in the corps who radiated joy through the brilliance of her dancing and the smile on her face. Yes, I thought, she's a special one. She was Merrill Ashley.

One day I received a beautiful fan letter and two jars of homemade jam (one broken) from a woman who signed herself Kitty Duell. She told me that her two sons, Daniel and Joe, were with City Ballet. Dan was in the corps, and Joe was still backstage, often carrying great bouquets onto the stage for the stars.

Kitty and I corresponded for a while, and in one letter she said that Joe was very lonely. So my husband and I invited the two young men for dinner, and found them delightful.

The Company was getting ready to go on tour, and Joe was feeling lost and unready, so we invited him to stay with us until he felt pulled together enough to go back to the Company. We were comfortable with Joe, and it was like having another son living with us. Before the company left for the tour,

we gave Joe a party for his twenty-first birthday, a gathering of little ballerinas, plus one of the priests from the great cathedral of St. John the Divine, with his long beard and staff, looking like a character from a Russian drama. And of course we, my actor husband and I, a writer, were their hosts, so it was an artistically eclectic group.

As the years went on, through Joe we came to know and love Lincoln Kirstein, and I remember an evening of good food and noisy conversation about life, with Lincoln, the bearded theologian from the cathedral, and Robert Giroux, one of the great editors in the world of publishing.

Going to the ballet, watching young dancers grow and develop, is a special pleasure. The company has kept its integrity through grief, the deaths of George Balanchine and Lincoln Kirstein, never letting down the effort to be the best, to keep the repertoire of the past with honor and delight, and to add new ballets, to keep growing. In the world of the arts as in the rest of life we grow through experience, and experience includes pain as well as pleasure.

I started going to the ballet with my husband. After his death, I continued to go with my granddaughters. We'll be heading for Lincoln Center and the State Theater tomorrow night, knowing that no matter how tired we are the ballet will energize us, for the dancers not only use energy, they also give energy.

There have been nights of bittersweet tears as one of the dancers is retiring; we are watching a last performance. At the end of the evening, when the great bouquets have been carried in and presented, then the stage is pelted with flowers, and tears of appreciation for what this dancer has given to the Company, and to us, the audience, flow spontaneously.

Occasionally I will be asked, "What are you seeing tonight?" And I will usually reply, "I don't know. Whatever it is, it will be wonderful."

1998

MADELEINE L'ENGLE
L'Engle is a longtime subscriber to NYCB who has drawn inspiration from NYCB's expressions of space and time.

COSTAS
Costas has taken pictures of NYCB since 1974. Here, Merrill Ashley's last bow.

Curtain Call

photograph, 1997

Somewhere Sometimes for New York City Ballet

Somewhere in that place we call space the universe is clashing bashing
banging ganging up on meteors falling up falling down making eagles in
the void dancing eagles rising tip toe jumping high jumping tall till a new
world can be found so they dance within that place we call space
        somewhere

Sometimes in gravity's world eagles fly on Fridays scoping out a place to
perch stopping at jazz clubs stopping at fish fries resting on zoo branches
hiding from hunters taking their children to see the ballet in gravity's
world

        sometimes

me? I arabesquely stretch to reach the chow chow for the pig feet
me? I dégagé second plié relevé the Ajax to clean
me? I grand plié while still in place and watch me move
        through time and space
I know I can dance I know I can dance I know I can dance
        but no one sees me

Someone in a city apartment or on a farm or in a small town where folk
go to church where folk go on hay rides where folks lean on fences and
gossip with neighbors while some dream of pizza and all night skates and
some are wishing for hot prom dates some boy or girl is bending and
stretching and standing on toes that reach up to Saturn and grabbing a ring
they hope to hold on to to lift them on stage where we all will applaud

and they dance and they dance and they love how they twirl and they dance
        for New York City Ballet

1998

NIKKI GIOVANNI
In 1974, Giovanni, who then lived
on the Upper West Side, took her
son to his first ballet.

RICHARD CORMAN
Corman photographed
Kyra Nichols in *Pavane* in lower
Manhattan, as part of NYCB's
advertising campaign of
the 1990s.

Pavane

photograph, 1997

Those Who Dance … and Wait

New York City Ballet's audience has always had its favorite dancers, those it liked, those it loved. Most, of course, were principals or soloists, but often—far more often than is usual in a dance company—these chosen few were members of the corps, or the ensemble, as we now know it, and most of them were women, very young ones.

I don't want to write about those who went on to become principals or soloists themselves—Merrill Ashley, Lourdes Lopez, Maria Calegari, Kyra Nichols, Darci Kistler, Suzanne Farrell, among others. We know their gifts, in many cases prodigal. (Has any company had such depths in the ranks of its ensemble, season after season? In some years, the progress of dancers from the corps to soloist to principal rank was like a benign tide in full flow.) I do want to remind us of those who danced and waited, who remained corps members, for whatever reason—injuries, of course, lack of drive, reticence (yes, it exists among performers), or perhaps an unwillingness to take on the responsibilities that come with dancing principal roles. Those, that is, who danced and waited, whom I loved.

I can start in the late 1940s and early 1950s, when the company was new and each performance was a revelation of Mr. Balanchine's choreography and the phenomenally high standard of dancing. Back then at the City Center, where the audience sat closer to the stage and were on intimate performance terms with the dancers, a dreamy-looking corps member named Barbara Bocher was a kind of epitome of the type. Onstage, she carried an otherworldly aura with her, a sense that her mind might be on matters besides the ballet she was dancing. Perhaps a poem (I'd like to think), or perhaps a new boyfriend, or even tomorrow's shopping list. For me, she was the perfect corps member, never pushing, never demanding attention, yet totally memorable in every ballet she danced—while still remaining an ineffable presence just out of reach.

And so was Irene Larsson, who was in the corps at the same time—tall, lush, with fine chiseled Scandinavian features that made her one of New York City Ballet's vamps. Mr. Balanchine seemed to like the type, and they have always had a place in the company. Witness Jillana and Karin von Aroldingen, for two irresistible examples.

As the years moved on, others of my favorites emerged. There was Muriel Aasen, for one, a sharp, flirtatious dancer whose double *A* assured her prime position in any listing of the corps. Aasen had a highly intelligent presence, self-aware and alert; with her sharp, black eyes (at least they were black to me) and knowing smile, she always suggested humor and irony. Clearly, she was a smart kid who knew what she was doing.

Aasen was joined by Deborah Flomine, an exquisitely feminine dancer, whose mere presence onstage gave off the aroma of a rose just coming into full bloom. Tall and supple, with a soft lyrical style that could take an audience off guard with its sweetness, she stayed with the company for several years, then, like Aasen, took off … where?

Around the same time, Virginia Stuart took her place in the company, a place marked by longevity, unwavering devotion to Mr. Balanchine's intentions, and a radiant blondness that reminded the audience of a silent screen star. Stuart was a direct, modest, and always reliable dancer, a kind of steady talisman of the company's ideals.

More recently, Renee Estopinal brought a kind of glittery street glamour and friendly exuberance to her performances that was quintessentially New York. Her nervous, skittering walk across the stage in *Danses Concertantes* was unforgettable. Even her name, with its soft rhythmic alternations of syllables and consonants, is unforgettable.

And I remember most of all, in recent years, Nina Fedorova, who was so tall that she was positioned at the rear of the stage for most ballets, where her admirers could keep an eye on her as she elegantly and often abstractedly stroked the music as though it were a bolt of gorgeous material. Fedorova was a riveting presence, if impassive and perhaps too quiet, even when dancing full out. That she was also one of the most beautiful women ever to be a part of the company certainly helped.

Mr. Balanchine seemed to love her as much as the rest of us did and for the same reasons. Fedorova returned the compliment to Mr. Balanchine by hand-painting Easter eggs for him each spring.

Of course, not every corps dancer has to aspire to principal status. How else would we have a corps? Those who choose to hold fast—for whatever reason—powerfully mark the company's identity, probably more so than the world acknowledges. They have always made up a golden cluster. Long may they dance for City Ballet.

1998

ROBERT KOTLOWITZ
Kotlowitz saw NYCB's very first performance at City Center in 1948, which featured *Orpheus, Concerto Barocco,* and *Symphony in C.*

DANIELLE FREEDMAN
A dancer herself, Freedman shot this photograph from the wings of the New York State Theater.

Monumentum Pro Gesualdo

photograph, 1998

Farewell Performance

Art. It cures affliction. As lights go down and
Maestro lifts his wand, the unfailing sea change
starts within us. Limber alembics once more
make of the common

lot a pure, brief gold. At the end our bravos
call them back, sweat-soldered and leotarded,
back, again back—anything not to face the
fact that it's over.

You are gone. You'd caught like a cold their airy
lust for essence. Now, in the furnace parched to
ten or twelve light handfuls, a mortal gravel
sifted through fingers,

coarse yet grayly glimmering sublimate of
palace days, Strauss, Sidney, the lover's plaintive
Can't we just be friends? which your breakfast phone call
clothed in amusement,

this is what we paddled a neighbor's dinghy
out to scatter—Peter who grasped the buoy,
I who held the box underwater, freeing
all it contained. Past

sunny, fluent soundings that gruel of selfhood
taking manlike shape for one last jeté on
ghostly—wait, ah!—point into darkness vanished.
High up, a gull's wings

clapped. The house lights (always supposing, caro,
Earth remains your house) at their brightest set the
scene for good: true colors, the sun-warm hand to
cover my wet one. . . .

Back they come. How you would have loved it. We in
turn have risen. Pity and terror done with,
programs furled, lips parted, we jostle forward
eager to hail them,

more, to join the troupe—will a friend enroll us
one fine day? Strange, though. For up close their magic
self-destructs. Pale, dripping, with downcast eyes they've
seen where it led you.

1995

JAMES MERRILL

This poem appeared in *Allegro*,
the publication of the School
of American Ballet.

STEVEN CARAS

On closing night of the 1982
spring season, Caras captured
Balanchine's last public
appearance—an uncharacter-
istic encore bow.

Last Bow

photograph, 1982

JASPER JOHNS

Numbers, commissioned by
Philip Johnson, was one
of Johns's first major commissions and has remained in the
same spot (north wall,
orchestra level) of the New York
State Theater since 1964.

Numbers, sculpmetal,
9 × 14 feet, 1964

New York City Ballet Repertory 1948–1998

1948

Concerto Barocco
Music: Johann Sebastian Bach
Choreography: George Balanchine
Scenery and Costumes: Eugene Berman
    (from 1951, performed in practice clothes
    and without scenery)
Lighting: Jean Rosenthal
New York City Ballet Premiere: October 11,
    1948
first presented June 27, 1941, American
    Ballet Caravan

Orpheus
Music: Igor Stravinsky (commissioned by
    Ballet Society)
Choreography: George Balanchine
Scenery and Costumes: Isamu Noguchi
Lighting: Jean Rosenthal
New York City Ballet Premiere: October 11,
    1948
first presented April 28, 1948, Ballet Society

Symphony in C
Music: Georges Bizet
Choreography: George Balanchine
Lighting: Jean Rosenthal
New York City Ballet Premiere: October 11,
    1948
presented March 22, 1948, Ballet Society; first
    produced as *Le Palais de Cristal*, July 28,
    1947, Paris Opera Ballet

Punch and the Child
Music: Richard Arnell
Choreography: Fred Danieli
Scenario: Fred Danieli, Richard Arnell
Scenery and Costumes: Horace Armistead
Lighting: Jean Rosenthal
New York City Ballet Premiere: October 18,
    1948
first presented November 12, 1947, Ballet
    Society

Symphonie Concertante
Music: Wolfgang Amadeus Mozart
Choreography: George Balanchine
Scenery and Costumes: James Stewart
    Morcom
Lighting: Jean Rosenthal
New York City Ballet Premiere: October 18,
    1948
first presented November 12, 1947, Ballet
    Society

The Four Temperaments
Music: Paul Hindemith (commissioned by
    George Balanchine)
Choreography: George Balanchine
Scenery and Costumes: Kurt Seligmann
    (from 1951, performed in practice clothes
    and without scenery)
Lighting: Jean Rosenthal
New York City Ballet Premiere: October 25,
    1948
first presented November 20, 1946, Ballet
    Society

Serenade
Music: Peter Ilyitch Tschaikovsky
Choreography: George Balanchine
Lighting: Jean Rosenthal
New York City Ballet Premiere: October 26,
    1948
originally presented March 1, 1935, American
    Ballet; originally performed by students of
    the School of American Ballet, June 10,
    1934

The Triumph of Bacchus and Ariadne
Music: Vittorio Rieti (commissioned by
    Ballet Society)
Choreography: George Balanchine
Scenery and Costumes: Corrado Cagli
Lighting: Jean Rosenthal
New York City Ballet Premiere: November 1,
    1948
first presented February 9, 1948, Ballet
    Society

Mother Goose Suite
Music: Maurice Ravel
Choreography: Todd Bolender
Scenery and Costumes: André Derain (from
    Dreams)
New York City Ballet Premiere: November 1,
    1948
first presented 1943, American Concert Ballet

Divertimento
Music: Alexei Haieff
Choreography: George Balanchine
Lighting: Jean Rosenthal
New York City Ballet Premiere: November 2,
    1948
first presented January 13, 1947, Ballet Society

1949

Time Table
Music: Aaron Copland
Choreography: Antony Tudor
Scenery and Costumes: James Stewart
    Morcom
Lighting: Jean Rosenthal
New York City Ballet Premiere: January 13,
    1949
first presented June 27, 1941, American Ballet
    Caravan

The Seasons
Music: John Cage
Choreography: Merce Cunningham
Scenery and Costumes: Isamu Noguchi
Lighting: Jean Rosenthal
New York City Ballet Premiere: January 14,
    1949
first presented May 18, 1947, Ballet Society

The Guests
Music: Marc Blitzstein
Choreography: Jerome Robbins
Lighting: Jean Rosenthal
Premiere: January 20, 1949

Jinx
Music: Benjamin Britten
Choreography: Lew Christensen
Scenario: Lew Christensen
Costumes: Russell Hartley
Scenery and Lighting: Jean Rosenthal
New York City Ballet Premiere: November
    24, 1949
first presented April 24, 1942, Dance Players

The Firebird
Music: Igor Stravinsky
Choreography: George Balanchine
(from 1970, choreography for *Monsters* by
    Jerome Robbins)
Scenery and Costumes: Marc Chagall
Lighting: Jean Rosenthal
Premiere: November 27, 1949

Bourrée Fantasque
Music: Emmanuel Chabrier
Choreography: George Balanchine
Costumes: Karinska
Lighting: Jean Rosenthal
Premiere: December 1, 1949

Ondine
Music: Antonio Vivaldi
Choreography: William Dollar

Scenery and Costumes: Horace Armistead
Lighting: Jean Rosenthal
Premiere: December 9, 1949

1950

Prodigal Son
Music: Sergei Prokofiev
Libretto: Boris Kochno
Choreography: George Balanchine
Scenery and Costumes: re-created by Esteban
  Francés from sketches by Georges Rouault
  (added July 1950)
Lighting: Jean Rosenthal
New York City Ballet Premiere: February 23,
  1950
first presented May 21, 1929, Diaghilev
  Ballets Russes

The Duel
Music: Raffaello de Banfield
Choreography: William Dollar
Costumes: Robert Stevenson
Lighting: Jean Rosenthal
Premiere: February 24, 1950
revision of Dollar's *Le Combat*, first presented
  February 24, 1949, Ballets de Paris de
  Roland Petit, London

Age of Anxiety
Music: Leonard Bernstein
Choreography: Jerome Robbins (based on
  the poem "The Age of Anxiety" by W. H.
  Auden)
Scenery: Oliver Smith
Costumes: Irene Sharaff
Lighting: Jean Rosenthal
Premiere: February 26, 1950

Illuminations
Music: Benjamin Britten
Choreography: Frederick Ashton (based on
  poems by Arthur Rimbaud)
Scenery and Costumes: Cecil Beaton
Lighting: Jean Rosenthal
Premiere: March 2, 1950

Pas de Deux Romantique
Music: Carl Maria von Weber
Choreography: George Balanchine
Costumes: Robert Stevenson
Premiere: March 3, 1950

Jones Beach
Music: Jurriaan Andriessen
Choreography: George Balanchine and
  Jerome Robbins
Costumes: Swimsuits by Jantzen
Lighting: Jean Rosenthal
Premiere: March 9, 1950

The Witch
Music: Maurice Ravel
Choreography: John Cranko
Scenery and Costumes: Dorothea Tanning
Premiere: August 18, 1950, Royal Opera
  House, Covent Garden, London

The Fairy's Kiss (Le Baiser de la Fée)
Music and Book: Igor Stravinsky
Choreography: George Balanchine
Scenery and Costumes: Alice Halicka (from
  1937 production)
Lighting: Jean Rosenthal
New York City Ballet Premiere: November
  28, 1950
first presented April 27, 1937, American Ballet

Mazurka from "A Life for the Tsar"
Music: Mikhail Glinka
Choreography: George Balanchine
Costumes: Karinska
Lighting: Jean Rosenthal
Premiere: November 30, 1950

Sylvia: Pas de Deux
Music: Léo Delibes
Choreography: George Balanchine
Costumes: Karinska
Lighting: Jean Rosenthal
Premiere: December 1, 1950

1951

The Card Game (The Card Party)
Music: Igor Stravinsky
Choreography: George Balanchine
Scenery and Costumes: Irene Sharaff
Premiere: February 15, 1951

Pas de Trois
Music: Léon Minkus
Choreography: George Balanchine
Costumes: Karinska
Lighting: Jean Rosenthal
New York City Ballet Premiere: February 18,
  1951
first presented 1948, Grand Ballet du Marquis
  de Cuevas

La Valse
Music: Maurice Ravel
Choreography: George Balanchine
Costumes: Karinska
Lighting: Jean Rosenthal
Premiere: February 20, 1951

Lady of the Camellias
Music: Giuseppe Verdi
Choreography: Antony Tudor
Scenario: after the novel by Alexandre
  Dumas *fils*
Scenery and Costumes: Cecil Beaton
Lighting: Jean Rosenthal
Premiere: February 28, 1951

Capriccio Brillant
Music: Felix Mendelssohn
Choreography: George Balanchine
Costumes: Karinska
Lighting: Jean Rosenthal
Premiere: June 7, 1951

Cakewalk
Music: Louis Moreau Gottschalk (adapted
  and orchestrated by Hershy Kay)
Choreography: Ruthanna Boris
Scenery and Costumes: Robert Drew and
  Keith Martin
Lighting: Jean Rosenthal
Premiere: June 12, 1951

The Cage
Music: Igor Stravinsky
Choreography: Jerome Robbins
Scenery and Lighting: Jean Rosenthal
Costumes: Ruth Sobotka
Premiere: June 14, 1951

The Miraculous Mandarin
Music: Béla Bartók
Choreography: Todd Bolender
Scenario: Melchior Lengyel
Scenery and Costumes: Alvin Colt
Lighting: Jean Rosenthal
Premiere: September 6, 1951

À la Françaix
Music: Jean Françaix
Choreography: George Balanchine
Scenery: Raoul Dufy
Lighting: Jean Rosenthal
Premiere: September 11, 1951

Tyl Ulenspiegel
Music: Richard Strauss
Choreography: George Balanchine
Scenery and Costumes: Esteban Francés
Lighting: Jean Rosenthal
Premiere: November 14, 1951

Apollo, Leader of the Muses
(later called *Apollo*)
Music and Scenario: Igor Stravinsky
Choreography: George Balanchine
Costumes: Karinska
Lighting: Jean Rosenthal
New York City Ballet Premiere: November
  15, 1951
revival from American Ballet, 1937; first
  presented June 12, 1928, Diaghilev Ballets
  Russes

Swan Lake
Music: Peter Ilyitch Tschaikovsky
Choreography: George Balanchine, after
  Ivanov
Scenery and Costumes: Cecil Beaton (from
  1964–1985, Rouben Ter-Arutunian;
  from 1986, Alain Vaës)

Lighting: Jean Rosenthal (from 1964–1977,
    Rouben Ter-Arutunian; from 1978, Ronald
    Bates)
Premiere: November 20, 1951

Lilac Garden
Music: Ernest Chausson
Choreography: Antony Tudor
Scenery: Horace Armistead
Costumes: Karinska
Lighting: Jean Rosenthal
New York City Ballet Premiere: November
    30, 1951
first presented as *Jardin aux Lilas*, January 26,
    1936, Ballet Rambert, London

The Pied Piper
Music: Aaron Copland
Choreography: Jerome Robbins
Lighting: Jean Rosenthal
Piper (solo clarinet): Edmund Wall
Premiere: December 4, 1951

1952

Ballade
Music: Claude Debussy
Choreography: Jerome Robbins
Scenery and Costumes: Boris Aronson
Lighting: Jean Rosenthal
Premiere: February 14, 1952

Caracole
Music: Wolfgang Amadeus Mozart
Choreography: George Balanchine
Costumes: Christian Bérard (from
    Mozartiana, Les Ballets 1933)
Lighting: Jean Rosenthal
Premiere: February 19, 1952

Bayou
Music: Virgil Thomson
Choreography: George Balanchine
Scenery and Costumes: Dorothea Tanning
Lighting: Jean Rosenthal
Premiere: February 21, 1952

La Gloire
Music: Ludwig van Beethoven
Choreography: Antony Tudor
Scenario: Lincoln Kirstein
Scenery: Gaston Longchamp
Costumes: Robert Fletcher
Lighting: Jean Rosenthal
Premiere: February 26, 1952

Picnic at Tintagel
Music: Arnold Bax
Choreography: Frederick Ashton
Scenery and Costumes: Cecil Beaton

Lighting: Jean Rosenthal
Premiere: February 28, 1952

Scotch Symphony
Music: Felix Mendelssohn
Choreography: George Balanchine
Scenery: Horace Armistead
Women's Costumes: Karinska
Men's Costumes: David Ffolkes
Lighting: Jean Rosenthal
Premiere: November 11, 1952

Metamorphoses
Music: Paul Hindemith
Choreography: George Balanchine
Scenery and Lighting: Jean Rosenthal
Costumes: Karinska
Premiere: November 25, 1952

Harlequinade Pas de Deux
Music: Riccardo Drigo
Choreography: George Balanchine
Costumes: Karinska
Lighting: Jean Rosenthal
Premiere: December 16, 1952

Kaleidoscope
Music: Dmitri Kabalevsky
Choreography: Ruthanna Boris
Scenery and Lighting: Jean Rosenthal
Costumes: Alvin Colt
Premiere: December 18, 1952

Interplay
Music: Morton Gould
Choreography: Jerome Robbins
Scenery and Costumes: Irene Sharaff (from
    1986, costumes, Santo Loquasto)
Lighting: Jean Rosenthal
New York City Ballet Premiere: December
    23, 1952
first performed June 1, 1945, Billy Rose's
    Concert Varieties

Concertino
Music: Jean Françaix
Choreography: George Balanchine
Costumes: Karinska
Lighting: Jean Rosenthal
Premiere: December 30, 1952

1953

Valse Fantaisie
Music: Mikhail Glinka
Choreography: George Balanchine
Costumes: Karinska
Lighting: Jean Rosenthal
Premiere: January 6, 1953

Will O'the Wisp
Music: Virgil Thomson
Choreography: Ruthanna Boris
Scenery and Costumes: Dorothea Tanning
    (from *Bayou*)
Premiere: January 13, 1953

The Five Gifts
Music: Ernö Dohnányi
Choreography: William Dollar
Scenario: after a story by Mark Twain
Costumes: Esteban Francés
Premiere: January 20, 1953

Filling Station
Music: Virgil Thomson
Choreography: Lew Christensen
Scenery and Costumes: Paul Cadmus
Lighting: Jean Rosenthal
New York City Ballet Premiere: May 12, 1953
first presented January 6, 1938, Ballet Caravan

Afternoon of a Faun
Music: Claude Debussy
Choreography: Jerome Robbins
Scenery and Lighting: Jean Rosenthal
Costumes: Irene Sharaff
Premiere: May 14, 1953

The Filly (or, A Stableboy's Dream)
Music: John Colman (commissioned by
    Ballet Society)
Choreography: Todd Bolender
Scenery and Costumes: Peter Larkin
Premiere: May 19, 1953

Fanfare
Music: Benjamin Britten
Choreography: Jerome Robbins
Scenery and Costumes: Irene Sharaff
Lighting: Jean Rosenthal
Premiere: June 2, 1953

Con Amore
Music: Gioacchino Rossini
Choreography: Lew Christensen
Scenario: James Graham-Lujan
Scenery and Costumes: James Bodrero (from
    March 1954, Esteban Francés)
Premiere: June 9, 1953

1954

Opus 34
Music: Arnold Schoenberg
Choreography: George Balanchine
Scenery and Lighting: Jean Rosenthal
Costumes: Esteban Francés
Premiere: January 19, 1954

The Nutcracker
Music: Peter Ilyitch Tschaikovsky
Choreography: George Balanchine
Scenario: after the tale by E. T. A. Hoffmann
Scenery: Horace Armistead (from 1964,
   Rouben Ter-Arutunian)
Costumes: Karinska
Masks: Lawrence Vlady
Lighting and Production: Jean Rosenthal
   (from 1964, Rouben Ter-Arutunian)
Premiere: February 2, 1954

Quartet
Music: Sergei Prokofiev
Choreography: Jerome Robbins
Scenery and Lighting: Jean Rosenthal
Costumes: Karinska
Premiere: February 18, 1954

Western Symphony
Music: Hershy Kay (commissioned by New
   York City Ballet)
Choreography: George Balanchine
Scenery: John Boyt (added in 1955)
Costumes: Karinska (added in 1955)
Lighting: Jean Rosenthal
Premiere: September 7, 1954

Ivesiana
Music: Charles Ives
Choreography: George Balanchine
Lighting: Jean Rosenthal
Premiere: September 14, 1954

1955

Roma
Music: Georges Bizet
Choreography: George Balanchine
Scenery and Costumes: Eugene Berman
Lighting: Jean Rosenthal
Premiere: February 23, 1955

Pas de Trois
Music: Mikhail Glinka
Choreography: George Balanchine
Costumes: Karinska
Lighting: Jean Rosenthal
Premiere: March 1, 1955

Pas de Dix
Music: Alexander Glazounov
Choreography: George Balanchine
Costumes: Esteban Francés
Lighting: Jean Rosenthal
Premiere: November 9, 1955

Souvenirs
Music: Samuel Barber
Choreography: Todd Bolender
Scenery and Costumes: Rouben Ter-
   Arutunian
Lighting: Jean Rosenthal
Premiere: November 15, 1955

Jeux d'Enfants
Music: Georges Bizet
Choreography: George Balanchine, Barbara
   Millberg, and Francisco Moncion
Scenery and Costumes: Esteban Francés
Lighting: Jean Rosenthal
Premiere: November 22, 1955

1956

Allegro Brillante
Music: Peter Ilyitch Tschaikovsky
Choreography: George Balanchine
Costumes: Karinska
Lighting: Jean Rosenthal
Premiere: March 1, 1956

The Concert (or, The Perils of Everybody)
Music: Frédéric Chopin
Choreography: Jerome Robbins
Scenery and Lighting: Jean Rosenthal (from
   1971, scenery, Saul Steinberg, lighting,
   Ronald Bates)
Costumes: Irene Sharaff
Premiere: March 6, 1956

The Still Point
Music: Claude Debussy (transcribed for
   orchestra by Frank Black)
Choreography: Todd Bolender
Lighting: Jean Rosenthal
Premiere: March 13, 1956

Divertimento No. 15
Music: Wolfgang Amadeus Mozart
Choreography: George Balanchine
Scenery: James Stewart Morcom (from
   Symphonie Concertante; from 1966, David
   Hays; from mid-1970s, performed without
   scenery)
Costumes: Karinska
Lighting: Jean Rosenthal (from 1966, David
   Hays)
New York City Ballet Premiere: December
   19, 1956
first presented May 31, 1956, American
   Shakespeare Festival, Stratford,
   Connecticut

1957

**The Unicorn, the Gorgon and the Manticore (or,
The Three Sundays of a Poet)**
Music and Scenario: Gian Carlo Menotti
Choreography: John Butler
Scenery and Lighting: Jean Rosenthal
Costumes: Robert Fletcher
Premiere: January 15, 1957

The Masquers
Music: Francis Poulenc
Choreography: Todd Bolender
Scenery and Costumes: David Hays
Lighting: Jean Rosenthal
Premiere: January 29, 1957

Pastorale
Music: Charles Turner
Choreography: Francisco Moncion
Scenery: David Hays
Costumes: Ruth Sobotka
Lighting: Jean Rosenthal
Premiere: February 14, 1957

Square Dance
Music: Antonio Vivaldi and Arcangelo
   Corelli
Choreography: George Balanchine
Lighting: Nananne Porcher (from 1976,
   Ronald Bates)
Caller: Elisha C. Keeler
Premiere: November 21, 1957
revived 1976 without caller

Agon
Music: Igor Stravinsky (commissioned by
   George Balanchine and Lincoln Kirstein)
Choreography: George Balanchine
Lighting: Nananne Porcher
Premiere: December 1, 1957

1958

Gounod Symphony
Music: Charles Gounod
Choreography: George Balanchine
Scenery: Horace Armistead (from *Lilac
   Garden*) (from 1985, Robin Wagner)
Costumes: Karinska
Lighting: Nananne Porcher (from 1985,
   Ronald Bates)
Premiere: January 8, 1958

Stars and Stripes
Music: John Philip Sousa (adapted and
   orchestrated by Hershy Kay)
Choreography: George Balanchine
Scenery: David Hays
Costumes: Karinska
Lighting: Nananne Porcher (from 1964,
   David Hays)
Premiere: January 17, 1958

Waltz-Scherzo
Music: Peter Ilyitch Tschaikovsky
Choreography: George Balanchine
Costumes: Karinska
Lighting: Nananne Porcher
Premiere: September 9, 1958

Medea
Music: Béla Bartók (orchestrated by Herbert
   Sandberg)
Choreography: Birgit Cullberg
Costumes: Lewis Brown
Lighting: David Hays
New York City Ballet Premiere: November
   26, 1958
first presented October 31, 1950, Rikstheatern
   Gaevle, Sweden

Octet
Music: Igor Stravinsky
Choreography: William Christensen
Costumes: Lewis Brown
Lighting: David Hays
Premiere: December 2, 1958

The Seven Deadly Sins
Music: Kurt Weill
Libretto: Bertolt Brecht (translated by W. H. Auden and Chester Kallman)
Choreography: George Balanchine
Scenery, Costumes, and Lighting: Rouben Ter-Arutunian
New York City Ballet Premiere: December 4, 1958
first presented as *Les Sept Péchés Capitaux*, June 7, 1933, Les Ballets 1933, Paris

1959

Native Dancers
Music: Vittorio Rieti
Choreography: George Balanchine
Scenery and Lighting: David Hays
Women's Costumes: Peter Larkin
Jockey silks: H. Kauffman & Sons Saddlery Company
Premiere: January 14, 1959

Episodes
Music: Anton von Webern
Choreography: Martha Graham (Part I) and George Balanchine (Part II) (Part I performed for two seasons only)
Scenery and Lighting: David Hays
Costumes: Karinska (Part I only)
Premiere: May 14, 1959

1960

Night Shadow (from November 1960 called *La Sonnambula*)
Music and Book: Vittorio Rieti
Choreography: George Balanchine, staged by John Taras
Scenery and Lighting: Esteban Francés
Costumes: André Levasseur (from 1987, Scenery and Costumes, Alain Vaës; Lighting, Mark Stanley)
New York City Ballet Premiere: January 6, 1960
first presented February 27, 1946, Ballet Russe de Monte Carlo, New York

Panamerica
Music: by Latin American composers, edited by Carlos Chávez (Carlos Chávez, Luis Escobar, Alberto Ginastera, Julián Orbón, Juan Orrego Salas, Silvestre Revueltas, Hector Tosa, Heitor Villa-Lobos)

Choreography: George Balanchine, Gloria Contreras, Francisco Moncion, John Taras, and Jacques d'Amboise
Scenery and Lighting: David Hays
Costumes: Karinska and Esteban Francés
Premiere: January 20, 1960

Theme and Variations
Music: Peter Ilyitch Tschaikovsky
Choreography: George Balanchine
Costumes: Karinska (from *Symphony in C*)
Lighting: David Hays
New York City Ballet premiere: February 5, 1960
first presented September 27, 1947, Ballet Theatre, Richmond, Virginia
from 1970, performed as part of *Tschaikovsky Suite No. 3*

Tschaikovsky Pas de Deux
Music: Peter Ilyitch Tschaikovsky
Choreography: George Balanchine
Costumes: Karinska
Lighting: Jack Owen Brown (subsequently by David Hays)
Premiere: March 29, 1960

The Figure in the Carpet
Music: George Frideric Handel
Book: George Lewis
Choreography: George Balanchine
Scenery, Costumes, and Lighting: Esteban Francés
Premiere: April 13, 1960

Monumentum Pro Gesualdo
Music: Igor Stravinsky
Choreography: George Balanchine
Scenery and Lighting: David Hays (from 1974, lighting, Ronald Bates)
Premiere: November 16, 1960

Donizetti Variations (originally called *Variations from "Don Sebastian"*)
Music: Gaetano Donizetti
Choreography: George Balanchine
Scenery and Lighting: David Hays (from 1971, lighting, Ronald Bates)
Women's Costumes: Karinska
Men's Costumes: Esteban Francés (from *Panamerica*) (from 1971, Karinska)
Premiere: November 16, 1960

Liebeslieder Walzer
Music: Johannes Brahms
Choreography: George Balanchine
Scenery and Lighting: David Hays (from 1984, scenery, David Mitchell; lighting, Ronald Bates)
Costumes: Karinska
Premiere: November 22, 1960

Jazz Concert
a four-part program consisting of the ballets *Creation of the World, Ragtime, Les Biches,* and *Ebony Concerto*

Creation of the World
Music: Darius Milhaud
Choreography: Todd Bolender
Scenery and Lighting: David Hays
Premiere: December 7, 1960

Ragtime
Music: Igor Stravinsky
Choreography: George Balanchine
Scenery: Robert Drew (from *Blackface*)
Costumes: Karinska
Lighting: David Hays
Premiere: December 7, 1960

Les Biches
Music: Francis Poulenc
Choreography: Francisco Moncion
Scenery and Lighting: David Hays
Costumes: Ruth Sobotka
Premiere: December 7, 1960

Ebony Concerto
Music: Igor Stravinsky
Choreography: John Taras
Scenery and Costumes: David Hays
Premiere: December 7, 1960

1961

Modern Jazz: Variants
Music: Gunther Schuller (commissioned by New York City Ballet)
Choreography: George Balanchine
Lighting: David Hays
Premiere: January 4, 1961

Electronics
Music: Electronic tape by Remi Gassmann in collaboration with Oskar Sala
Choreography: George Balanchine
Scenery and Lighting: David Hays
Premiere: March 22, 1961

Valses et Variations (from 1963 called *Raymonda Variations*)
Music: Alexander Glazounov
Choreography: George Balanchine
Scenery: Horace Armistead (from *Lilac Garden*)
Costumes: Karinska
Lighting: David Hays
Premiere: December 7, 1961

1962

A Midsummer Night's Dream
Music: Felix Mendelssohn
Choreography: George Balanchine
Scenery and Lighting: David Hays, assisted
by Peter Harvey
Costumes: Karinska
Premiere: January 17, 1962

1963

Bugaku
Music: Toshiro Mayuzumi (commissioned
by New York City Ballet)
Choreography: George Balanchine
Scenery and Lighting: David Hays
Costumes: Karinska
Premiere: March 20, 1963

Arcade
Music: Igor Stravinsky
Choreography: John Taras
Scenery and Lighting: David Hays
Costumes: Ruth Sobotka
Premiere: March 28, 1963

Movements for Piano and Orchestra
Music: Igor Stravinsky
Choreography: George Balanchine
Lighting: Peter Harvey
Premiere: April 9, 1963

The Chase (or, The Vixen's Choice)
Music: Wolfgang Amadeus Mozart
Choreography: Jacques d'Amboise
Scenery and Lighting: David Hays
Costumes: Karinska
Premiere: September 18, 1963

Fantasy
Music: Franz Schubert
Choreography: John Taras
Premiere: September 24, 1963

Meditation
Music: Peter Ilyitch Tschaikovsky
Choreography: George Balanchine
Costumes: Karinska
Premiere: December 10, 1963

1964

Tarantella
Music: Louis Moreau Gottschalk (recon-
structed and orchestrated by Hershy Kay)
Choreography: George Balanchine
Costumes: Karinska
Premiere: January 7, 1964

Quatuor
Music: Dmitri Shostakovich
Choreography: Jacques d'Amboise
Premiere: January 16, 1964

Clarinade
Music: Morton Gould
Clarinet Solo: Benny Goodman
Choreography: George Balanchine
Costumes: Karinska
Premiere: April 29, 1964

Dim Lustre
Music: Richard Strauss
Choreography: Antony Tudor
Scenery, Costumes, and Lighting: Beni
Montresor
New York City Ballet Premiere: May 6, 1964
first presented October 20, 1943, Ballet
Theatre, New York

Irish Fantasy
Music: Camille Saint-Saëns
Choreography: Jacques d'Amboise
Scenery and Lighting: David Hays
Costumes: Karinska
Premiere: August 12, 1964, Greek Theater,
Los Angeles

Piège de Lumière
Music: Jean-Michel Damase
Choreography: John Taras
Scenario: Philippe Hériat
Scenery: Felix Labisse
Costumes: André Levasseur
Supervision and Lighting: David Hays
New York City Ballet Premiere: October 1,
1964
first presented December 23, 1952, Grand
Ballet du Marquis de Cuevas, Paris

**Tschaikovsky Piano Concerto No. 2 (originally
called *Ballet Imperial*)**
Music: Peter Ilyitch Tschaikovsky
Choreography: George Balanchine
Scenery: Rouben Ter-Arutunian (from 1973,
no scenery)
Costumes: Karinska (from 1973: new
costumes, Karinska; lighting, Ronald Bates;
from 1985: costumes, Ben Benson; from
1990: costumes, Gary Lisz; from 1991:
lighting, Mark Stanley)
New York City Ballet Premiere: October 15,
1964
first presented 1941, American Ballet
Caravan, Rio de Janeiro

1965

Pas de Deux and Divertissement
Music: Léo Delibes
Choreography: George Balanchine
Costumes: Karinska
Lighting: David Hays
Premiere: January 14, 1965

Shadow'd Ground
Music: Aaron Copland
Choreography: John Taras
Libretto and Epitaphs: Scott Burton
Costumes and Production Design: John
Braden
Premiere: January 21, 1965

Harlequinade
Music: Riccardo Drigo
Choreography: George Balanchine
Scenery, Costumes, and Lighting: Rouben
Ter-Arutunian
Premiere: February 4, 1965

Don Quixote
Music: Nicolas Nabokov (commissioned by
New York City Ballet)
Choreography: George Balanchine
Scenery, Costumes, and Lighting: Esteban
Francés, assisted by Peter Harvey
Giant: Kermit Love and Peter Saklin
Masks and Armor: Lawrence Vlady
Premiere: May 28, 1965

1966

Variations
Music: Igor Stravinsky
Choreography: George Balanchine
Lighting: Ronald Bates
Premiere: March 31, 1966

Summerspace
Music: Morton Feldman
Choreography: Merce Cunningham
Scenery and Costumes: Robert Rauschenberg
Lighting: Ronald Bates
Production Supervisor: John Braden
New York City Ballet Premiere: April 14,
1966
first presented 1958, Merce Cunningham and
Dance Company, American Dance
Festival, New London, Connecticut

Brahms-Schoenberg Quartet
Music: Johannes Brahms (orchestrated by
Arnold Schoenberg)
Choreography: George Balanchine
Scenery: Peter Harvey (from 1986, David
Mitchell)
Costumes: Karinska
Lighting: Ronald Bates
Premiere: April 21, 1966

Jeux
Music: Claude Debussy
Choreography: John Taras
Libretto: after Vaslav Nijinsky
Scenery and Costumes: Raoul Pène du Bois
Lighting: Jules Fisher
Premiere: April 28, 1966

Narkissos
Music: Robert Prince
Choreography: Edward Villella (from an idea by William D. Roberts)
Scenery, Costumes, and Lighting: John Braden
Premiere: July 21, 1966, Saratoga Performing Arts Center

Élégie
Music: Igor Stravinsky
Choreography: George Balanchine
Premiere: July 28, 1966, Saratoga Performing Arts Center
first presented July 15, 1966, Philharmonic Hall, New York

La Guirlande de Campra
Music: Georges Auric, Arthur Honegger, Francis Poulenc, Germaine Tailleferre, Daniel Lesur, Alexis Roland-Manuel, and Henri Sauguet (after a theme by André Campra)
Choreography: John Taras
Scenery: Peter Harvey
Costumes: Peter Harvey and Esteban Francés (from *The Figure in the Carpet*)
Premiere: December 1, 1966

1967

Prologue
Music: selected keyboard works of William Byrd, Giles Farnaby, and others (arranged and orchestrated by Robert Irving)
Choreography: Jacques d'Amboise
Scenery, Costumes, and Lighting: Peter Larkin
Premiere: January 12, 1967

Ragtime
Music: Igor Stravinsky
Choreography: George Balanchine
Lighting: Ronald Bates
New York City Ballet Premiere: January 17, 1967
first presented July 15, 1966, Philharmonic Hall, New York

Trois Valses Romantiques
Music: Emmanuel Chabrier (orchestrated by Felix Mottl)
Choreography: George Balanchine
Costumes: Karinska
Lighting: Ronald Bates
Premiere: April 6, 1967

Jewels
Music: "Emeralds": Gabriel Fauré, "Rubies": Igor Stravinsky, "Diamonds": Peter Ilyitch Tschaikovsky
Choreography: George Balanchine
Scenery: Peter Harvey (from 1983, Robin Wagner)
Costumes: Karinska
Lighting: Ronald Bates
Premiere: April 13, 1967

Glinkiana (later called *Glinkaiana*)
Music: Mikhail Glinka
Choreography: George Balanchine
Scenery, Costumes, and Lighting: Esteban Francés
Premiere: November 23, 1967

1968

Metastaseis & Pithoprakta
Music: Iannis Xenakis
Choreography: George Balanchine
Lighting: Ronald Bates
Premiere: January 18, 1968

Haydn Concerto
Music: Franz Joseph Haydn
Choreography: John Taras
Scenery and Costumes: Raoul Pène du Bois
Lighting: Jules Fisher
Premiere: January 25, 1968

Slaughter on Tenth Avenue
Music: Richard Rodgers (from *On Your Toes*, 1936, with new orchestration by Hershy Kay)
Choreography: George Balanchine
Scenery and Lighting: Jo Mielziner
Costumes: Irene Sharaff
Premiere: May 2, 1968

Requiem Canticles
In Memoriam: Martin Luther King Jr. (1929–1968)
Music: Igor Stravinsky
Choreography: George Balanchine
Costumes and Candelabra: Rouben Ter-Arutunian
Lighting: Ronald Bates
Premiere and only performance: May 2, 1968

Stravinsky: Symphony in C
Music: Igor Stravinsky
Choreography: John Clifford
Costumes and Lighting: John Braden
New York City Ballet Premiere: May 9, 1968
first presented May 1967, School of American Ballet

La Source
Music: Léo Delibes
Choreography: George Balanchine
Costumes: Karinska
Lighting: Ronald Bates
Premiere: November 23, 1968

1969

Tschaikovsky Suite (later called *Tschaikovsky Suite No. 2*)
Music: Peter Ilyitch Tschaikovsky
Choreography: Jacques d'Amboise
Costumes and Production Design: John Braden
Premiere: January 9, 1969

Fantasies
Music: Ralph Vaughan Williams
Choreography: John Clifford
Costumes: Robert O'Hearn
Lighting: Ronald Bates
Premiere: January 23, 1969

Prelude, Fugue and Riffs
Music: Leonard Bernstein
Choreography: John Clifford
Lighting: Ronald Bates
Premiere: May 15, 1969

Dances at a Gathering
Music: Frédéric Chopin
Choreography: Jerome Robbins
Costumes: Joe Eula
Lighting: Thomas Skelton
Premiere: May 22, 1969

Pas de Deux
Music: Anton von Webern
Choreography: Jacques d'Amboise
Production Design: John Braden
Premiere: May 29, 1969

Valse Fantaisie
(Formerly the second section of *Glinkiana*)
Music: Mikhail Glinka
Choreography: George Balanchine
Scenery, Costumes, and Lighting: Esteban Francés
Premiere: June 1, 1969

Reveries (from 1971, called *Tschaikovsky Suite No. 1*)
Music: Peter Ilyitch Tschaikovsky
Choreography: John Clifford
Costumes: Joe Eula
Lighting: Ronald Bates
Premiere: December 4, 1969

1970

In the Night
Music: Frédéric Chopin
Choreography: Jerome Robbins
Costumes: Joe Eula (from 1980, Anthony Dowell)
Lighting: Thomas Skelton (from 1990, Jennifer Tipton)
Premiere: January 29, 1970

Who Cares?
Music: George Gershwin (orchestrated by Hershy Kay)
Choreography: George Balanchine
Scenery: Jo Mielziner (from November 1970)
Costumes: Karinska (from 1983, Ben Benson)
Lighting: Ronald Bates
Premiere: February 5, 1970

Sarabande and Danse
Music: Claude Debussy (orchestration by Maurice Ravel)
Choreography: John Clifford
Costumes: Joe Eula
Lighting: Ronald Bates
Premiere: May 21, 1970

Tschaikovsky Suite No. 3
Music: Peter Ilyitch Tschaikovsky
Choreography: George Balanchine
Scenery and Costumes: Nicolas Benois
Lighting: Ronald Bates
Premiere: December 3, 1970

1971

Kodály Dances
Music: Zoltán Kodály
Choreography: John Clifford
Costumes: Stanley Simmons
Lighting: Ronald Bates
Premiere: January 14, 1971

Four Last Songs
Music: Richard Strauss
Choreography: Lorca Massine
Scenery: John Braden
Costumes: Joe Eula
Lighting: Ronald Bates
Premiere: January 21, 1971

Concerto for Two Solo Pianos
Music: Igor Stravinsky
Choreography: Richard Tanner
Costumes: Stanley Simmons
Lighting: Ronald Bates
Premiere: January 21, 1971

Concerto for Jazz Band and Orchestra
Music: Rolf Liebermann (performed by "Doc" Severinsen and the *Tonight Show* orchestra)
Choreography: George Balanchine and Arthur Mitchell
Performed with The Dance Theatre of Harlem

Lighting: Ronald Bates
Premiere and only performance: May 6, 1971

Octandre
Music: Edgar Varèse
Choreography: Richard Tanner
Lighting: Ronald Bates
Premiere: May 13, 1971

The Goldberg Variations
Music: Johann Sebastian Bach
Choreography: Jerome Robbins
Costumes: Joe Eula
Lighting: Thomas Skelton
Premiere: May 27, 1971

PAMTGG
Music: Roger Kellaway (based on themes by Stan Applebaum and Sid Woloshin)
Choreography: George Balanchine
Scenery and Lighting: Jo Mielziner
Costumes: Irene Sharaff
Premiere: June 17, 1971

1972

Printemps
Music: Claude Debussy
Choreography: Lorca Massine
Costumes: Irene Sharaff
Lighting: Ronald Bates
Premiere: January 13, 1972

Chopiniana
Music: Frédéric Chopin
Choreography: Staged by Alexandra Danilova, after Michel Fokine
Lighting: Ronald Bates
Premiere: January 20, 1972

Watermill
Music: Teiji Ito
Choreography: Jerome Robbins
Scenery: Jerome Robbins, in association with David Reppa
Costumes: Patricia Zipprodt
Lighting: Ronald Bates
Premiere: February 3, 1972

STRAVINSKY FESTIVAL, JUNE 18–25, 1972

Sonata
Music: Igor Stravinsky
Choreography: George Balanchine
Premiere: June 18, 1972

Scherzo Fantastique
Music: Igor Stravinsky
Choreography: Jerome Robbins
Lighting: Ronald Bates
Premiere: June 18, 1972

Symphony in Three Movements
Music: Igor Stravinsky
Choreography: George Balanchine
Lighting: Ronald Bates
Premiere: June 18, 1972

Violin Concerto (from 1973 called *Stravinsky Violin Concerto*)
Music: Igor Stravinsky
Choreography: George Balanchine
Lighting: Ronald Bates
Premiere: June 18, 1972

Symphony in E Flat
Music: Igor Stravinsky
Choreography: John Clifford
Costumes: Stanley Simmons
Lighting: Ronald Bates
Premiere: June 20, 1972

Concerto for Piano and Winds
Music: Igor Stravinsky
Choreography: John Taras
Costumes: Rouben Ter-Arutunian
Lighting: Ronald Bates
Premiere: June 20, 1972

Danses Concertantes
Music: Igor Stravinsky
New Choreography: George Balanchine
Scenery and Costumes: Eugene Berman (from the Ballet Russe de Monte Carlo production)
New York City Ballet Premiere: June 20, 1972
first presented September 10, 1944, Ballet Russe de Monte Carlo, with similar choreography

Octuor
Music: Igor Stravinsky
Choreography: Richard Tanner
Lighting: Ronald Bates
Premiere: June 21, 1972

Serenade in A
Music: Igor Stravinsky
Choreography: Todd Bolender
Costumes: Stanley Simmons
Lighting: Ronald Bates
Premiere: June 21, 1972

Divertimento from "Le Baiser de la Fée"
Music: Igor Stravinsky
Choreography: George Balanchine
Costumes: Eugene Berman (from *Roma*)
Lighting: Ronald Bates
Premiere: June 21, 1972

Scherzo à la Russe
Music: Igor Stravinsky
Choreography: George Balanchine
Costumes: Karinska
Lighting: Ronald Bates
Premiere: June 21, 1972

Circus Polka
Music: Igor Stravinsky
Choreography: Jerome Robbins
Lighting: Ronald Bates
Premiere: June 21, 1972

Scènes de Ballet
Music: Igor Stravinsky
Choreography: John Taras
Costumes: Karinska
Lighting: Ronald Bates
Premiere: June 22, 1972

Duo Concertant
Music: Igor Stravinsky
Choreography: George Balanchine
Lighting: Ronald Bates
Premiere: June 22, 1972

The Song of the Nightingale
Music: Igor Stravinsky
Choreography: John Taras
Costumes and Props: Rouben Ter-Arutunian
Lighting: Ronald Bates
Premiere: June 22, 1972

Piano-Rag-Music
Music: Igor Stravinsky
Choreography: Todd Bolender
Costumes: Stanley Simmons
Lighting: Ronald Bates
Premiere: June 23, 1972

Dumbarton Oaks
Music: Igor Stravinsky
Choreography: Jerome Robbins
Costumes: Patricia Zipprodt
Lighting: Ronald Bates
Premiere: June 23, 1972

Ode
Music: Igor Stravinsky
Choreography: Lorca Massine
Lighting: Ronald Bates
Premiere: June 23, 1972

Pulcinella
Music: Igor Stravinsky
Choreography: George Balanchine and
  Jerome Robbins
Scenery and Costumes: Eugene Berman
Lighting: Ronald Bates
Masks and Props: Kermit Love
Premiere: June 23, 1972

Choral Variations on Bach's "Vom Himmel Hoch"
Music: Igor Stravinsky
Choreography: George Balanchine
Chorus: Gregg Smith Singers
Scenery: Rouben Ter-Arutunian
Lighting: Ronald Bates
Premiere: June 25, 1972

Requiem Canticles
Music: Igor Stravinsky
Choreography: Jerome Robbins
Lighting: Ronald Bates
Premiere: June 25, 1972

1973

Cortège Hongrois
Music: Alexander Glazounov
Choreography: George Balanchine
Scenery and Costumes: Rouben
  Ter-Arutunian
Lighting: Ronald Bates
Premiere: May 17, 1973

An Evening's Waltzes
Music: Sergei Prokofiev
Choreography: Jerome Robbins
Scenery and Costumes: Rouben
  Ter-Arutunian
Lighting: Ronald Bates
Premiere: May 24, 1973

1974

Four Bagatelles
Music: Ludwig van Beethoven
Choreography: Jerome Robbins
Costumes: Florence Klotz
Lighting: Ronald Bates
Premiere: January 10, 1974
gala benefit preview as *A Beethoven Pas de
  Deux*, May 16, 1973

Variations Pour une Porte et un Soupir
Music: Pierre Henry
Choreography: George Balanchine
Scenery and Costumes: Rouben Ter-
  Arutunian
Lighting: Ronald Bates
Premiere: February 17, 1974

Dybbuk (later called *The Dybbuk Variations*)
Music: Leonard Bernstein (commissioned
  by New York City Ballet)
Choreography: Jerome Robbins
Scenery: Rouben Ter-Arutunian
Costumes: Patricia Zipprodt
Lighting: Jennifer Tipton
Premiere: May 17, 1974

Bartók No. 3
Music: Béla Bartók
Choreography: John Clifford
Costumes: Ardith Haddow
Lighting: Ronald Bates
New York City Ballet Premiere: May 23, 1974
first presented March 27, 1974, Los Angeles
  Ballet Theater

Saltarelli
Music: Antonio Vivaldi
Choreography: Jacques d'Amboise
Scenery and Costumes: John Braden
Lighting: Ronald Bates
Premiere: May 30, 1974

Coppélia
Music: Léo Delibes
Choreography: George Balanchine and
  Alexandra Danilova, after Marius Petipa
Book: Charles Nuitter, after E. T. A.
  Hoffmann
Scenery and Costumes: Rouben
  Ter-Arutunian
Lighting: Ronald Bates
Premiere: July 17, 1974, Saratoga Performing
  Arts Center

1975

Sinfonietta
Music: Paul Hindemith
Choreography: Jacques d'Amboise
Production Design: John Braden
Lighting: Ronald Bates
Premiere: January 9, 1975

RAVEL FESTIVAL, MAY 14–31, 1975

Sonatine
Music: Maurice Ravel
Choreography: George Balanchine
Lighting: Ronald Bates
Premiere: May 15, 1975

In G Major (originally called *Concerto in G*)
Music: Maurice Ravel
Choreography: Jerome Robbins
Scenery and Costumes: Rouben
  Ter-Arutunian (from 1984, Erté)
Lighting: Ronald Bates
Premiere: May 15, 1975

L'Enfant et les Sortilèges
Music: Maurice Ravel
Choreography: George Balanchine
Libretto: Colette (translated by Catherine
  Wolff)
Scenery and Costumes: Kermit Love
Supervising Designer: David Mitchell
Lighting: Ronald Bates
Premiere: May 15, 1975
first version by Balanchine presented
  March 21, 1925, Diaghilev Ballets Russes;
  second version presented November 20,
  1946, Ballet Society

Introduction and Allegro for Harp
Music: Maurice Ravel
Choreography: Jerome Robbins
Costumes: Arnold Scaasi
Lighting: Ronald Bates
Premiere: May 22, 1975

Shéhérazade
Music: Maurice Ravel
Choreography: George Balanchine
Lighting: Ronald Bates
Premiere: May 22, 1975

Alborada del Gracioso
Music: Maurice Ravel
Choreography: Jacques d'Amboise
Costumes: John Braden
Lighting: Ronald Bates
Premiere: May 22, 1975

**Ma Mère L'Oye (Fairy Tales for Dancers) (later
called *Mother Goose*)**
Music: Maurice Ravel
Choreography: Jerome Robbins
Scenario: Maurice Ravel, based on fairy tales
   by Charles Perrault and others
Costumes: Stanley Simmons
Lighting: Ronald Bates
Premiere: May 22, 1975

Daphnis and Chloé
Music: Maurice Ravel
Choreography: John Taras
Costumes and Production Design: Joe Eula
Lighting: Ronald Bates
Premiere: May 22, 1975

Le Tombeau de Couperin
Music: Maurice Ravel
Choreography: George Balanchine
Lighting: Ronald Bates
Premiere: May 29, 1975

Pavane
Music: Maurice Ravel
Choreography: George Balanchine
Lighting: Ronald Bates
Premiere: May 29, 1975

Une Barque sur l'Océan
Music: Maurice Ravel
Choreography: Jerome Robbins
Costumes: Parmalee Welles
Lighting: Ronald Bates
Premiere: May 29, 1975

Tzigane
Music: Maurice Ravel
Choreography: George Balanchine
Costumes: Joe Eula and Stanley Simmons
   (from *Kodály Dances*)
Lighting: Ronald Bates
Premiere: May 29, 1975

Gaspard de la Nuit
Music: Maurice Ravel
Choreography: George Balanchine
Scenery and Costumes: Bernard Daydé
   (execution supervised by David Mitchell)
Lighting: Bernard Daydé, in association
   with Ronald Bates
Premiere: May 29, 1975

Sarabande and Danse
Music: Claude Debussy (orchestrated by
   Maurice Ravel)
Choreography: Jacques d'Amboise
Costumes: John Braden
Lighting: Ronald Bates
Premiere: May 29, 1975

Chansons Madécasses
Music: Maurice Ravel
Choreography: Jerome Robbins
Lighting: Ronald Bates
Premiere: May 29, 1975

Rapsodie Espagnole
Music: Maurice Ravel
Choreography: George Balanchine
Costumes: Michael Avedon
Lighting: Ronald Bates
Premiere: May 29, 1975

————————————

The Steadfast Tin Soldier
Music: Georges Bizet
Choreography: George Balanchine
Scenery and Costumes: David Mitchell
Lighting: Ronald Bates
Premiere: July 30, 1975, Saratoga Performing
   Arts Center

1976

Chaconne
Music: Christoph Willibald von Gluck
Choreography: George Balanchine
Costumes: Karinska (added Spring 1976)
Lighting: Ronald Bates
Premiere: January 22, 1976

Union Jack
Music: Hershy Kay (adapted from traditional
   British sources) (commissioned by New
   York City Ballet)
Choreography: George Balanchine
Scenery and Costumes: Rouben
   Ter-Arutunian
Scottish Costumes: Sheldon M. Kasman
Lighting: Ronald Bates
Premiere: May 13, 1976

Other Dances
Music: Frédéric Chopin
Choreography: Jerome Robbins
Costumes: Santo Loquasto
Lighting: Ronald Bates

New York City Ballet Premiere:
   November 26, 1976
first presented May 9, 1976, Metropolitan
   Opera House, Gala Benefit for the Library
   of the Performing Arts at Lincoln Center

1977

Bournonville Divertissements
Music: S. Holger Paulli, Hans Christian
   Lumbye, Edvard Helsted, J. Paulli
Choreography: August Bournonville, staged
   by Stanley Williams
Scenery: Alain Vaës (from 1987)
Costumes: Ben Benson (after original
   designs)
Lighting: Ronald Bates (from 1987, Mark
   Stanley)
Premiere: February 3, 1977

Étude for Piano
Music: Alexander Scriabin
Choreography: George Balanchine
Costumes: Christina Giannini
Lighting: Ronald Bates
New York City Ballet Premiere: June 12, 1977
first presented June 4, 1977, Spoleto Festival,
   Charleston, SC

Vienna Waltzes
Music: Johann Strauss II, Franz Lehár,
   Richard Strauss
Choreography: George Balanchine
Scenery: Rouben Ter-Arutunian
Costumes: Karinska
Lighting: Ronald Bates
Premiere: June 23, 1977

1978

Ballo della Regina
Music: Giuseppe Verdi
Choreography: George Balanchine
Costumes: Ben Benson
Lighting: Ronald Bates
Premiere: January 12, 1978

Calcium Light Night
Music: Charles Ives
Choreography: Peter Martins
Scenery: Steven Rubin
Lighting: Ronald Bates
New York City Ballet Premiere: January 19,
   1978
first presented November 15, 1977, Spokane,
   Washington

Kammermusik No. 2
Music: Paul Hindemith
Choreography: George Balanchine
Costumes: Ben Benson
Lighting: Ronald Bates
Premiere: January 26, 1978

Tricolore
Music: Georges Auric (commissioned by New York City Ballet)
Ballet conceived and supervised by George Balanchine
Choreography: Peter Martins, Jean-Pierre Bonnefoux, Jerome Robbins
Scenery and Costumes: Rouben Ter-Arutunian
Lighting: Ronald Bates
Premiere: May 18, 1978

A Sketch Book
Music: George Frideric Handel, Heinrich von Biber, Gioacchino Rossini, Georg Philipp Telemann, Giuseppe Verdi
Choreography: Jerome Robbins and Peter Martins
Lighting: Ronald Bates
Premiere: June 8, 1978

1979

The Four Seasons
Music: Giuseppe Verdi
Choreography: Jerome Robbins
Scenery and Costumes: Santo Loquasto
Lighting: Ronald Bates
Premiere: January 18, 1979

Opus 19/The Dreamer
Music: Sergei Prokofiev
Choreography: Jerome Robbins
Costumes: Ben Benson
Lighting: Ronald Bates
Premiere: June 14, 1979

Giardino di Scarlatti (later called _Sonate di Scarlatti_)
Music: Domenico Scarlatti
Choreography: Peter Martins
Costumes: Ben Benson
Lighting: Ronald Bates
Premiere: July 13, 1979, Saratoga Performing Arts Center

1980

Suite of Dances (from _The Dybbuk Variations_)
Music: Leonard Bernstein
Choreography: Jerome Robbins
Costumes: Ben Benson
Lighting: Ronald Bates
Premiere: January 17, 1980

Eight Easy Pieces
Music: Igor Stravinsky
Choreography: Peter Martins
New York City Ballet Premiere: January 24, 1980

first presented June 16, 1980, Alice Tully Hall, Gala Benefit for the Library of the Performing Arts at Lincoln Center

Fancy Free
Music: Leonard Bernstein
Choreography: Jerome Robbins
Scenery: Oliver Smith
Costumes: Kermit Love
Lighting: Ronald Bates
New York City Ballet Premiere: January 31, 1980
first presented April 18, 1944, Ballet Theatre

Ballade
Music: Gabriel Fauré
Choreography: George Balanchine
Scenery and Costumes: Rouben Ter-Arutunian (from _Tricolore_) (from 1982, costumes, Ben Benson)
Lighting: Ronald Bates
Premiere: May 8, 1980

Walpurgisnacht Ballet
Music: Charles Gounod
Choreography: George Balanchine, staged by Brigitte Thom
Costumes: Karinska (from 1984)
Lighting: Ronald Bates
New York City Ballet Premiere: May 15, 1980
first presented June 3, 1975, Paris Opera Ballet

Le Bourgeois Gentilhomme
Music: Richard Strauss
Choreography: George Balanchine
Scenery and Costumes: Rouben Ter-Arutunian
Lighting: Ronald Bates
New York City Ballet Premiere: May 22, 1980
first presented April 8, 1979, New York City Opera

Robert Schumann's "Davidsbündlertänze"
Music: Robert Schumann
Choreography: George Balanchine
Scenery and Costumes: Rouben Ter-Arutunian
Lighting: Ronald Bates
Premiere: June 19, 1980

Lille Suite
Music: Carl Nielsen
Choreography: Peter Martins
Costumes: Ben Benson (after a concept by Otto Nielsen)
Lighting: Ronald Bates
New York City Ballet Premiere: October 10, 1980, John F. Kennedy Center, Washington, D.C.
first presented August 23, 1980, Tivoli Concert Hall, Copenhagen

Rondo
Music: Wolfgang Amadeus Mozart
Choreography: Jerome Robbins
Lighting: Ronald Bates
Premiere: November 11, 1980

1981

Suite from Histoire du Soldat
Music: Igor Stravinsky
Choreography: Peter Martins
Costumes: Ben Benson
Lighting: Ronald Bates
Premiere: January 29, 1981

TSCHAIKOVSKY FESTIVAL, JUNE 4–14, 1981
* Throughout the Festival and until the end of the New York season on June 28, the scenery was an architectural structure with movable ranks of translucent plastic cylinders by Philip Johnson and John Burgee, in arrangements and with lighting designs by Ronald Bates.

Mozartiana
Music: Peter Ilyitch Tschaikovsky
New Choreography: George Balanchine
Costumes: Rouben Ter-Arutunian
Lighting: Ronald Bates
New York City Ballet Premiere: June 4, 1981

Capriccio Italien
Music: Peter Ilyitch Tschaikovsky
Choreography: Peter Martins
Lighting: Ronald Bates
New York City Ballet Premiere: June 4, 1981
(performed by students from the School of American Ballet)
first presented May 9, 1981, School of American Ballet

Andantino
Music: Peter Ilyitch Tschaikovsky
Choreography: Jerome Robbins
Costumes: Ben Benson
Lighting: Ronald Bates
Premiere: June 4, 1981

Souvenir de Florence
Music: Peter Ilyitch Tschaikovsky
Choreography: John Taras
Costumes: Rouben Ter-Arutunian
Lighting: Ronald Bates
Premiere: June 5, 1981

Concert Fantasy
Music: Peter Ilyitch Tschaikovsky
Choreography: Jacques d'Amboise
Costumes: Ben Benson
Lighting: Ronald Bates
Premiere: June 5, 1981

Symphony No. 1
Music: Peter Ilyitch Tschaikovsky
Choreography: Peter Martins
Costumes: Ben Benson
Lighting: Ronald Bates
Premiere: June 6, 1981

Scherzo: Opus 42
Music: Peter Ilyitch Tschaikovsky
Choreography: Jacques d'Amboise
Costumes: Ben Benson
Lighting: Ronald Bates
Premiere: June 7, 1981

Tempo di Valse

1. Garland Dance from *The Sleeping Beauty*, Act II
Music: Peter Ilyitch Tschaikovsky
Choreography: George Balanchine
Costumes: Karinska and Rouben
  Ter-Arutunian
Lighting: Ronald Bates

2. Valse Scherzo
Music: Peter Ilyitch Tschaikovsky
Choreography: Jacques d'Amboise
Costumes: Rouben Ter-Arutunian
Lighting: Ronald Bates

3. *"Waltz of the Flowers"* from *The Nutcracker*
Music: Peter Ilyitch Tschaikovsky
Choreography: George Balanchine (from
  The Nutcracker, first presented February 2,
  1954)
Costumes: Karinska
Lighting: Ronald Bates

4. Valse à Cinq Temps
Music: Peter Ilyitch Tschaikovsky
Choreography: Jerome Robbins
Lighting: Ronald Bates

5. *Variation VI* from *Trio in A Minor*
Music: Peter Ilyitch Tschaikovsky
Choreography: John Taras
Lighting: Ronald Bates

6. *Waltz* from *Eugen Onegin*, Act I
Music: Peter Ilyitch Tschaikovsky
Choreography: John Taras
Lighting: Ronald Bates
Premiere: June 9, 1981

Piano Pieces
Music: Peter Ilyitch Tschaikovsky
Choreography: Jerome Robbins
Costumes: Ben Benson
Lighting: Ronald Bates
Premiere: June 11, 1981

Introduction and Fugue from Suite No. 1
Music: Peter Ilyitch Tschaikovsky
Choreography: Joseph Duell
Costumes: Ben Benson
Lighting: Ronald Bates
Premiere: June 12, 1981

Hungarian Gypsy Airs
Music: Sophie Menter (orchestrated by Peter
  Ilyitch Tschaikovsky)
Choreography: George Balanchine
Costumes: Ben Benson
Lighting: Ronald Bates
Premiere: June 13, 1981

Allegro con Gracia
Music: Peter Ilyitch Tschaikovsky
Choreography: Jerome Robbins
Costumes: Ben Benson
Lighting: Ronald Bates
Premiere: June 14, 1981

Adagio Lamentoso
Music: Peter Ilyitch Tschaikovsky
Choreography: George Balanchine
Costumes: Rouben Ter-Arutunian
Lighting: Ronald Bates
Premiere: June 14, 1981
(one performance only)

1982

The Magic Flute
Music: Riccardo Drigo
Choreography: Peter Martins
Scenery: David Mitchell
Costumes: Ben Benson
Lighting: Ronald Bates
New York City Ballet Premiere: January 21,
  1982
first presented May 9, 1981, School of
  American Ballet

Gershwin Concerto
Music: George Gershwin
Choreography: Jerome Robbins
Scenery and Costumes: Santo Loquasto
Lighting: Ronald Bates
Premiere: February 4, 1982

STRAVINSKY CENTENNIAL
CELEBRATION, JUNE 10–18, 1982

*Throughout the Stravinsky Centennial, the
  scenery was an architectural structure with
  movable ranks of translucent plastic cylinders
  by Philip Johnson and John Burgee, in
  arrangements and with lighting designs by
  Ronald Bates, originally created for the
  Tschaikovsky Festival in 1981.

Tango
Music: Igor Stravinsky
Choreography: George Balanchine
Lighting: Ronald Bates
Premiere: June 10, 1982

Piano-Rag-Music
Music: Igor Stravinsky
Choreography: Peter Martins
Costumes: Ben Benson
Lighting: Ronald Bates
Premiere: June 10, 1982

Pastorale
Music: Igor Stravinsky
Choreography: Jacques d'Amboise
Costumes: Ben Benson
Lighting: Ronald Bates
Premiere: June 10, 1982

Concerto for Piano and Wind Instruments
Music: Igor Stravinsky
Choreography: John Taras
Costumes: Rouben Ter-Arutunian
Lighting: Ronald Bates
Premiere: June 10, 1982

Noah and the Flood
Music: Igor Stravinsky
Choreography: George Balanchine, assisted
  by Jacques d'Amboise
Production Design: Rouben Ter-Arutunian
Lighting: Ronald Bates
Premiere: June 11, 1982
first staging of production for CBS-TV June
  14, 1962

Serenade en La
Music: Igor Stravinsky
Choreography: Jacques d'Amboise
Costumes: Ben Benson
Lighting: Ronald Bates
Premiere: June 12, 1982

Norwegian Moods
Music: Igor Stravinsky
Choreography: Lew Christensen
Costumes: Ben Benson
Lighting: Ronald Bates
New York City Ballet Premiere: June 12, 1982
first presented April 10, 1976, San Francisco
  Ballet

Concerto for Two Solo Pianos
Music: Igor Stravinsky
Choreography: Peter Martins
Costumes: Ben Benson
Lighting: Ronald Bates
Premiere: June 13, 1982

Élégie
Music: Igor Stravinsky
New Choreography: George Balanchine
Lighting: Ronald Bates
Premiere: June 13, 1982
first presented July 28, 1966, Saratoga
    Performing Arts Center

Four Chamber Works
Music: Igor Stravinsky
Choreography: Jerome Robbins
Scenery: Lawrence Wilder
Lighting: Ronald Bates
Premiere: June 16, 1982

Perséphone
Music: Igor Stravinsky
Choreography: George Balanchine, John
    Taras, Vera Zorina
Text: André Gide
Production Design: Kermit Love
Lighting: Ronald Bates
Premiere: June 18, 1982

Variations for Orchestra
Music: Igor Stravinsky
Choreography: George Balanchine
Lighting: Ronald Bates
Premiere: July 2, 1982

La Création du Monde
Music: Darius Milhaud
Choreography: Joseph Duell
Costumes: Ben Benson (set and costumes by
    David Mitchell for New York Premiere,
    November 18, 1982)
Lighting: Ronald Bates
New York City Ballet Premiere: July 14, 1982,
    Saratoga Performing Arts Center
(performed by students from the School of
    American Ballet)
first presented June 2, 1981, School of
    American Ballet

1983

Celebration
Music: Felix Mendelssohn
Choreography: Jacques d'Amboise
Costumes: Ben Benson
Production Design: Ronald Bates
Premiere: January 20, 1983

Delibes Divertissement
Music: Léo Delibes
Choreography: Peter Martins
Costumes: Ben Benson
Lighting: Ronald Bates

New York City Ballet Premiere: February 3,
    1983
first presented May 1, 1982, School of
    American Ballet

Rossini Quartets
Music: Gioacchino Rossini
Choreography: Peter Martins
Scenery: David Mitchell
Costumes: Ben Benson
Lighting: Ronald Bates
Premiere: February 10, 1983

Glass Pieces
Music: Philip Glass
Choreography: Jerome Robbins
Production Design: Jerome Robbins and
    Ronald Bates
Costumes: Ben Benson
Lighting: Ronald Bates
Premiere: May 12, 1983

Ballet d'Isoline
Music: André Messager
Choreography: Helgi Tomasson
Costumes: Ben Benson
Lighting: Ronald Bates
New York City Ballet Premiere: June 9, 1983
first presented April 30, 1981, School of
    American Ballet

I'm Old Fashioned
Music: Morton Gould (based on a theme by
    Jerome Kern)
Choreography: Jerome Robbins
Costumes: Florence Klotz
Lighting: Ronald Bates
Premiere: June 16, 1983

Tango
Music: Igor Stravinsky
Choreography: Peter Martins
Costumes: Ben Benson
Lighting: Ronald Bates
Premiere: September 14, 1983, Tivoli Concert
    Hall, Copenhagen (conceived for "A
    Choreographer's Notebook: Stravinsky
    Piano Ballets by Peter Martins" on *Dance
    in America*)

1984

A Schubertiad
Music: Franz Schubert
Choreography: Peter Martins
Scenery: Federico Pallavicini
Costumes: Ben Benson
Lighting: Chenault Spence
Production Supervisor: Ronald Bates
Premiere: January 26, 1984

Antique Epigraphs
Music: Claude Debussy
Choreography: Jerome Robbins
Costumes: Florence Klotz
Lighting: Jennifer Tipton
Premiere: February 2, 1984

Moves
Choreography: Jerome Robbins
Lighting: Jennifer Tipton
New York City Ballet Premiere: May 2, 1984
first presented July 3, 1959, Ballets: USA

Réjouissance
Music: Johann Sebastian Bach
Choreography: Peter Martins
Lighting: Ronald Bates
Premiere: May 17, 1984

Brahms/Handel
Music: Johannes Brahms/ *Variations and
    Fugue on a Theme by Handel* (orchestrated
    by Edmund Rubbra)
Choreography: Jerome Robbins and Twyla
    Tharp
Costumes: Oscar de la Renta
Lighting: Jennifer Tipton
Premiere: June 7, 1984

Menuetto
Music: Wolfgang Amadeus Mozart
Choreography: Helgi Tomasson
Costumes: Jose Verona
Lighting: Ronald Bates
Premiere: July 17, 1984, Saratoga Performing
    Arts Center

Seven by Five
Music: Camille Saint-Saëns
Choreography: Bart Cook
Lighting: Ronald Bates
Premiere: July 17, 1984, Saratoga Performing
    Arts Center

1985

Poulenc Sonata
Music: Francis Poulenc
Choreography: Peter Martins
Lighting: Ronald Bates
Premiere: January 17, 1985

Eight Lines
Music: Steve Reich
Choreography: Jerome Robbins
Costumes: Florence Klotz
Lighting: Ronald Bates
Premiere: February 14, 1985

Valse Triste
Music: Jean Sibelius
Choreography: Peter Martins
Lighting: Ronald Bates
Premiere: May 23, 1985

Eight More
Music: Igor Stravinsky
Choreography: Peter Martins
Lighting: Ronald Bates
Premiere: May 23, 1985

In Memory Of . . .
Music: Alban Berg
Choreography: Jerome Robbins
Scenery: David Mitchell
Costumes: Dain Marcus
Lighting: Jennifer Tipton
Premiere: June 13, 1985

Eight Miniatures
Music: Igor Stravinsky
Choreography: Peter Martins
Lighting: Ronald Bates
Premiere: July 17, 1985, Saratoga Performing
   Arts Center

Shadows
Music: Frank Martin
Choreography: Jean-Pierre Bonnefoux
Scenery and Costumes: Alain Vaës
Lighting: Ronald Bates
Premiere: November 21, 1985

1986

Songs of the Auvergne
Music adapted and orchestrated:
   Marie-Joseph Canteloube
Choreography: Peter Martins
Scenery and Costumes: Alain Vaës
Lighting: Ronald Bates
Singer: Frederica von Stade
Premiere: February 6, 1986

Quiet City
Music: Aaron Copland
Choreography: Jerome Robbins
Lighting: Jennifer Tipton
Premiere: May 8, 1986

Piccolo Balletto
Music: Igor Stravinsky
Choreography: Jerome Robbins
Scenery and Costumes: Santo Loquasto
Lighting: Ronald Bates
Premiere: June 5, 1986

1987

Les Petits Riens
Music: Wolfgang Amadeus Mozart
Choreography: Peter Martins
Costumes: Barbara Matera
Lighting: Mark Stanley
Premiere: January 15, 1987

Ecstatic Orange
Music: Michael Torke ("Green" and
   "Purple" added June 11, 1987; "Purple"
   commissioned by New York City Ballet)
Choreography: Peter Martins
Costumes: Stephen Sprouse
Lighting: Mark Stanley
Premiere: January 15, 1987

Sinfonia Mistica
Music: Andrezej Panufnik
Choreography: Paul Mejia
Costumes: Barbara Matera
Lighting: Mark Stanley
Premiere: February 5, 1987

Les Gentilhommes
Music: George Frideric Handel
Choreography: Peter Martins
Costumes: Alain Vaës
Lighting: Mark Stanley
Premiere: May 14, 1987

1988

Ives, Songs
Music: Charles Ives
Choreography: Jerome Robbins
Scenery: David Mitchell
Costumes: Florence Klotz
Lighting: Jennifer Tipton
Singer: Timothy Nolan
Premiere: February 4, 1988

AMERICAN MUSIC FESTIVAL, APRIL
26–MAY 15, 1988

Sophisticated Lady
Music: Duke Ellington (orchestrated by
   André Kostelanetz)
Choreography: Peter Martins
Costumes: Karinska
Miss Farrell's Dress: Barbara Matera
Miss Farrell's Jewelry: Van Cleef and Arpels
Lighting: Mark Stanley
Premiere: April 26, 1988

Tanzspiel
Music: Ellen Taaffe Zwilich (commissioned
   by New York City Ballet)
Choreography: Peter Martins
Costumes: Barbara Matera
Lighting: Mark Stanley
Premiere: April 27, 1988

Jubilee!
Music: Hershy Kay (after Louis Moreau
   Gottschalk)
Choreography: Joseph Duell (staged by
   Leslie Peck)
Costumes: Mimi Maxmen
Lighting: Mark Stanley
New York City Ballet Premiere: April 28, 1988
(performed by students from the School of
   American Ballet)
first presented May 12, 1980, School of
   American Ballet

Five
Music: Charles Wuorinen (commissioned by
   New York City Ballet)
Choreography: Jean-Pierre Bonnefoux
Scenery: Gary Stephan
Scenery Supervision: Mark Stanley
Costumes: Barbara Matera
Lighting: Mark Stanley
Premiere: April 28, 1988

Archetypes
Music: Paul Schwartz (commissioned by
   New York City Ballet)
Choreography: Robert Weiss
Scenery and Costumes: Steven Rubin, based
   on images of artist Jonathan Borofsky
Lighting: Mark Stanley
Premiere: April 29, 1988

Rhapsody in Blue
Music: George Gershwin (arranged by
   Ferde Grofe)
Choreography: Lar Lubovitch
Costume Supervision: Barbara Matera
Lighting: Mark Stanley
Premiere: April 29, 1988

Into the Hopper
Music: William Bolcom
Choreography: Bart Cook
Scenery: Huck Snyder
Film Sequence: Dennis Diamond and
   Edward M. Greenberg
Costume Supervision: Holly Hynes
Lighting: Mark Stanley
Premiere: April 30, 1988

The Unanswered Question
Music: Charles Ives
Choreography: Eliot Feld
Properties: Eliot Feld and Peter Hauser
Costumes: Willa Kim
Lighting: Allen Lee Hughes
Guest Violinist: Paul Zucofsky
Guest Pianist: Jeananne Albee
Guest Performers: James Sewell and
   Buffy Miller
Premiere: April 30, 1988

Woodland Sketches
Music: Edward MacDowell, orchestrated by
    Camarata
Choreography: Robert La Fosse
Scenery: David Mitchell
Costumes: Gary Lisz
Costume Supervision: Holly Hynes
Lighting: Mark Stanley
Premiere: May 5, 1988

Sonatas and Interludes
Music: John Cage
Choreography: Richard Tanner
Lighting: Mark Stanley
New York City Ballet Premiere: May 5, 1988
first presented April 17, 1982, by the Eglevsky
    Ballet

The Waltz Project
Music: Milton Babbitt, John Cage, Tom
    Constanten, Joseph Fennimore, Peter
    Gena, Philip Glass, Morton Gould, Lou
    Harrison, Robert Moran, Roger Sessions,
    Ivan Tcherepnin, Virgil Thomson, Joan
    Tower
Choreography: Peter Martins
Drawings: Andy Warhol
Scenery and Costumes: Alain Vaës
Lighting: Mark Stanley
Premiere: May 5, 1988

Space
Music: Steve Reich
Choreography: ©Laura Dean
Costume Supervision: Holly Hynes
Lighting: Mark Stanley
Premiere: May 5, 1988

The Newcomers
Music: David Diamond
Choreography: Miriam Mahdaviani
Costume Supervision: Holly Hynes
Lighting: Mark Stanley
Premiere: May 7, 1988

Black & White
Music: Michael Torke (commissioned by
    New York City Ballet)
Choreography: Peter Martins
Lighting: Mark Stanley
Guest Conductor: David Alan Miller
Premiere: May 7, 1988

Behind the China Dogs
Music: Leslie Stuck (commissioned by New
    York City Ballet)
Choreography: William Forsythe
China Dogs: Cara Perlman
Costumes: Barbara Matera/William Forsythe
Lighting: Mark Stanley
Premiere: May 7, 1988

Set of Seven
Music: Mary Jeanne van Appledorn
Choreography: Violette Verdy
Costumes: Alain Vaës
Lighting: Mark Stanley
Guest Pianist: Virginia Eskin
Premiere: May 10, 1988

Tea-Rose
Music: George Gershwin (orchestrated by
    Michael Tilson Thomas, Larry Moore, and
    George Gershwin)
Choreography: Peter Martins
Costumes: Oscar de la Renta
Lighting: Mark Stanley
Guest Conductor/Pianist: Michael Tilson
    Thomas
Premiere: May 10, 1988

Barber Violin Concerto
Music: Samuel Barber
Choreography: Peter Martins
Costumes: William Ivey Long
Lighting: Jennifer Tipton
Guest Violinist: Nadja Salerno-Sonnenberg
Guest Performers: Kate Johnson and David
    Parsons
Premiere: May 12, 1988

Danbury Mix
Music: Charles Ives
Choreography: Paul Taylor
Scenery: David Gropman
Costumes: William Ivey Long
Lighting: Jennifer Tipton
Guest Performers: The Paul Taylor Dance
    Company
Premiere: May 12, 1988

Baroque Variations
Music: Lukas Foss
Choreography: Ib Andersen
Costume Supervision: Barbara Matera
Lighting: Mark Stanley
Premiere: May 14, 1988

The Chairman Dances
Music: John Adams
Choreography: Peter Martins
Scenery and Costumes: Rouben
    Ter-Arutunian
Lighting: Mark Stanley
Premiere: May 14, 1988

The Bounding Line
Music: Aaron Copland
Choreography: Christopher d'Amboise
Scenery: April Gornik
Costumes: Mary Jane Marcasiano
Costume Supervision: Holly Hynes
Lighting: Mark Stanley
Premiere: May 14, 1988

A Fool for You
Music: Ray Charles, Hoagy
    Carmichael/Stuart Gorrell, Memphis
    Curtis, Henry Glover, Oscar
    Hammerstein/Jerome Kern, Percy
    Mayfield, A. Nugetre
Choreography: Peter Martins
Costume Supervision: Barbara Matera
Lighting: Mark Stanley
Guest Artists: Ray Charles, The Original Ray
    Charles Orchestra and the Raeletts
Premiere: May 14, 1988

Fred and George
Part I
Music: Fred Astaire and Van Phillips
Lyrics: Desmond Carter
Choreography: Peter Martins
Miss Nichols's Dress: Oscar de la Renta
Lighting: Mark Stanley
Part II
Music and Lyrics: George Balanchine
Choreography: Peter Martins
Lighting: Mark Stanley
Piano Solo: George Balanchine
Premiere: May 15, 1988

1989

Beethoven Romance
Music: Ludwig van Beethoven
Choreography: Peter Martins
Costumes: Heather Watts
Lighting: Mark Stanley
Premiere: February 2, 1989

Mozart Serenade
Music: Wolfgang Amadeus Mozart
Choreography: Peter Martins
Costumes: Barbara Matera
Lighting: Mark Stanley
Premiere: February 2, 1989

Echo
Music: Michael Torke (commissioned by
    New York City Ballet)
Choreography: Peter Martins
Costumes: Gary Lisz
Lighting: Mark Stanley
Premiere: June 15, 1989

1990

Four Gnossiennes
Music: Erik Satie
Choreography: Peter Martins
Lighting: Mark Stanley
New York City Ballet Premiere: February 25,
    1990
first presented May 17, 1986, School of
    American Ballet

Prague Symphony
Music: Wolfgang Amadeus Mozart
Choreography: Richard Tanner
Costumes: Steven Rubin
Lighting: Mark Stanley
Premiere: February 8, 1990

Fearful Symmetries
Music: John Adams
Choreography: Peter Martins
Costumes: Steven Rubin
Lighting: Mark Stanley
Premiere: May 3, 1990

A Mass (Missa Sicca)
Music: Michael Torke (commissioned by
    Lincoln Kirstein)
Baritone: William Stone
Staged by: Peter Martins and Robert La Fosse
Architecture: Philip Johnson (rendered for
    stage by Alain Vaës)
Lighting: Mark Stanley
Premiere: June 27, 1990

1991

Waltz Trilogy
Music: Carl Maria von Weber
Choreography: Robert La Fosse
Costumes: Gary Lisz
Lighting: Stan Pressner
Premiere: February 7, 1991

Salome Dances for Peace
Music: Terry Riley
Guest performers: Kronos Quartet
Choreography: Alexandre Proia
Premiere and only performance: February 24,
    1991, Dancers' Emergency Fund Benefit

Gretry Pas de Deux
Music: Andre Ernest Modeste Gretry
Choreography: Robert La Fosse
Premiere and only performance: February 24,
    1991, Dancers' Emergency Fund Benefit

Dance Preludes
Music: Witold Lutoslawski
Choreography: Miriam Mahdaviani
Premiere and only performance: February 24,
    1991, Dancers' Emergency Fund Benefit

Romeo and Juliet
(Balcony scene)
Music: Sergei Prokofiev
Choreography: Sean Lavery
Scenery: Drew Miller
Lighting: Mark Stanley
Premiere: February 24, 1991

The Sleeping Beauty
Libretto: Marius Petipa and I. A.
    Vsevolozhsky (after stories by Charles
    Perrault and others)
Music: Peter Ilyitch Tschaikovsky
Choreography: Peter Martins (after Marius
    Petipa)
("Garland Dance" by George Balanchine)
Scenery: David Mitchell
Costume Design: Patricia Zipprodt
Costume Execution: Barbara Matera, Ltd.
Makeup, Hair, and Wig Design: Michael
    Avedon
Lighting: Mark Stanley
Premiere: April 25, 1991

Ash
Music: Michael Torke
Choreography: Peter Martins
Costumes: Steven Rubin
Lighting: Mark Stanley
Premiere: June 20, 1991

A Musical Offering
Music: Johann Sebastian Bach
Choreography: Peter Martins
Costumes: Barbara Matera
Lighting: Mark Stanley
Premiere: November 21, 1991

1992

Delight of the Muses
Music: Charles Wuorinen (commissioned by
    New York City Ballet)
Choreography: Peter Martins
Costumes: Barbara Matera and Steven Rubin
Lighting: Mark Stanley
Premiere: January 29, 1992

THE DIAMOND PROJECT I

Reunions
Music: Ernest Bloch
Choreography: David Allan
Costumes: Holly Hynes
Lighting: Mark Stanley
Premiere: May 27, 1992

I Have My Own Room
Music: Eve Beglarian
Choreography: Robert La Fosse
Lighting: Mark Stanley
Guest Artist: Jeffrey Krieger
Premiere: May 27, 1992

Mercury
Music: Joseph Haydn
Choreography: Lynne Taylor-Corbett
Costumes: Holly Hynes
Lighting: Mark Stanley
Premiere: May 27, 1992

Herman Schmerman
Music: Thom Willems (commissioned for
    The Diamond Project I)
Choreography: William Forsythe
Production Design: William Forsythe
Women's Leotards Courtesy of Gianni
    Versace
Lighting: Mark Stanley
Premiere: May 28, 1992

Jeu de Cartes
Music: Igor Stravinsky
Choreography: Peter Martins
Costumes: Barbara Matera and Holly Hynes
Lighting: Mark Stanley
Premiere: May 28, 1992

Ancient Airs and Dances
Music: Ottorino Respighi
Choreography: Richard Tanner
Costumes: Barbara Matera
Lighting: Mark Stanley
Premiere: May 29, 1992

Bet Ann's Dance
Music: Jean Piché (Part I); Gary Kulesha
    (Part II)
Choreography: John Alleyne
Lighting: Mark Stanley
Premiere: May 29, 1992

Flötezart
Music: Wolfgang Amadeus Mozart
Choreography: Bart Cook
Costumes: Holly Hynes
Lighting: Mark Stanley
Premiere: May 30, 1992

Images
Music: Claude Debussy
Choreography: Miriam Mahdaviani
Lighting: Mark Stanley
Premiere: May 30, 1992

Two's Company
Music: Antonin Dvořák
Choreography: Toni Pimble
Costumes: Holly Hynes
Lighting: Mark Stanley
Premiere: May 30, 1992

Refractions
Music: Kamran Ince
Choreography: Alexandre Proia
Costumes: Holly Hynes
Lighting: Mark Stanley
Premiere: May 30, 1992

Three Preludes
Music: George Gershwin
Choreography: Mark Morris
Costumes: Isaac Mizrahi
Lighting: James F. Ingalls

Guest Performer: Mikhail Baryshnikov
New York City Ballet Premiere:
  June 16, 1992

Zakouski
Music: Sergei Rachmaninoff, Igor Stravinsky,
  Sergei Prokofiev, Peter Ilyitch
  Tschaikovsky
Choreography: Peter Martins
Costumes: Barbara Matera
Lighting: Mark Stanley
Premiere: November 17, 1992

1993

Jazz (Six Syncopated Movements)
Music: Wynton Marsalis
Choreography: Peter Martins
Costumes: Peter Martins and Barbara Matera
Lighting: Mark Stanley
Guest Performers: Wynton Marsalis and
  eleven-piece band
Premiere: January 14, 1993

Sinfonia
Music: Igor Stravinsky
Choreography: Peter Martins
Lighting: Mark Stanley
Premiere: February 21, 1993, Dancers'
  Emergency Fund Benefit

Zenobia Pas de Deux
(from the musical *On Your Toes*)
Music: Richard Rodgers
Choreography: George Balanchine
Lighting: Mark Stanley
New York City Ballet Premiere:
  November 23, 1993
first presented April 11, 1936, Imperial
  Theater, New York

1994

Symphonic Dances
Music: Sergei Rachmaninoff
Choreography: Peter Martins
Costumes: Santo Loquasto
Lighting: Mark Stanley
Premiere: February 3, 1994

A Schubert Sonata
Music: Franz Schubert
Choreography: Richard Tanner
Costumes: Holly Hynes
Lighting: Mark Mongold
Premiere: February 10, 1994

Papillons
Music: Robert Schumann
Choreography: Peter Martins
Premiere and only performance: February 27,
  1994, Dancers' Emergency Fund Benefit

A Suite of Dances
Music: Johann Sebastian Bach
Choreography: Jerome Robbins
Costumes: Santo Loquasto
Lighting: Jennifer Tipton
Guest Performer: Mikhail Baryshnikov
Premiere: May 10, 1994
first presented March 3, 1994, White Oak
  Dance Project

THE DIAMOND PROJECT II

Viola Alone . . . (with One Exception)
Music: Paul Hindemith
Choreography: Kevin O'Day
Costumes: Holly Hynes
Lighting: Mark Stanley
Guest Artist: Paul Neubauer
Premiere: May 18, 1994

Ebony Concerto
Music: Igor Stravinsky
Choreography: Damian Woetzel
Costumes: Heather Watts
Lighting: Mark Stanley
Premiere: May 18, 1994

Steel and Rain
Music: Béla Bartók
Choreography: Trey McIntyre
Costumes: Holly Hynes
Lighting: Mark Stanley
Premiere: May 18, 1994

Pastoral Dances
Music: Erik-Lars Larsson, Kurt Atterberg,
  Hugo Alfvén
Choreography: David Allan
Costumes: Holly Hynes
Lighting: Mark Stanley
Premiere: May 18, 1994

Mozart Piano Concerto
Music: Wolfgang Amadeus Mozart
Choreography: Peter Martins
Costumes: Holly Hynes
Lighting: Mark Stanley
Premiere: May 19, 1994

Red Angels
Music: Richard Einhorn
Choreography: Ulysses Dove
Costumes: William Ivey Long
Lighting: Jennifer Tipton
Guest Artist: Mary Rowell (electronic violin)
Premiere: May 19, 1994

Chiaroscuro
Music: Francesco Geminiani, edited by
  Walter Kolneder

Choreography: Lynne Taylor-Corbett
Artwork: Michael Zansky (courtesy of
  Berry Hill Gallery)
Costumes: Holly Hynes
Lighting: Mark Stanley
Premiere: May 21, 1994

In the Blue
Music: Johannes Brahms
Choreography: Anna Laerkesen
Costumes: Holly Hynes
Lighting: Mark Stanley
Premiere: May 26, 1994

Correlazione
Music: Arcangelo Corelli
Choreography: Miriam Mahdaviani
Costumes: Holly Hynes
Lighting: Mark Stanley
Premiere: May 26, 1994

Episodes & Sarcasms
Music: Sergei Prokofiev
Choreography: Richard Tanner
Costumes: Holly Hynes
Lighting: Mark Stanley
Premiere: May 31, 1994

The New Blondes
Music: Johann Pachelbel
Choreography: John Alleyne
Costumes: Holly Hynes
Lighting: Mark Stanley
Premiere: May 31, 1994

Danses de Cour
Music: Richard Strauss
Choreography: Robert La Fosse
Costumes: Gary Lisz
Lighting: Mark Stanley
Premiere: June 3, 1994

Glazounov Pas de Deux
Music: Alexander Glazounov
Choreography: Damian Woetzel
Costumes: Heather Watts
Lighting: Mark Stanley
Premiere: July 16, 1994, Saratoga Performing
  Arts Center

Untitled
Music: Charles Wuorinen (commissioned by
  New York City Ballet)
Choreography: Peter Martins
Costumes: Holly Hynes
Lighting: Mark Stanley
Premiere: November 22, 1994

X-Ray
Music: John Adams
(commissioned by The Minnesota Orchestra,
   The London Symphony Orchestra, and
   New York City Ballet)
Choreography: Peter Martins
Lighting: Mark Stanley
Premiere: November 22, 1994
   (from June 1, 1995, performed as third
   movement of *Adams Violin Concerto*)

1995

2 & 3 Part Inventions
Music: Johann Sebastian Bach
Choreography: Jerome Robbins
Lighting: Jennifer Tipton
New York City Ballet Premiere: January 19,
   1995
first presented June 4, 1994, School of
   American Ballet

Operetta Affezionata
Music: Carl Maria von Weber
Choreography: Richard Tanner
Costumes: Holly Hynes
Lighting: Mark Mongold
Premiere: February 2, 1995

Huoah
Music: Graham Fitkin
Choreography: Kevin O'Day
Costumes: Gary Lisz
Lighting: Mark Stanley
Premiere: February 9, 1995

West Side Story Suite
Music: Leonard Bernstein
Lyrics: Stephen Sondheim
Original Book: Arthur Laurents
Choreography: Jerome Robbins
   (Co-choreographer: Peter Gennaro)
Costumes: Irene Sharaff
Scenery: Oliver Smith
Lighting: Jennifer Tipton
New York City Ballet Premiere:
   May 18, 1995

Adams Violin Concerto
Music: John Adams
Choreography: Peter Martins
Costumes: Holly Hynes
Lighting: Mark Stanley
Premiere: June 1, 1995
(third movement originally appeared as
   X-Ray, first presented opening night gala
   November 22, 1994)

Dvořák Bagatelles
Music: Antonin Dvořák
Choreography: Kevin O'Day
Costumes: Carole Divet
Lighting: Mark Stanley
Premiere: November 21, 1995

Reliquary
Music: Charles Wuorinen
Choreography: Peter Martins
Lighting: Mark Stanley
Premiere: January 4, 1996

Touch
Music: Richard Peaslee
Choreography: David Parsons
Costumes: William Ivey Long
Lighting: Howell Binkley
Premiere: February 15, 1996

Twilight
Music: Michael Torke
Choreography: Ulysses Dove
Costumes: Holly Hynes
Lighting: Mark Stanley
Premiere: May 23, 1996

Tschaikovsky Pas de Quatre
Music: Peter Ilyitch Tschaikovsky
Choreography: Peter Martins
Costumes: Barbara Matera
Lighting: Mark Stanley
Premiere: May 30, 1996

Badchonim (Merry-Makers)
Music: Sergei Prokofiev (orchestrated by
   Mack Schlefer)
Choreography: Kevin O'Day
Costumes: Carole Divet
Lighting: Mark Stanley
Premiere: June 6, 1996

Schoenberg/Wuorinen Variations
Music: Arnold Schoenberg (arranged for two
   pianos by Charles Wuorinen)
Choreography: Richard Tanner
Costumes: Holly Hynes
Lighting: Mark Stanley
Premiere: July 24, 1996, Saratoga Performing
   Arts Center

1997

Brandenburg
Music: Johann Sebastian Bach
Choreography: Jerome Robbins
Costumes: Holly Hynes
Lighting: Jennifer Tipton
Premiere: January 22, 1997

THE DIAMOND PROJECT III

Open Strings
Music: John King (commissioned by
   New York City Ballet)
Choreography: Kevin O'Day
Costumes: Carole Divet
Lighting: Mark Stanley
Premiere: May 17, 1997

La Stravaganza
Music: Antonio Vivaldi, Evelyn Ficarra,
   Robert Normandeau, Serge Morand,
   Ake Parmerud
Choreography: Angelin Preljocaj
Scenery: Maya Schweizer
Scenery Supervision: Mark Stanley
Costumes: Herve-Pierre
Costume Supervision: Holly Hynes
Lighting: Mark Stanley
Premiere: May 22, 1997

Circle of Fifths
Music: Philip Glass
Choreography: Christopher d'Amboise
Costumes: Holly Hynes
Lighting: Mark Stanley
Premiere: May 30, 1997

Urban Dances
Music: Richard Danielpour (commissioned
   by New York City Ballet)
Choreography: Miriam Mahdaviani
Costumes: Holly Hynes
Lighting: Mark Stanley
Premiere: June 4, 1997

Slavonic Dances
Music: Antonin Dvořák
Choreography: Christopher Wheeldon
Costumes: Angela Kostrizky
Costume Supervision: Holly Hynes
Photography: Josef Sudek
Projections: Mark Mongold
Lighting: Mark Stanley
Premiere: June 12, 1997

Concerto in Five Movements
Music: Sergei Prokofiev
Choreography: Robert La Fosse
Costumes: Gary Lisz
Lighting: Mark Stanley
Premiere: June 17, 1997

Variations on a Nursery Song
Music: Ernst von Dohnányi
Choreography: Richard Tanner
Scenery and Costumes: Alain Vaës
Lighting: Mark Stanley
Premiere: January 22, 1998

Concerti Armonici
Music: Unico Wilhelm Graf van Wassenaer
Choreography: Peter Martins
Costumes: William Ivey Long
Lighting: Mark Stanley
Premiere: January 22, 1998

Stabat Mater
Music: Giovanni Battista Pergolesi
Choreography: Peter Martins
Scenery and Costumes: Alain Vaës
Lighting: Mark Stanley
Premiere: February 20, 1998

New York City Ballet Chronology

1948

With commissioned music by Igor Stravinsky, and sets and costumes by Isamu Noguchi, Ballet Society presents the premiere of George Balanchine's *Orpheus* at City Center on April 28. Morton Baum, Chairman of the Finance Committee of City Center of Music & Drama, invites Balanchine and Lincoln Kirstein to establish a permanent ballet company to be called New York City Ballet.

New York City Ballet's first season opens on October 11 with three George Balanchine ballets: *Concerto Barocco, Orpheus,* and *Symphony in C.* The original roster reads: George Balanchine, Artistic Director; Lincoln Kirstein, General Director; Leon Barzin, Musical Director; Lighting by Jean Rosenthal; Frances Hawkens, General Manager. Principal dancers: Maria Tallchief, Marie-Jeanne, Tanaquil Le Clercq, Beatrice Tompkins, Jocelyn Vollmar, Nicholas Magallanes, Francisco Moncion, Herbert Bliss, and Todd Bolender.

1949

The company presents its first independent season in January, consisting of ten performances, including Antony Tudor's revival of *Time Table* (originally created for American Ballet Caravan in 1941), Merce Cunningham's *The Seasons,* and Lew Christensen's *Jinx.*

In January, Jerome Robbins joins the Company and is named associate artistic director by George Balanchine. His first ballet for the Company, *The Guests,* premieres on January 14.

Melissa Hayden, Yvonne Mounsey, Janet Reed, and Frank Hobi join the company as principal dancers.

Barbara Karinska begins her long association with the Company as costume maker and designer.

Firebird premieres in November and *Bourrée Fantasque* premieres in December, George Balanchine's first restudies of ballets that have already become classics.

1950

British choreographer Frederick Ashton is invited to create a new ballet, *Illuminations,* the first of two works he creates for New York City Ballet.

Diana Adams, Hugh Laing, Harold Lang, and Patricia Wilde join the Company as principal dancers.

Venturing abroad for the first time, the Company presents a five-week season at London's Royal Opera House, Covent Garden, followed by a three-week tour of the English provinces.

Lew Christensen is named ballet master.

In February, George Balanchine revives *Prodigal Son,* his last ballet for Diaghilev, and in the same month, Jerome Robbins's *Age of Anxiety* premieres.

In November, George Balanchine revives *The Fairy's Kiss,* first done for American Ballet in 1937.

Frances Hawkens retires as general manager. Betty Cage assumes the position, which she holds for thirty-five years.

1951

The Company's first American performances outside of New York take place at the Chicago Civic Opera House from late April to early May.

Ruthanna Boris, Nora Kaye, and André Eglevsky join the Company as principal dancers.

Antony Tudor creates *Lady of the Camellias,* his first original ballet for New York City Ballet. In November, he mounts and performs in his earliest work, *Lilac Garden.*

Jerome Robbins choreographs *The Cage,* which premieres in June. In the same month, Ruthanna Boris's *Cakewalk* also premieres.

George Balanchine creates *Tyl Ulenspiegel* and his own version of *Swan Lake (Act II),* with designs by Cecil Beaton. He also revives *Apollo,* which he originally made for Diaghilev in 1928.

George Balanchine's new version of *La Valse* appears on television, in CBS's first commercial color telecast.

George Balanchine eliminates the sets and costumes of *Concerto Barocco* and *The Four Temperaments,* and both are now performed in practice clothes. In the future, he will continue to produce ballets on a bare stage with dancers dressed in leotards, to reveal the shape of the choreography and also for considerations of expense.

1952

New ballets by George Balanchine, Jerome Robbins, Antony Tudor, Frederick Ashton, and Ruthanna Boris premiere.

Michael Maule and Roy Tobias are promoted to the rank of principal dancer.

The Company makes its debut in continental Europe with a five-month tour, participating in several major festivals. Cities visited are Barcelona, Paris, Florence, Lausanne, Zürich, The Hague, London, Edinburgh, and Berlin.

1953

After dancing in Baltimore and Washington, D.C., the Company makes the first of a continuing series of cross-country tours, performing in Red Rocks, Colorado; the Greek Theatre in Los Angeles (the first of many summer seasons there); and San Francisco's War Memorial Opera House. Under the sponsorship of the International Exchange program of the United States Department of State, administered through the American National Theater and Academy (ANTA), the Company appears at Milan's Teatro de la Scala and in Venice, Como, Naples, Rome, Florence, Trieste, Bologna, Genoa, Munich, Stuttgart, and Brussels.

Jacques d'Amboise is promoted to the rank of principal dancer.

Jerome Robbins creates *Afternoon of a Faun* and *Fanfare.*

Lew Christensen's *Filling Station* from Ballet Caravan is added to the repertory. Christensen, now director of the San Francisco Ballet, restages his *Con Amore* for the Company, in exchange for George Balanchine's *Serenade.*

The Rockefeller Foundation awards City Center a grant-in-aid of $100,000 to cover artistic and production costs of new works. It is the largest contribution so far to have been received for the benefit of New York City Ballet.

1954

George Balanchine choreographs *Western Symphony, Ivesiana,* and a full-length version of *The Nutcracker.* The Company's most lavish ballet to date, Balanchine's *The Nutcracker* is mounted in February at City Center. The large cast includes thirty-nine children from the School of American Ballet. This is the first of a number of ballets that will employ students.

Special holiday seasons are devoted to Balanchine's *The Nutcracker,* thus beginning a Christmas tradition that will be emulated by many ballet companies across the country. Its popularity provides major support for New York City Ballet through the coming years of growth and increasing expenses.

During the summer the Company appears for the first time in Seattle.

1955

ANTA sponsors a summer tour of Europe, which includes the cities of Monte Carlo, Marseilles, Lyons, Florence, Rome, Bordeaux, Lisbon, Paris, Lausanne, Zürich, Stuttgart, Amsterdam, and The Hague.

Beginning this year, City Center initiates annual three-month winter seasons running from November or December to January or February of the following year.

1956

Jerome Robbins choreographs *The Concert*, which premieres in March.

Company members perform George Balanchine's new *A Musical Joke* and *Divertimento No. 15* in May at the bicentennial Mozart Festival at the American Shakespeare Festival Theatre in Stratford, Connecticut. *Divertimento No. 15* then enters the New York City Ballet repertory.

A ten-week European tour beginning in August encompasses Salzburg, Vienna, Zürich, Venice, Berlin, Munich, Frankfurt, Brussels, Antwerp, Paris, Cologne, Copenhagen, and Stockholm.

1957

George Balanchine works closely with Igor Stravinsky on the structure of a commissioned score for *Agon*, which premieres in December.

Reactivated as a sponsor of new works with gifts from individuals, Ballet Society underwrites ballets by Todd Bolender, John Butler, and Francisco Moncion.

Allegra Kent is promoted to the rank of principal dancer.

In Montreal, the Canadian Broadcasting Company makes the first films of New York City Ballet works.

The Company makes its first appearance in Philadelphia.

The first full-length television version of George Balanchine's *The Nutcracker* is broadcast on CBS-TV's *Seven Lively Arts* program.

1958

Under the auspices of the United States Department of State and ANTA, the Company embarks upon a five-month tour of Japan, Australia, and the Philippines.

Domestic appearances take place in Indiana and Michigan. The Swedish choreographer Birgit Cullberg restages her dramatic ballet *Medea;* its cast includes French ballerina Violette Verdy, a new principal.

Lotte Lenya, who sang in the first version of George Balanchine's *The Seven Deadly Sins* for Les Ballets 1933, appears in his new production for New York City Ballet.

George Balanchine choreographs *Gounod Symphony* and *Stars and Stripes*, both of which premiere in January.

Balanchine stages a special television version of *The Nutcracker* for CBS-TV's *Playhouse 90* in which he performs the role of Herr Drosselmeyer.

George Balanchine implements alphabetical listing of principal dancers and soloists.

Robert Irving, of England's Royal Ballet, assumes the post of musical director.

1959

The new year begins with a performance of *Stars and Stripes* at the inauguration of New York's Governor Nelson A. Rockefeller in Albany. At the invitation of Lincoln Kirstein, the Gagaku troupe of musicians and dancers from the Imperial Household of Japan appear as guests during the spring season.

Episodes, the collaboration between Martha Graham and George Balanchine, is presented in May.

In August, the Company makes the first of its many summer appearances at the Ravinia Festival in Illinois.

Jillana, Edward Villella, and Jonathan Watts are promoted to the rank of principal dancer.

1960

Danish dancer Erik Bruhn first appears as guest artist, which he continues to do for two seasons.

George Balanchine's *The Figure in the Carpet* premieres in May and is performed in honor of the Fourth International Congress of Iranian Art and Archeology.

George Balanchine's *Liebeslieder Walzer* premieres in November.

In November, John Taras choreographs *Ebony Concerto*, which premieres in November with three other ballets in the four-part program *Jazz Concert*. It is his first ballet for the Company.

A series of free Saturday matinees is inaugurated by George Balanchine for New York City's public school children. Sponsored by Ballet Society, they take place at City Center during regular seasons.

1961

United States tours include first visits to Ohio and North Carolina.

New York City Ballet makes its Canadian debut as part of the Vancouver International Festival.

The newly created New York State Council on the Arts awards its first grant to a performing arts organization in support of the Company's appearance at the Empire State Festival at Bear Mountain.

Patricia McBride and Conrad Ludlow are promoted to the rank of principal dancer.

1962

The New York State Council on the Arts sponsors the first Company tour in upstate New York, where it also presents lecture-demonstrations in twelve cities. George Balanchine then establishes ongoing programs of lecture-demonstrations for New York City public schools.

Company members accompany George Balanchine to Hamburg, West Germany, for a celebration of Igor Stravinsky's eightieth birthday. Members also appear in *Noah and the Flood*, a dance-drama by Balanchine and Stravinsky created especially for television.

Arthur Mitchell is promoted to the rank of principal dancer.

New York City Ballet dances in the summer at the Seattle World's Fair.

In the fall, the Company makes a tour of Hamburg, Berlin, Zürich, Stuttgart, Cologne, Frankfurt, Vienna, and later, Moscow, Leningrad, Kiev, Tbilisi, and Baku. The trip marks George Balanchine's first return to his native Russia since his departure in 1924.

The production of *A Midsummer Night's Dream* is the first new full-length ballet by George Balanchine. Its premiere is also the occasion for the first annual gala to benefit the New York City Ballet.

1963

New York City Ballet establishes its own costume shop under the direction of Mme. Karinska.

The Company participates in the Kennedy Administration's Second Anniversary Inaugural Salute in Washington, D.C.

In July the Company appears at the Long Island Festival of the Arts.

Jacques d'Amboise choreographs his first ballet, *The Chase (or, The Vixen's Choice)*, which premieres in September.

André Prokovsky joins the Company as principal dancer.

The Ford Foundation, through its Humanities and the Arts program headed by W. McNeil Lowry, awards the Company a grant of $2,500,000, to be paid over a ten-year period. The School of American Ballet is awarded $2,425,000 for an equal term. Grants are given to seven recipients; it is the largest sum ever dedicated to dance from a single source.

NEW YORK STATE THEATER

1964

January 26 marks the last performance of New York City Ballet at City Center.

On April 20 the Company dances at the gala opening of the New York State Theater, which is to be its new home. Built by Lincoln Center for the State of New York in time for participation in the 1964 New York World's Fair, the theater is to become the property of New York City at the fair's closing in 1966. According to terms of an enabling act of the New York State Legislature, the city is then to lease the theater to City Center, thereby fulfilling the act's specification of occupancy by a popularly priced nonprofit organization offering a variety of cultural presentations. The city pledges to provide ongoing support for the new facility. Throughout the World's Fair, the New York City Ballet shares the theater with the Music Theater of Lincoln Center, founded by Richard Rodgers and Oscar Hammerstein II. Architect Philip Johnson works closely with Lincoln Kirstein on the unique public spaces and with George Balanchine on meeting the stage requirements of dance, including the development of a plan to build a stage floor of unusual resilience.

George Balanchine's *The Nutcracker* is redesigned by Rouben Ter-Arutunian to fit the much larger stage. It is the first of a number of such readjustments.

New York City Ballet is now comprised of sixty-six dancers. Lincoln Kirstein is general director, George Balanchine and John Taras are ballet masters, Betty Cage is general manager, Ronald Bates is production stage manager, Robert Irving is music director and principal conductor, and Hugo Fiorato is associate conductor. Principal dancers are Jacques d'Amboise, Melissa Hayden, Jillana, Allegra Kent, Conrad Ludlow, Nicholas Magallanes, Patricia McBride, Arthur Mitchell, Francisco Moncion, André Prokovsky, Maria Tallchief, Violette Verdy, Edward Villella, and Patricia Wilde.

1965

In February and March, the Company makes a southwestern United States tour: Houston, San Antonio, Austin, Dallas, Bloomington, St. Louis, and Urbana.

George Balanchine creates the full-length *Don Quixote*, which premieres in May. He dances the title role in the Company's gala preview and in several performances thereafter.

Suzanne Farrell is promoted to the rank of principal dancer.

A tour of Europe and the Middle East takes the Company to Paris, Milan, Spoleto (Festival of Two Worlds), Venice, Dubrovnik, Athens, Jerusalem, Tel Aviv, Salzburg (Salzburg Festival), Amsterdam, and London, from June to September.

1966

The City Center of Music & Drama, of which New York City Ballet continues to be a part, assumes the lease for the New York State Theater. The theater is now to be the official home of New York City Ballet and New York City Opera. The introduction of a subscription plan significantly increases regular audience attendance.

As a constituent of Lincoln Center, City Center joins the Lincoln Center Student Program, through which the Company continues its public service programs in city schools.

On July 8, the Company makes its debut at the new Saratoga Performing Arts Center in Saratoga Springs, New York. Built in consultation with George Balanchine and Ronald Bates, it is to be a permanent home during July of each year. The opening performance is *A Midsummer Night's Dream*.

The Company pays its first visits to Newark, Montreal, and Toronto.

Merce Cunningham, who had previously done choreography for Ballet Society, restages his *Summerspace*, earlier made for his own company.

Mimi Paul and Anthony Blum are promoted to the rank of principal dancer.

Under George Balanchine's direction and supervision, the Company films *A Midsummer Night's Dream*, the first full-length ballet movie made in the United States.

1967

In April, George Balanchine's three-part, full-length ballet *Jewels* premieres.

American tours include a first appearance at the new Merriweather Post Pavilion of Music in Columbia, Maryland.

During the Company's return engagement at the Edinburgh Festival, Peter Martins dances as a guest artist in *Apollo*.

1968

Beginning this year, the Company presents a regular spring season at the New York State Theater, running from April or May to June or early July. The standard year is to contain a fourteen-week winter season, with four weeks of George Balanchine's *The Nutcracker*, and a nine-week spring season.

Requiem Canticles, with music by Igor Stravinsky, is staged by George Balanchine for one performance in memory of Martin Luther King Jr.

1969

As part of Monte Carlo's Diaghilev Festival, commemorating the sixtieth anniversary of the founding of his Ballets Russes, the Company dances George Balanchine's *Apollo* and *Prodigal Son*.

Jerome Robbins returns to the Company after a twelve-year absence, assuming the title of ballet master, which he shares with George Balanchine and John Taras. He creates *Dances at a Gathering*, which premieres in May.

Kay Mazzo and Suki Schorer are promoted to the rank of principal dancer.

The National Endowment for the Arts Dance Program makes its first grant to the New York City Ballet.

1970

Jean-Pierre Bonnefoux, Peter Martins, and Helgi Tomasson join the company as principal dancers.

George Balanchine's *Who Cares?* premieres in February.

1971

Dance Theatre of Harlem, founded by former principal Arthur Mitchell, shares the stage with the Company for a one-time-only gala performance of *Concerto for Jazz Band and*

Orchestra, jointly choreographed by George Balanchine and Arthur Mitchell.

1972

George Balanchine presents an eight-day Stravinsky Festival as a tribute to the composer, who died the previous year. Twenty-two new works are presented by George Balanchine, Todd Bolender, John Clifford, Lorca Massine, Jerome Robbins, Richard Tanner, and John Taras, along with repertory ballets by Balanchine and Robbins. Balanchine's new ballets include *Symphony in Three Movements, Duo Concertant*, and *Violin Concerto*. Balanchine and Robbins co-choreograph and appear in *Pulcinella*.

In August, New York City Ballet represents the United States in cultural presentations at the Olympic Games in Munich. Upon its return, the Company dances for the first time at the new Wolf Trap Farm Park for the Performing Arts in Vienna, Virginia.

A second visit to the Soviet Union is followed by a first appearance in Poland, where the Company dances in Lodz and Warsaw.

Karin von Aroldingen, Gelsey Kirkland, and Sara Leland are promoted to the rank of principal dancer.

Friends of the Company formalize their efforts for support by creating the New York City Ballet Guild.

The Saratoga Performing Arts Center receives a major touring grant from the National Endowment for the Arts to support the Company's summer performances.

1973

Company members go to Berlin to film fifteen George Balanchine ballets for RM Productions.

Lincoln Kirstein publishes *New York City Ballet* (Alfred A. Knopf) in commemoration of the Company's twenty-fifth anniversary, with photographs by George Platt Lynes and Martha Swope.

John Clifford is promoted to the rank of principal dancer.

1974

The New York City Ballet performs for the first time at the John F. Kennedy Center for the Performing Arts in Washington, D.C.

George Balanchine and ballerina Alexandra Danilova collaborate on a new production of *Coppélia*, which is given its premiere at the Saratoga Performing Arts Center.

Peter Schaufuss, an alumnus of the Royal Danish Ballet, joins the Company as principal dancer.

The Ford Foundation awards the Company a seven-year challenge grant of $2,700,000 intended to stabilize its financial position.

1975

George Balanchine pays homage to composer Maurice Ravel and to France with a two-week Ravel Festival. It includes sixteen new ballets by Jacques d'Amboise, George Balanchine, Jerome Robbins, and John Taras as well as repertory ballets. Highlights include *Le Tombeau de Couperin* by George Balanchine and Jerome Robbins's *Mother Goose*.

Adam Lüders, a principal dancer with the Royal Danish Ballet, joins the Company as principal dancer.

There are now eighty-five members of the Company.

While remaining under the purview of City Center, New York City Ballet establishes its own board of directors.

1976

The Company celebrates the United States Bicentennial with George Balanchine's *Union Jack*, a tribute to America's British heritage, underwritten by The Fan Fox and Leslie R. Samuels Foundation.

The Company also participates in the International Festival de Danse in Paris as part of a French salute to the United States Bicentennial.

The Andrew W. Mellon Foundation inaugurates a renewable three-year cycle of significant support to be used at the discretion of the artistic

director. Important individual gifts continue to be made for commissioning of new works.

1977

In Nashville, Tennessee, the Company films its first two of a number of *Dance in America* programs for the Public Broadcasting System (PBS), featuring works by George Balanchine: *Tzigane, Andante* from *Divertimento No. 15*, and *The Four Temperaments*.

The Canadian Broadcasting System also films George Balanchine's *Bugaku* and *Chaconne*.

Merrill Ashley and Robert Weiss are promoted to the rank of principal dancer.

Mme. Karinska retires after designing and making the costumes for George Balanchine's *Vienna Waltzes*.

Stanley Williams stages *Bournonville Divertissements*, using a selection of works by August Bournonville.

A first visit is made to Santo Domingo in the Dominican Republic.

The Company is awarded its first $1,000,000 Challenge Grant from the National Endowment for the Arts.

1978

Peter Martins's first ballet, *Calcium Light Night*, premieres in January.

The year's engagements include first visits to West Palm Beach, Florida, and Copenhagen's Tivoli Gardens.

Mikhail Baryshnikov makes his debut as a member of the Company at the Saratoga Performing Arts Center after dancing in *Prodigal Son* for a *Dance in America* program with New York City Ballet.

The television series *Live from Lincoln Center* presents *Coppélia*.

Sean Lavery is promoted to the rank of principal dancer.

1979

Grants from the New York State Council on the Arts, the National Endowment for the Arts, and local presenters enable performances in the upstate New York cities of Rochester, Syracuse, and Buffalo.

Jerome Robbins creates *Opus 19/The Dreamer*, which premieres in June.

The Company returns to London for the first time in fourteen years, for two weeks of performances at the Royal Opera House, Covent Garden in September.

A New York City Ballet Education Department is formally appointed.

Organized by George Balanchine, the Company inaugurates its annual "Ballet for Young People" matinees at the New York State Theater.

Bart Cook, Daniel Duell, Kyra Nichols, and Heather Watts are promoted to the rank of principal dancer.

1980

The Company participates in Stravinsky festivals in Berlin and Paris.

Ib Andersen, formerly of the Royal Danish Ballet, joins as principal dancer.

New ballets include Jerome Robbins's *Suite of Dances* and *Rondo*, Peter Martins's *Eight Easy Pieces* and *Lille Suite*, and George Balanchine's *Robert Schumann's Davidsbündlertänze*.

At the instigation of George Balanchine, New York City Ballet donates the proceeds of its April 29 benefit performance to assist in the purchase of protective vests for New York City police officers.

George Balanchine, Ronald Bates, and Perry Silvey, stage manager, with financial assistance from the Kresge Foundation, develop an innovative, widely copied portable dance floor for touring.

1981

The Company makes its first visit to Fort Worth, Texas.

In June, New York City Ballet honors Russian composer Peter Ilyitch Tschaikovsky with a two-week Tschaikovsky Festival, which, in addition to repertory ballets, includes twelve new works by George Balanchine, Jacques d'Amboise, Joseph Duell, Peter Martins, Jerome Robbins, and John Taras. The stage setting for the entire festival is made

of translucent tubing designed by Philip Johnson and John Burgee to be hung and lit in different architectural configurations.

For the Tschaikovsky festival, George Balanchine rechoreographs his 1933 *Mozartiana*.

For a *Dance in America* telecast, George Balanchine, in collaboration with Kermit Love, reconceives *L'Enfant et les Sortilèges*, which he had set as his first commission from Diaghilev (1925), for the opening of Ballet Society (1946), and again for the Ravel Festival (1975).

Peter Martins is named ballet master, joining George Balanchine, Jerome Robbins, and John Taras.

1982

The hundredth anniversary of Stravinsky's birth inspires George Balanchine to present a Stravinsky Centennial Celebration. It comprises ten evenings of past masterworks as well as new ballets by Balanchine, Lew Christensen, Jacques d'Amboise, Peter Martins, Jerome Robbins, and John Taras. The Philip Johnson–John Burgee tubing created for the Tschaikovsky Festival is used again. *Noah and the Flood* is given its first stage presentation by Balanchine, assisted by Jacques d'Amboise. The ballerina Vera Zorina collaborates with Balanchine and Taras on *Perséphone*, in which she also plays the title role.

Live from Lincoln Center telecasts *Apollo* and *Orpheus*.

Darci Kistler is promoted to the rank of principal dancer.

The New York State Theater undergoes a major acoustical renovation made possible by The Fan Fox and Leslie R. Samuels Foundation.

1983

George Balanchine dies on April 30 in New York at the age of seventy-nine, following a long illness.

Jerome Robbins and Peter Martins assume positions of ballet masters in chief.

The Company dances in London, Copenhagen, and Paris.

Jerome Robbins's *Glass Pieces* premieres in May.

December 6 marks the one thousandth performance of George Balanchine's *The Nutcracker*, and Peter Martins dances his final performance.

Maria Calegari is promoted to the rank of principal dancer. Valentina Kozlova and Leonid Kozlov, both formerly with the Bolshoi Ballet, join the Company as principal dancers.

The National Endowment for the Arts awards the Company a Challenge Grant of $1,000,000, to be matched in the ensuing three years.

The Lila Acheson and DeWitt Wallace Fund for Lincoln Center, established by the cofounders of *Reader's Digest*, makes the first of its annual leadership grants to the Company in support of new productions.

1984

Liebeslieder Walzer, absent for some time, is reintroduced on May 24. New designs by David Mitchell follow ideas discussed by George Balanchine and Lincoln Kirstein many years earlier; Karinska's costumes are retained. It is the first of five productions of Balanchine ballets to be restudied at the behest of Kirstein. Others are *Gounod Symphony*, *Brahms-Schoenberg Quartet*, *Swan Lake*, and *La Sonnambula*.

A special two-part *Dance in America* telecast commemorates George Balanchine's life and achievements. Works by Peter Martins (*Concerto for Two Solo Pianos*, *Eight Easy Pieces*, and *The Magic Flute*) are also televised.

Jerome Robbins choreographs *Antique Epigraphs*, which premieres in February.

Twyla Tharp collaborates with Jerome Robbins on *Brahms/Handel*, which premieres in June.

Helgi Tomasson choreographs *Menuetto* for New York City Ballet.

Joseph Duell, Lourdes Lopez, and Stephanie Saland are promoted to the rank of principal dancer.

The Company pays its first visit to Minneapolis.

1985

This year marks the anniversary of *Serenade*, which has been in continuous performance for fifty years.

Never before seen at the New York State Theater, George Balanchine's *Gounod Symphony* is reconstructed for revival by former ballet mistress Vida Brown. Robin Wagner designs the new set, and the original Karinska costumes are reproduced.

New ballets are created by Peter Martins (*Poulenc Sonata*, *Valse Triste*, *Eight More*, and *Eight Miniatures*), Jean-Pierre Bonnefoux (*Shadows*), and Jerome Robbins (*Eight Lines* and *In Memory of . . .*)

Christopher d'Amboise and Jock Soto are promoted to the rank of principal dancer.

At Jerome Robbins's initiative, New York City Ballet establishes a Dancers' Emergency Fund, for which there is to be a closing night benefit at the end of the winter season.

In April, Peter Martins stages a special performance of *We Are the World* in support of USA for Africa.

1986

Settings for two ballets by George Balanchine are redesigned: *Brahms-Schoenberg Quartet* by David Mitchell, and *Swan Lake* by Alain Vaës, who works closely with Lincoln Kirstein, again following ideas projected by Balanchine.

Peter Martins creates *Songs of the Auvergne*, which premieres in February.

Judith Fugate is promoted to the rank of principal dancer. Robert La Fosse, formerly with American Ballet Theatre, joins the Company as a principal dancer.

Special grants from AT&T, corporate sponsor of the tour, the National

Endowment for the Arts, and Lawrence A. Wien enable New York City Ballet to travel to the West Coast for the first time in fourteen years. The Company appears in Berkeley and Costa Mesa, California, and Seattle, Washington.

Dance in America produces *Choreography by Jerome Robbins with the New York City Ballet*, which is broadcast in May.

1987

On May 18, New York City Ballet and the School of American Ballet join in celebrating Lincoln Kirstein's eightieth birthday with a special performance at the New York State Theater.

Peter Martins choreographs *Ecstatic Orange*. George Balanchine's *La Sonnambula* is revived and given a new production by Alain Vaës, who also provides new decor for *Bournonville Divertissements*.

On October 4 the Company participates in *Dancing for Life*, a benefit to help victims of AIDS.

Peter Frame is promoted to the rank of principal dancer. Lindsay Fischer, formerly a member of the Dutch National Ballet, joins the Company as a principal dancer.

Following a three-year sponsorship of "Ballet for Young People" matinee performances, New York Telephone becomes the corporate sponsor of Balanchine's *The Nutcracker*, ensuring preservation of this work and allowing its presentation to one thousand New York City schoolchildren each year. It is the largest corporate contribution the Company has received.

1988

Bolshoi Ballet principal dancers Nina Ananiashvili and Andris Liepa perform as guest artists in February, in the first such collaboration between the Soviet Union and the United States.

Under the direction of Peter Martins, a three-week American Music Festival in honor of New York City Ballet's fortieth anniversary is

presented during the spring season, from April 26 to May 15. Twenty-two world premieres are offered, including five ballets to newly commissioned scores, along with ballets in repertory, among them Jerome Robbins's *Ives, Songs*, presented earlier in the year. Choreographers represented are Christopher d'Amboise, Ib Andersen, George Balanchine, Jean-Pierre Bonnefoux, Bart Cook, Laura Dean, Joseph Duell, Eliot Feld, William Forsythe, Robert La Fosse, Lar Lubovitch, Miriam Mahdaviani, Peter Martins, Jerome Robbins, Richard Tanner, Paul Taylor, Violette Verdy, and Robert Weiss. Composers are drawn from the entire spectrum of nineteenth- and twentieth-century music. Merrill Lynch & Co., Inc., is the corporate sponsor of the Company's fortieth-anniversary American Music Festival.

The National Endowment for the Arts, the Lila Acheson and DeWitt Wallace Fund for Lincoln Center, and The Fan Fox and Leslie R. Samuels Foundation award leadership grants to the festival; other major contributions are made to the festival.

As New York City Ballet celebrates forty years of existence, it begins its eighty-ninth New York season on November 22, 1988, with the original opening night program, consisting of George Balanchine's *Concerto Barocco*, *Orpheus*, and *Symphony in C*. It numbers 104 dancers.

In July, fifteen American Music Festival ballets premiere at Saratoga, along with Jerome Robbins's *Ives, Songs*.

In September, the Company departs for its first tour to east Asia since 1958, two weeks and thirteen performances at Tokyo Bay N.K. Hall in Japan.

For the 1988–89 Winter Season, the Company initiates the NYCB Discovery Series to encourage children and their parents to explore the world of ballet.

1989

Two new Peter Martins ballets premiere in February: *Beethoven Romance* and *Mozart Serenade.*

Also in February, New York City Ballet holds the fifth Dancers' Emergency Fund Benefit. The fortieth anniversary program, "Forty Carats," is comprised of excerpts from twelve ballets spanning the Company's forty-year history.

May marks the tenth anniversary of Ballet for Young People, celebrated with a free matinee for 2,500 students from thirty-two New York school districts.

Ray Charles and the Raeletts return to New York City Ballet to perform Peter Martins's American Music Festival ballet *A Fool for You.* The live performance was telecast on *Live from Lincoln Center* and was viewed by over 2.7 million households.

In June, Patricia McBride makes her farewell performance at the New York State Theater.

The Spring Gala performance honors Jerome Robbins's seventieth birthday. The all-Robbins program includes *The Concert*, with six principals in the "Mistake Waltz," and a special version of *Circus Polka* that concludes with forty-eight students forming the initials "J.R." in a floor pattern.

Echo, a new work by Peter Martins, premieres in June, with music by composer Michael Torke. The Saratoga season features local premieres of Peter Martins's *Beethoven Romance, Mozart Serenade*, and *Echo.*

Patricia McBride dances her farewell performance at the Saratoga Performing Arts Center in *Valse Triste.*

In August, the Company embarks on a European tour, with one week in each of the following cities: Copenhagen, Glasgow, The Hague (Holland Dance Festival), and Paris (Festival International de Danse de Paris). After completing the tour, members of the Company return to Denmark for the filming of two *Dance in America* (PBS) segments, including George Balanchine's *Serenade* and *Western Symphony*, and Peter Martins's *Sophisticated Lady* and *Valse Triste.*

Peter Boal, Heléne Alexopoulos, Damian Woetzel, and Gen Horiuchi are promoted to the rank of principal dancer. Robert Hill, formerly of American Ballet Theatre, joins the company as principal dancer.

In November, Suzanne Farrell dances her final performance with New York City Ballet in *Vienna Waltzes* and *Sophisticated Lady.*

1990

The *Dance in America* segments taped in 1989 are broadcast in January.

Richard Tanner's *Prague Symphony* premieres in February.

Also in February, the annual Dancers' Emergency Fund Benefit closes the season, featuring the premiere of Peter Martins's *Four Gnossiennes*, with music by Erik Satie.

In June, West Sixty-third Street between Broadway and Columbus Avenue is named Balanchine Way.

Nichol Hlinka is promoted to the rank of principal dancer.

In June, the company celebrates the work of Jerome Robbins with *A Festival of Jerome Robbins' Ballets*, three weeks of performances of twenty-seven of the fifty-four works Jerome Robbins has made for New York City Ballet. The program includes two major revivals, *Mother Goose* and *Watermill*, and a special closing night features guest artists from the Paris Opera Ballet and American Ballet Theatre.

At the Spring Gala in May, Peter Martins's *Fearful Symmetries* premieres, with music by John Adams.

In late June and early July, Peter Martins and Robert La Fosse stage performances of *A Mass (Missa Sicca)*, performed by fifty Company members and fifty students from the School of American Ballet. The score, commissioned by Lincoln Kirstein, is by Michael Torke. The chapel architecture, by Philip Johnson, is rendered for the stage by Alain Vaës.

In June, Ib Andersen dances his final performance with New York City Ballet in *Apollo.*

This summer marks the twenty-fifth-anniversary season of the Saratoga Performing Arts Center.

In September, the company departs for one week of performances at the Orange County Performing Arts Center.

In honor of the 150th anniversary of the composer's birth, opening night of the winter season features Balanchine/Tschaikovsky ballets: *Serenade, Tschaikovsky Pas de Deux*, and *Diamonds.*

1991

In February, Robert La Fosse's *Waltz Trilogy* premieres. In the same month, soloist Shaun O'Brien retires after a final performance as Dr. Coppélius in *Coppélia.*

The annual Dancers' Emergency Fund Benefit, on closing night of the winter season, features four *pas de deux* premieres by Miriam Madhaviani, Robert La Fosse, Alexandre Proia, and Sean Lavery.

In April, *The Sleeping Beauty* premieres. The full-length production features choreography by Peter Martins (after Marius Petipa), with George Balanchine's *Garland Dance*, music by Tschaikovsky, costume design by Patricia Zipprodt, and sets by David Mitchell.

In June, Peter Martins's *Ash* premieres, with music by Michael Torke.

The summer season features Saratoga premieres of *The Sleeping Beauty, Ash, Waltz Trilogy*, and Sean Lavery's *Romeo and Juliet Pas de Deux.*

Robert Irving, principal conductor and music director of New York City Ballet for more than thirty years, dies in England on September 13.

This year, underwriting from The Fan Fox and Leslie R. Samuels Foundation, Inc., establishes the Robert Irving Guest Conductor's Chair. The three-year gift enables the Company to engage such artists as Maurice Kaplow and Donald York to perform with the New York City Ballet orchestra.

Margaret Tracey and Wendy Whelan are promoted to the rank of principal dancer.

The November Opening Night Gala features the premiere of Peter Martins's *A Musical Offering*, with music by Johann Sebastian Bach.

1992

In January, Peter Martins's *Delight of the Muses* premieres, with music by Charles Wuorinen.

In February, the eighth annual Dancers' Emergency Fund Benefit closes the season. This one-time-only program features excerpts from "story ballets," including *A Midsummer Night's Dream, Swan Lake, Romeo and Juliet, The Sleeping Beauty*, Balanchine's *The Nutcracker, Apollo*, and *Prodigal Son.*

May 27 marks the inaugural Diamond Project performance, made possible by the Aaron Diamond Foundation. Created to foster works by new choreographers, the project features a total of eleven new ballets. The choreographers are David Allen, John Alleyne, Bart Cook, William Forsythe, Robert La Fosse, Miriam Mahdaviani, Peter Martins, Toni Pimble, Alexandre Proia, Richard Tanner, and Lynne Taylor-Corbett.

In June, New York City Ballet presents three performances of *Duo Concertant*, danced by Mikhail Baryshnikov and Yvonne Borree. Baryshnikov also dances the New York premiere of *Three Preludes*, choreographed by Mark Morris and with music by George Gershwin.

The premiere of Peter Martins's *Zakouski* opens the 1992–93 winter season in November. On this occasion, Nikolaj Hübbe, former principal dancer with the Royal Danish Ballet, makes his debut with the Company as a principal dancer.

1993

In January, New York City Ballet presents the world premiere of Peter Martins's *Jazz*, to a commissioned score by Wynton Marsalis, who performs with his ensemble at each performance.

Nilas Martins and Philip Neal are promoted to the rank of principal dancer.

In May, an eight-week Balanchine Celebration opens on Lincoln Kirstein's eighty-sixth birthday. The celebration marks ten years since George Balanchine's death in April 1983 and offers an unprecedented overview of his works in chronological order. The Company presents several refurbished productions, including *Serenade, Firebird, Union Jack, Bourrée Fantasque,* and *Harlequinade.* In total, seventy-three ballets are performed.

In June, the Company hosts *Dinner with Balanchine,* a performance that lasts nearly six hours, with guest artists from American and European companies. During the three intermissions, hors d'oeuvres, entrée, and dessert are served. The evening finishes with a toast to Mr. B with Absolut vodka.

The Balanchine Celebration is featured on the PBS *Dance in America* series and airs on December 25.

In early September, the Company returns to Copenhagen for seven performances during the 150th anniversary of Tivoli Gardens.

In October, the Company performs for a two-week engagement at the Orange County Performing Arts Center.

On November 24, the film version of George Balanchine's *The Nutcracker* opens in movie theaters across the country.

1994

Peter Martins's *Symphonic Dances* premieres in February, with music by Rachmaninoff. Richard Tanner's *A Schubert Sonata* premieres.

The second Diamond Project takes place during the spring season, and provides the company with twelve new works by David Allan, John Alleyne, Ulysses Dove, Anna Laerkesen, Robert La Fosse, Miriam Mahdaviani, Trey McIntyre, Kevin O'Day, Peter Martins, Richard Tanner, Lynne Taylor-Corbett, and Damian Woetzel.

For selected performances in May, Mikhail Baryshnikov appears as a guest artist in Jerome Robbins's *A Suite of Dances.*

In June, Adam Lüders and Gen Horiuchi dance their farewell performances.

In July, Damian Woetzel's *Glazounov Pas de Deux* premieres, with costumes designed by Heather Watts.

For ten days in August, the Company travels to Italy, performing at Teatro di Verdura in Palermo.

November 22, opening night, marks the premiere of two Peter Martins ballets: *Untitled,* with music by Charles Wuorinen, and *X-Ray,* with music by John Adams. November also sees the Company premiere of *2 & 3 Part Inventions,* previously created for School of American Ballet students by Jerome Robbins and with music by Johann Sebastian Bach.

1995

In January, Heather Watts dances her final performance with New York City Ballet, in *Bugaku* and *Valse Triste.*

In February, Richard Tanner's *Operetta Affezionata* and Kevin O'Day's *Huoah* premiere.

Albert Evans and Ethan Stiefel are promoted to the rank of principal dancer.

In May, Jerome Robbins's *West Side Story Suite* premieres, with music from the Broadway show by Leonard Bernstein, lyrics by Stephen Sondheim, set designs by Oliver Smith, costume designs by Irene Sharaff, and lighting designs by Jennifer Tipton. The conductor is Paul Gemignani.

In June, Peter Martins's *Adams Violin Concerto* premieres.

From late September to early October, the Company dances for two weeks at the Theatre du Châtelet in Paris as part of the International Festival de Danse de Paris.

At the November Opening Night Gala, Kevin O'Day's *Dvořák Bagatelles* premieres.

1996

In January, Peter Martins's *Reliquary* premieres, with music by Charles Wuorinen. The ballet is a tribute to George Balanchine's choreography, and the score is based on fragments of Stravinsky's compositions that were given to Wuorinen by the late composer's wife. David Parsons's *Touch,* set to a commissioned score by composer Richard Peaslee, also premieres in January.

On January 5, Lincoln Kirstein dies at the age of eighty-eight.

On February 18, a memorial service for Lincoln Kirstein is held at the New York State Theater. Excerpts of *Mozartiana* and *Orpheus* are performed by Kyra Nichols and Peter Boal. Speakers include Paul Cadmus, Philip Johnson, Beverly Sills, and Jamie Wyeth.

Miranda Weese is promoted to the rank of principal dancer.

During the spring season, Ulysses Dove's *Twilight,* Peter Martins's *Tschaikovsky Pas de Quatre,* and Kevin O'Day's *Badchonim (Merry-Makers)* premiere.

1997

On January 22, Jerome Robbins's *Brandenburg* premieres, with music by Johann Sebastian Bach. With this performance the New Combinations Evening is inaugurated: from this year forward, New York City Ballet will celebrate the anniversary of George Balanchine's birthday with a new choreographic work.

Judith Fugate retires from the Company.

The third Diamond Project ushers in the spring season, with six new works by Christopher d'Amboise, Robert La Fosse, Miriam Mahdaviani, Kevin O'Day, Angelin Preljocaj, and Christopher Wheeldon.

In July, three Diamond Project ballets premiere at the Saratoga Performing Arts Center: *La Stravaganza, Open Strings,* and *Slavonic Dances.*

In September and October, the Company is divided for the first time into two touring groups: one group departs for Brazil for two weeks of performances in São Paulo, Rio de Janeiro, and Salvador. The second group spends three weeks in the Pacific Rim, with performances in Seoul, Taipei, and Melbourne.

On opening night of the 1997–98 winter season, Merrill Ashley dances in her final performance with New York City Ballet.

1998

On January 22, George Balanchine's birthday and New Combinations Evening, two new works premiere: Peter Martins's *Concerti Armonici* and Richard Tanner's *A Nursery Song.*

In February, Peter Martins's *Stabat Mater* premieres, with music by Pergolesi.

For the Spring Gala, Jerome Robbins revives *Les Noces,* originally choreographed in 1965 for American Ballet Theatre.

New York City Ballet Dancers 1948–1998

Muriel Aasen
Dena Abergel
Diana Adams
Jade Adams
Wendy Ahearn
Heléne Alexopoulos
Audrey Allen
Samantha Allen
Christopher d'Amboise
Jacques d'Amboise
Ninette d'Amboise
Ib Andersen
Bengt Anderson
Charles Anderson
Alexandra Ansanelli
Manola Ansensio
Arlene
Michael Arshansky
Karin von Aroldingen
Jukka Aromaa
Aesha Ash
Merrill Ashley
Charles Askegard
Debra Austin
Doria Avila

Michelle Bailey
Alan Baker
Stephanie Balling
Robert Barnett
Beverly Barsanti
Mikhail Baryshnikov
John Bass
Karen Batizi
Dick Beard
Sant'gria Bello
Charles Bennett
Tracy Bennett
Toni Bentley
Valentina Bertran
Saskia Beskow
Lois Bewley
Rex Bickmore
Edward Bigelow
Jenny Blascovich
Herbert Bliss
Anthony Blum
Peter Boal
Barbara Bocher
Christopher Boehmer

James Bogan
Todd Bolender
Jean-Pierre Bonnefoux
Joan Bonomo
Paul Boos
Ruthanna Boris
Bonita Borne
Elyse Borne
Yvonne Borree
Susan Borree
Mary Helen Bowers
Benjamin Bowman
Joan Bowman
Diane Bradshaw
Doris Breckenridge
Marjorie Bresler
Barbara Britton
Victoria Bromberg
Allison Brown
Vida Brown
Leslie Brown
Edith Brozak
Erik Bruhn
James Brusock
Lynn Bryson
Wilhelm Burmann
Anne Burton
Jilise Bushling
Val Buttignol
Michael Byars

Stacy Caddell
Maria Calegari
Stacey Calvert
Stuart Capps
Paula Caputo
Steven Caras
Bill Carter
Evelyn Carton
Bruce Cartwright
Arlouine Case
Kelly Cass
Victor Castelli
Alfonso Catá
Marisa Cerveris
Lisa Chalmers
Jennifer Chipman
Lew Christensen
Thordal Christensen
Zbigniew Cichocki
Ivy Clear
John Clifford

Emily Coates
Janice Cohen
Shelly Cohn
Elaine Comsudi
Hermes Condé
Diane Consoer
Bart Cook
Lucile Collins
Ronald Colton
Cara Copeland
Beatriz Costa
Cornel Crabtree
Darius Crenshaw
Gail Crisa
Ann Crowell
Wilma Curley

James DeBolt
Rebecca Dempster
Elena Diner
Carole Divet
Aura Dixon
Joan Djorup
William Dollar
Geralyn Donald
Edward Dragon
Richard Dryden
Penelope Dudleston
Daniel Duell
Joseph Duell
Rosemary Dunleavy
Victor Duntiere
Richard Duse
Dorothy Dushock

Bill Earl
Gerard Ebitz
Amanda Edge
Jeffrey Edwards
André Eglevsky
Lois Ellyn
Suzanne Erlon
Renee Estópinal
Albert Evans

Barbara Fallis
Suzanne Farrell
James Fayette
Nina Fedorova
Joyce Feldman
Kristina Fernandez
Royes Fernandez
Carole Fields

Toby Fine
Truman Finney
Lindsay Fischer
Hester FitzGerald
Florence Fitzgerald
Elise Flagg
Laura Flagg
Christopher Fleming
Deborah Flomine
Edwina Fontaine
Jason Fowler
Timothy Fox
Paul Frame
Peter Frame
Antonia Franceschi
Wilhelmina Frankfurt
Susan Freedman
Pinkey Freyman
Judith Friedman
Jean-Pierre Frohlich
Kurt Froman
Kyle Froman
Jennifer Fuchs
Judith Fugate

Myrna Galle
Heidi Gans
Ana Garcia
Tatiana Garcia-
    Stefanovich
Constance Garfield
Penelope Gates
Gene Gavin
Carolyn George
Walter Georgov
Elizabeth Geyer
Michele Gifford
Ruth Gilbert
Espen Giljane
Tanya Gingerich
Susan Gluck
Nanette Glushak
Pauline Golbin
Tom Gold
Mary Jean Golden
Ann Goldstein
Erica Goodman
Gloria Govrin
Meg Gordon
Judith Green
John Grensback
Janet Greschler

Kenneth Greve
Janice Groman
Leo Guerard

Kathleen Haigney
Victoria Hall
Stephen Hanna
Peter Hansen
Dana Hanson
Lydia Harmsen
Lauren Hauser
Heather Hawk
Douglas Hay
Melissa Hayden
Julie Hays
Andrea Hecker
Susan Hendl
Jessy Hendrickson
Sharon Hershfield
Alexia Hess
Lisa Hess
Gloriann Hicks
Georgia Hiden
Arch Higgins
Robert Hill
Mary Hinkson
Patrick Hinson
Nichol Hlinka
Frank Hobi
Linda Homek
Darla Hoover
Gen Horiuchi
Marian Horosko
Richard Hoskinson
Dolores Houston
Kipling Houston
Alan Howard
Nikolaj Hübbe
Ben Huys
Eric Hyrst

Elise Ingalls
William Inglis
Elizabeth Irwin
Alexandre Iziliaev

Brooks Jackson
Lisa Jackson
Janice James
Sandra Jennings
Jillana
William Johnson
Jay Jolley

Harry Jones
Heather Jurgensen

Gail Kachadurian
Una Kai
Russell Kaiser
Myrna Kamara
Rita Karlin
Peggy Karlson
Romy Karz
Zippora Karz
Jack Kauflin
Nora Kaye
David Keary
Susan Kenniff
Allegra Kent
Katrina Killian
Isabel Kimmel
Ruth Ann King
Jerome Kipper
Gelsey Kirkland
Johnna Kirkland
Julie Kirsten
Darci Kistler
Deborah Koolish
Alex Kotymski
Maria Kowroski
Leonid Kozlov
Valentina Kozlova
Helen Kramer
Margo Krody
Jerri Kumery

Robert La Fosse
Hugh Laing
Deni Lamont
Harold Lang
Irene Larsson
Charles Laskey
Sean Lavery
Yurek Lazowski
Gerard Leavitt
Sherri LeBlanc
Tanaquil Le Clercq
Sara Leland
Sara Letton
Daniel Levans
Mindy Levine
Dana Lewis
Edward Liang
Anna Liceica
Robert Lindgren
Michael Lland

Cynthia Lochard
Andrea Long
Lourdes Lopez
Riolama Lorenzo
Roberta Lubell
Adam Lüders
Conrad Ludlow
Robert Lyon

Linda MacArthur
Christopher MacDougall
Nicholas Magallanes
Miriam Mahdaviani
Robert Maiorano
Tania Makaroff
John Mandia
Sebastien Marcovici
Marie-Jeanne
Richard Marsden
Eloise Martin
Nilas Martins
Peter Martins
Jane Mason
Lorca Massine
Carmen Mathe
Laurence Matthews
Michael Maule
Christine Mayer
Kay Mazzo
Deanna McBrearty
Patricia McBride
Teena McConnell
Janey McGeary
David McNaughton
Roberta Meier
Paul Mejia
Jean Mercier
Carlo Merlo
Linda Merrill
Marlene Mesavage
Rebecca Metzger
Monique Meunier
Julie Michael
Barbara Milberg
Benjamin Millepied
Arthur Mitchell
Janice Mitoff
Afshin Mofid
Cora Monahan
Francisco Moncion
David Moore
Aubrey Morgan
Karen Morrell

Catherine Morris
Marnee Morris
Francesca Mosarra
Yvonne Mounsey
Jeppe Mydtskov

Janice Nagley
Ivan Nagy
Jennifer Nairn-Smith
Eva Natanya
Peter Naumann
Philip Neal
Colleen Neary
Patricia Neary
Otto Neubert
Tange Nicelli
Kyra Nichols
Rusty Nickel
Rita Norona
Cynthia Nystrom

Larry O'Brien
Shaun O'Brien
Frank Ohman
Catherine Oppenheimer
Alice Orel
Karen O'Sullivan
David Otto
William Otto

Bruce Padgett
Gretchen Patchell
Alice Patelson
Mimi Paul
Moira Paul
Laura Paulus
Elizabeth Pawluk
Leslie Peck
François Perron
Delia Peters
Kenneth Petersen
Carolyn Peterson
Roger Peterson
Roger Pietrucha
Susan Pilarre
Sabrina Pillars
Bryan Pitts
Lila Popper
Terri Lee Port
Jennifer Porteous
Marilyn Poudrier
John Prinz
Alexandre Proia
André Prokovsky

Michael Puleo

James Radich
Richard Rapp
Charlotte Ray
Mavis Ray
Christine Redpath
Janet Reed
Brian Reeder
Nanette Reedy
Elise Reiman
Hanne-Marie Reiner
Teresa Reyes
Nancy Reynolds
Marsha Reynolds
Nadine Revene
Lisa de Ribere
Virginia Rich
David Richardson
Mandy-Jane Richardson
Carrie Lee Riggins
Julien Ringdahl
Jenifer Ringer
Alexander Ritter
Jerome Robbins
Giselle Roberge
Andrew Robertson
Robert Rodham
Leda Roffi
Cam la Rondeau
Leslie Roy
Melinda Roy
Leslie Ruchala
Francia Russell
Rachel Rutherford
Catherine Ryan

Donna Sackett
Francis Sackett
Paul Sackett
Stephanie Saland
Philip Salem
Lilly Samuels
Kaye Sargent
Patricia Savoia
Sean Savoye
Dido Sayers
Peter Schaufuss
Luis Schaw
Peter Schetter
Suki Schorer
Chrissy Schultz
Simone Schumacher
Dorothy Scott

Shelley Scott
Grant Scruggs
Marisa Seelos
Ramon Segarra
Barbara Seibert
Henry Seth
Noelle Shader
Polly Shelton
Karel Shimoff
Ellen Shire
Karel Shook
Joysanne Sidimus
Earle Sieveling
Bettijane Sills
Victoria Simon
Ruth Sobotka
Jennie Somogyi
Roma Sosenko
Jock Soto
Marjorie Spohn
Peter Stark
Zoya Staskevich
Michael Steele
Lynne Stetson
Gordon Stevens
Shawn Stevens
Ethan Stiefel
Marilee Stiles
Kent Stowell
Sally Streets
Carol-Marie Strizak
Virginia Stuart
Carol Sumner
Kaja Sundsten
Martha Swope

Harriet Talbot
Maria Tallchief
Eugene Tanner
Richard Tanner
John Taras
Richard Thomas
Jennifer Tinsley
Roy Tobias
Caroline Todd
Beatrice Tompkins
Helgi Tomasson
Mel A. Tomlinson
Kathleen Tracey
Margaret Tracey
Ulrik Trojaborg
Nolan T'sani
Santhe Tsetsilas

Beverly Tucker
Sonja Tyven

Pascale van Kipnis
Joan Van Orden
Joseph Varcasia
Gloria Vauges
Roland Vazquez
Inmaculada Velez
Violette Verdy
Edward Villella
Joanna Vischer
Jocelyn Vollmar

Barbara Walczak
Elizabeth Walker
Margaret Walker
Melissa Walter
Jian Wang
Sheryl Ware
Heather Watts
Jonathan Watts
Miranda Weese
Robert Weiss
Bruce Wells
Robert Wersinger
William Weslow
Christopher Wheeldon
Wendy Whelan
Diana White
Garielle Whittle
Kay Wilcoxson
Patricia Wilde
Jacqueline Williams
Todd Williams
Sallie Wilson
Deborah Wingert
Ulrik Wivel
Damian Woetzel
Jamie Wolf
Margaret Wood
Tomi Wortham

Runsheng Ying
Lynda Yourth

Igor Zelensky
Erlends Zieminch
Sandra Zigars
Stanley Zompakos
Neima Zweili

New York City Ballet Music

Adagio Lamentoso
Music: *Symphony No. 6 in B Minor, Op. 74 ("Pathétique")* (fourth movement) (1893)
Peter Ilyitch Tschaikovsky

Adams Violin Concerto
Music: *Violin Concerto* (1994) (commissioned by New York City Ballet, London Symphony Orchestra, and Minnesota Orchestra)
John Adams

Afternoon of a Faun
Music: *Prélude à l'Après Midi d'un Faune* (1892–94)
Claude Debussy

Age of Anxiety
Music: *Symphony No. 2 for Piano and Orchestra ("The Age of Anxiety")* (1949)
Leonard Bernstein

Agon
Music: *Agon* (1953–56)
Igor Stravinsky

À La Françaix
Music: *Serenade for Small Orchestra* (1934)
Jean Françaix

Alborada del Gracioso
Music: *Alborada del Gracioso* (orchestral version of piece originally for piano) (1905)
Maurice Ravel

Allegro Brillante
Music: *Piano Concerto No. 3 in E-Flat Major, Op. 75* (1892) (unfinished)
Peter Ilyitch Tschaikovsky

Allegro con Grazia
Music: *Symphony No. 6 in B Minor, Op. 74 ("Pathétique")* (second movement) (1893)
Peter Ilyitch Tschaikovsky

Ancient Airs and Dances
Music: *Ancient Airs and Dances* (1917–1931)
Ottorino Respighi

Andantino
Music: *Piano Concerto No. 1 in B flat Minor, Op. 23* (1875) (second movement)
Peter Ilyitch Tschaikovsky

Antique Epigraphs
Music: *Six Épigraphes Antiques* (1915) (orchestrated by Ernest Ansermet); and *Syrinx, for solo flute* (1912)
Claude Debussy

Apollo
Music: *Apollon Musagète* (1928)
Igor Stravinsky

Arcade
Music: *Concerto for Piano and Winds* (1924)
Igor Stravinsky

Archetypes
Music: *Archetypes* (1988) (commissioned by New York City Ballet)
Paul Schwartz

Ash
Music: *Ash* (1991)
Michael Torke

Badchonim (Merry-Makers)
Music: *Overture on Hebrew Themes* (1919); *Quintet for Oboe, Clarinet, Violin, Viola, Double Bass, Op. 39* (1924) (orchestrated by Mack Schlefer)
Sergei Prokofiev

Le Baiser de la Fée
See *The Fairy's Kiss*

Ballade
Music: *Ballade in F for Piano and Orchestra, Op. 19* (1881)
Gabriel Fauré

Ballade
Six Épigraphes Antiques (1915) (orchestrated by Ernest Ansermet); and *Syrinx, for solo flute* (1912)
Claude Debussy

Ballet d'Isoline
Music: Ballet music from the opera *Isoline* (1888)
André Messager

Ballet Imperial
See *Tschaikovsky Piano Concerto No. 2*

Ballo della Regina
Music: From the opera *Don Carlo* (1867)
Giuseppe Verdi

Barber Violin Concerto
Music: *Concerto for Violin and Orchestra, Op. 14* (1941)
Samuel Barber

Baroque Variations
Music: *Baroque Variations* (1967)
Lukas Foss

Une Barque sur l'Océan
Music: *Une Barque sur l'Océan*, orchestral version (1907) of a piece originally for piano (1905)
Maurice Ravel

Bartók No. 3
Music: *Piano Concerto No. 3* (1945)
Béla Bartók

Bayou
Music: *Acadian Songs and Dances* (1947)
Virgil Thomson

Beethoven Romance
Music: *Romance in F for Violin and Orchestra, Op. 50* (1805)
Ludwig van Beethoven

Behind the China Dogs
Music: *Behind the China Dogs* (1988) (commissioned by New York City Ballet)
Leslie Stuck

Bet Ann's Dance
Music: *Steal the Thunder* (1984)
Jean Piché
Angels (1983)
Gary Kulesha

Les Biches
Music: From *Les Biches* (1923)
Francis Poulenc

Black & White
Music: *Black & White* (1988)
Michael Torke

Le Bourgeois Gentilhomme
Music: *Le Bourgeois Gentilhomme* (orchestral suite), *Op. 60* (ca. 1917)
Richard Strauss

The Bounding Line
Music: *Short Symphony ("Symphony No. 2")* (1932–33)
Aaron Copland

Bournonville Divertissements
Music:
"Ballabile" from Act I and "Tarantella" from Act II, *Napoli* (1842); Pas de Deux from Act I, *Kermesse in Bruges* (1851); Pas de Six from *Abdallah*
S. Holger Paulli
Pas de Trois from *La Ventana* (1854)
Hans Christian Lumbye
Pas de Deux from *Flower Festival in Genzano* (1858)
Edvard Helsted, J. Paulli

Bourrée Fantasque
Music: *Marche Joyeuse* (1888); *Bourrée Fantasque* (1891); *"Prélude"* from *Gwendoline* (1885), *"Fête Polonaise"* from *Le Roi Malgré Lui* (1887)
Emmanuel Chabrier

Brahms/Handel
Music: *Variations and Fugue on a Theme by Handel, Op. 24* (1861) (orchestrated by Edmund Rubbra)
Johannes Brahms

Brahms-Schoenburg Quartet
Music: *Piano Quartet No. 1 in G Minor, Op. 25* (1861)
Johannes Brahms, orchestrated by Arnold Schoenberg (1937)

Brandenburg
Music: *Brandenburg Concertos* (1711–1720)
Johann Sebastian Bach

Bugaku
Music: *Bugaku* (1962)
Toshiro Mayuzumi

The Cage
Music: *Concerto in D for String Orchestra ("Basler")* (1946)
Igor Stravinsky

N E W   Y O R K   C I T Y   B A L L E T   M U S I C

Cakewalk
Music: *"Grand Introductory Walkaround"; "Wallflower Waltz"; "Sleight of Feet"; "Perpendicular Points"; "Freebee"; "Skipaway"; "Cakewalk"* (1951) (adapted and orchestrated by Hershy Kay)
Louis Moreau Gottschalk

Calcium Light Night
Music: *The Seer* (1908); *The New River* (1913)/(1921); *Incantations, At Sea* (1912); *Ann Street* (1921); *Gyp the Blood or Hearst? Which Is Worst?* (1912); *Halloween* (1906); and *Calcium Light Night* (1911)
Charles Ives

Capriccio Brillant
Music: *Capriccio Brillant for Piano and Orchestra, Op. 22* (1825–26)
Felix Mendelssohn

Capriccio Italien
Music: *Capriccio Italien, Op. 45* (1880)
Peter Ilyitch Tschaikovsky

Caracole
Music: *Divertimento No. 15 in B Flat Major, K. 287* (1777)
Wolfgang Amadeus Mozart

The Card Game (The Card Party)
Music: *Jeu de Cartes* (1936) (commissioned by Lincoln Kirstein and Edward M. M. Warburg)
Igor Stravinsky

Celebration
Music: *Symphony No. 4 "Italian," Op. 90* (first movement) (1833); *Lieder Ohne Worte, Op. 19, Nos. 1* (1829), *3* (1829), *6* (1830); *Op. 30, No. 2* (1834) *and Op. 62, Nos. 1* (1844) *and 2* (1843) (*Op. 30, No. 2* and *Op. 62, No. 2* orchestrated by Robert Irving); adagio from *Violin Sonata in F* (1820); *Capriccio Brillante in B Minor for Piano and Orchestra, Op. 22* (1825–26)
Felix Mendelssohn

Chaconne
Music: Ballet music from the opera *Orfeo ed Euridice* (Paris version, 1774)
Christoph Willibald Gluck

The Chairman Dances
Music: *The Chairman Dances* (1925–26)
John Adams

Chansons Madècasses
Music: *Chansons Madècasses* (1925–26)
Maurice Ravel

The Chase (or, The Vixen's Choice)
Music: *Horn Concerto No. 3, K. 447* (1783)
Wolfgang Amadeus Mozart

Chiaroscuro
Music: *Concerto Grosso "La Follia" after Arcangelo Corelli's Op. 5, No. 12*
Francesco Geminiani

Chopiniana
Music: *Nocturne in A flat Major, Op. 32, No. 2* (1836–37); *Waltz in G flat Major, Op. 70, No. 1* (1833); *Mazurka in D Major, Op. 33, No. 2* (1837–38); *Mazurka in C Major, Op. 67, No. 3* (1835); *Prelude in A Major, Op. 28, No. 7* (1836–39); *Waltz in C sharp Minor, Op. 64, No. 2* (1846–47); *Waltz in E flat Major, Op. 18, No. 1* (1834)
Frédéric Chopin

Choral Variations on Bach's "Vom Himmel Hoch"
Music: *Chorale Variations on "Vom Himmel Hoch da komm ich her" for Chorus and Orchestra* (after Bach) (1956)
Igor Stravinsky

Circle of Fifths
Music: *Concerto for Violin and Orchestra* (1987)
Philip Glass

Circus Polka
Music: *Circus Polka for Wind Symphony* (1942) (written at the request of George Balanchine)
Igor Stravinsky

Clarinade
Music: *Derivations for Clarinet and Jazz Band* (1954–55) (composed for Benny Goodman)
Morton Gould

Con Amore
Music: Overtures: *La Scala di Seta* (1812); *Il Signor Bruschino* (1812); and *La Gazza Ladra* (1817)
Gioacchino Rossini

The Concert (or, The Perils of Everybody)
Music: *Polonaise "Militaire"; Berceuse, Op. 57* (1843–44); *Prelude Op. 28, No. 18* (1836–39); *Prelude Op. 28, No. 16* (1836–39); *Waltz in E Minor (Posth.); Prelude Op. 28, No. 7* (1836); *Prelude Op. 28, No. 4* (1838); *Mazurka in G Major (Posth.); Ballade Op. 47, No. 3* (1831–42)
Frédéric Chopin

Concert Fantasy
Music: *Concert-Fantasia for Piano and Orchestra, Op. 56* (1884)
Peter Ilyitch Tschaikovsky

Concerti Armonici
Music: *Concerto I in G Major; Concerto II in G Major; Concertino VI in E-Flat Major; Concerto III in A Major; Concerto V in B-Flat Major* (1725–40)
Unico Wilhelm Graf van Wassenaer

Concertino
Music: *Concertino for Piano and Orchestra* (1932)
Jean Françaix

Concertino
Music: *Concertino for Twelve Instruments* (1952) and *Three Pieces for Solo Clarinet* (1919)
Igor Stravinsky

Concerto Barocco
Music: *Concerto in D Minor for Two Violins and Orchestra, BWV 1043* (1717–23)
Johann Sebastian Bach

Concerto for Jazz Band and Orchestra
Music: *Concerto for Jazz Band and Orchestra* (1954)
Rolf Lieberman

Concerto for Piano and Wind Instruments
Music: *Concerto for Piano and Wind Instruments* (1924)
Igor Stravinsky

Concerto for Two Solo Pianos
Music: *Concerto for Two Solo Pianos* (1935)
Igor Stravinsky

Concerto in Five Movements
Music: *Concerto No. 5 in G for Piano and Orchestra, Op. 55* (1931–32)
Sergei Prokofiev

Coppélia
Music: *Coppélia, ou La Fille aux Yeux d'Émail* (1876), with excerpts from *Sylvia* (1876) and *La Source* (Naïla) (1866)
Léo Delibes

Correlazione
Music: *Concerto Grosso, Op. 6, No. 1 in D* (1714), *No. 3 in C Minor* (1714), *No. 8 in G Minor (Christmas Concerto)* (1714); *"La Follia" Sonata for Violin in D Minor, Op. 5, No. 12* (1700)
Arcangelo Corelli

Cortége Hongrois
Music: Excerpts from *Raymonda* (1896–97)
Alexander Glazounov

La Création du Monde
Music: *La Création du Monde* (1923)
Darius Milhaud

Creation of the World
Music: *La Création du Monde* (1923)
Darius Milhaud

Danbury Mix
Music: *Orchestral Set No. 2* (first and second movements) (1909–15); *Circus Band March* (1894); *Three Places in New England* (second and third movements) (1903–14)
Charles Ives

Dance Preludes
Music: *Dance Preludes for Clarinet and Orchestra* (1954, orchestrated 1955)
Witold Lutoslawski

144   145

Dances at a Gathering
Music: (in order of performance) *Mazurka, Op. 63, No. 3* (1847); *Waltz, Op. 69, No. 2* (1829); *Mazurka, Op. 33, No. 3* (1837–38); *Mazurka, Op. 6, No. 2* and *No. 4* (1830); *Mazurka, Op. 7, No. 5* (1831) and *No. 4* (1824); *Mazurka, Op. 24, No. 2* (1834–35); *Waltz, Op. 42* (1840); *Waltz, Op. 34, No. 2* (1831); *Mazurka, Op. 56, No. 2* (1843); *Étude, Op. 25, No. 4* (1832–36); *Waltz, Op. 34, No 1* (1835); *Waltz, Op. 70, No. 2* (1841); *Étude, Op. 25, No. 5* (1832–36); *Étude, Op. 10, No. 2* (1829–32); *Scherzo, Op. 20* (1831–32); *Nocturne, Op. 15, No. 1* (1830–31)
Frédéric Chopin

Danses Concertantes
Music: *Danses Concertantes* (1941–42)
Igor Stravinsky

Danses de Cour
Music: *Divertimento for Small Orchestra, Op. 86* (1940–41)
Richard Strauss

Daphnis and Chloé
Music: *Daphnis et Chloé* (1910–12)
Maurice Ravel

Delibes Divertissement
Music: Excerpts from *Sylvia* (1876)
Léo Delibes

Delight of the Muses
Music: *Delight of the Muses* (1991) (commissioned by New York City Ballet)
Charles Wuorinen

Dim Lustre
Music: *Burlesque for Piano and Orchestra* (1885)
Richard Strauss

Divertimento
Music: *Divertimento for Small Orchestra* (1944)
Alexei Haieff

Divertimento No. 15
Music: *Divertimento No. 15 in B-flat Major, K. 287 (1777)*
Wolfgang Amadeus Mozart

Divertimento from "Le Baiser de la Fée"
Music: *Divertimento from "Le Baiser de la Fée"* (1928)
Igor Stravinsky

Donizetti Variations
Music: Excerpts from the opera *Don Sebastian* (1843)
Gaetano Donizetti

Don Quixote
Music: *Don Quixote* (1965) (commissioned by New York City Ballet)
Nicolas Nabokov

The Duel
Music: *Le Combat* (1949)
Raffaello de Banfield

Dumbarton Oaks
Music: *Concerto in E-flat for Chamber Orchestra ("Dumbarton Oaks")* (1938)
Igor Stravinsky

Duo Concertant
Music: *Duo Concertant* (1931–32)
Igor Stravinsky

Dvorák Bagatelles
Music: *Bagatelles for Two Violins, Cello and Harmonium, Op. 47* (1878)
Anton Dvorák

Dybbuk (later called The Dybbuk Variations)
Music: *The Dybbuk Variations* (1974) (commissioned by New York City Ballet)
Leonard Bernstein

Ebony Concerto
Music: *Ebony Concerto for Clarinet and Jazz Ensemble* (1945)
Igor Stravinsky

Ebony Concerto
Music: *Ebony Concerto for Clarinet and Jazz Band* (1946)
Igor Stravinsky

Echo
Music: *Slate* (1989) (commissioned by New York City Ballet)
Michael Torke

Ecstatic Orange
Music: *Verdant Music* (1985); *Purple* (1987); *Ecstatic Orange* (1985)
Michael Torke

Eight Easy Pieces
Music: *Eight Easy Pieces* (1915)
Igor Stravinsky

Eight Lines
Music: *Eight Lines* (1979) (orchestrated version of Octet for chamber group)
Steve Reich

Eight Miniatures
Music: *Eight Instrumental Miniatures* (1963)
Igor Stravinsky

Eight More
Music: *Suites 1 and 2 for Small Orchestra* (1917–25)
Igor Stravinsky

Electronics
Music: Electronic tape by Remi Gassmann in collaboration with Oskar Sala

Élégie
Music: *Elegy for solo viola* (1944)
Igor Stravinsky

Episodes
Music: *Symphony, Op. 21* (1928); *Five Pieces, Op. 10* (1911–13); *Concerto, Op. 24* (1934); *Ricercata in Six Voices from Bach's Musical Offering* (1934–35)
Anton von Webern

Episodes & Sarcasms
Music: *Pieces, Op. 12 ("Episodes")* (1913) and *Sarcasms, Op. 17* (1912)
Sergei Prokofiev

Étude for Piano
Music: *Étude for C-Sharp Minor, Op. 8, No. 1* (1894)
Alexander Scriabin

An Evening's Waltzes
Music: *Suite of Waltzes, Op. 110* (1946) (waltzes from *Cinderella, War and Peace, Lermontov*)
Sergei Prokofiev

The Fairy's Kiss (Le Baiser de la Fée)
Music: *Le Baiser de la Fée* (1928)
Igor Stravinsky

Fancy Free
Music: *Fancy Free* (1944)
Leonard Bernstein

Fanfare
Music: *The Young Person's Guide to the Orchestra, Op. 34* (1945)
Benjamin Britten

Fantasies
Music: *Fantasia on a Theme of Thomas Tallis* (1910)
Ralph Vaughan Williams

Fantasy
Music: *Fantaisie in F Minor for Piano, Four Hands, D.940, Op. 103* (1828) (orchestrated by Felix Mottl)
Franz Schubert

Fearful Symmetries
Music: *Fearful Symmetries* (1988)
John Adams

The Figure in the Carpet
Music: From the *Royal Fireworks Music* (1749) and *Water Music* (ca. 1717)
George Frideric Handel

Filling Station
Music: *Filling Station* (1937) (commissioned by Ballet Caravan)
Virgil Thomson

The Filly (or, A Stableboy's Dream)
Music: *The Filly (or, A Stableboy's Dream)* (1953) (commissioned by Ballet Society)
John Colman

The Firebird
Music: *Firebird Suite* (1945), from *Firebird* (1910)
Igor Stravinsky

The Five
Music: *Five* (1988) (commissioned by New York City Ballet)
Charles Wuorinen

The Five Gifts
Music: *Variations on a Nursery Song, for Piano and Orchestra, Op. 25* (1913)
Ernö Dohnányi

Flötezart
Music: *Flute Concerto No. 2 in D Major, K. 314 (1778)* and *Andante in C Major for Flute and Orchestra, K. 315 (1778)*
Wolfgang Amadeus Mozart

A Fool for You
Music: *Georgia on My Mind* (1930); *Ain't That Love* (1957); *Don't You Know* (1954); *It Should've Been Me* (1954); *Hit the Road Jack* (1961); *Rockhouse* (1958); *Mess Around* (1954); *A Fool for You* (1955); *I've Got a Woman* (1955); *Drown in My Tears* (1956); *What'd I Say* (1959); *Ol' Man River* (1927); *America the Beautiful* (music, 1882; words, 1895)
Ray Charles and various composers

Four Bagatelles
Music: *Bagatelles, Op. 33, Nos. 4, 5, 2* (1823); *Op. 126, No. 4* (1825)
Ludwig van Beethoven

Four Chamber Works
Music: *Septet* (1952–53); *Ragtime for Eleven Instruments* (1918); *Concertino for Twelve Instruments* (1952) and *Three Pieces for Solo Clarinet* (1919); *Octet for Wind Instruments* (1922)
Igor Stravinsky

Four Gnossiennes
Music: *Four Gnossiennes* (1890–97)
Erik Satie

Four Last Songs
Music: *Four Last Songs (Vier Letzte Lieder)* (1948)
Richard Strauss

The Four Seasons
Music: *The Four Seasons* from *Les vêpres siciliennes* (1855), ballet music from *I Lombardi* (1843) and *Il Trovatore* (1853)
Giuseppe Verdi

The Four Temperaments
Music: *The Four Temperaments: Theme with Variations for Piano and Strings* (1940)
Paul Hindemith

Fred and George
Music:
Part I: *Not My Girl*
Fred Astaire and Van Phillips
Part II: *Love Is a Simple Thing*
George Balanchine

Garland Dance (*from* The Sleeping Beauty)
Music: *Garland Dance* from *The Sleeping Beauty* (produced 1890)
Peter Ilyitch Tschaikovsky

Gaspard de la Nuit
Music: *Gaspard de la Nuit* (1908)
Maurice Ravel

Les Gentilhommes
Music: *Concerto Grosso, Op. 6, No. 9* and *Concerto Grosso, Op. 6, No. 2 (largo)* (1739)
George Frideric Handel

Gershwin Concerto
Music: *Piano Concerto in F* (1925)
George Gershwin

Giardino di Scarlatti (*later called* Sonate di Scarlatti)
Music: *Sonatas K.491 (L.164); K.33 (L.424); K.159 (l.104); K.525 (L.188); K.55 (L.335); K.146 (L.349); K.502 (L.3); K.380 (L.23); K.322 (L.483)*
Domenico Scarlatti

Glass Pieces
Music: *"Rubric"; "Façades"* from *Glassworks* (1981); *"Funeral March"* from *Akhnaten* (1983)
Philip Glass

Glazounov Pas de Deux
Music: *Les Ruses d'Amour, Op. 61* (1898)
Alexander Glazounov

Glinkiana (*later called* Glinkaiana)
Music: *Polka* (1849); *Valse Fantaisie in B Minor* (1839; orchestrated 1856); *Jota Aragonese* (1845); *Divertimento Brilliante* (1832)
Mikhail Glinka

La Gloire
Music: Overtures: *Leonora III* (1806); *Coriolanus* (1807); *Egmont* (1810)
Ludwig van Beethoven

The Goldberg Variations
Music: *Goldberg Variations, BWV 988* (1742)
Johann Sebastian Bach

Gounod Symphony
Music: *Symphony No. 1 in D Major* (1855)
Charles Gounod

Grétry Pas de Deux
Music: excerpts from *Zémire et Azor* (1771); *Céphale et Procris* (1773); *L'Embarras des richesses* (1782)
André Ernest Modeste Grétry

The Guests
Music: *The Guests* (1949)
Marc Blitzstein

La Guirlande de Campra
Music: Georges Auric, Arthur Honegger, Daniel Lesur, Alexis Roland-Manuel, Francis Poulenc, Henri Sauguet, Germaine Tailleferre (1954); after a theme by André Campra (1717)

Harlequinade
Music: *Les Millons d'Arlequin* (produced 1900)
Riccardo Drigo

Harlequinade: Pas de Deux
Music: from *Les Millons d'Arlequin*, Act I (produced 1900)
Riccardo Drigo

Haydn Concerto
Music: *Concerto No. 1 in C Major for Flute, Oboe, and Orchestra* (1786)
Franz Joseph Haydn

Herman Schmerman
Music: *Just Ducky* (1992) (commissioned by New York City Ballet)
Thom Willems

Hungarian Gypsy Airs
Music: *Ungarische Zigeunerweisen* (1895)
(orchestrated by Peter Ilyitch Tschaikovsky)
Franz Liszt, probable composer

Huoah
Music: *Huoah* (1988)
Graham Fitkin

I Have My Own Room
Music: *Born Dancin'* (1991) and *Eloise* (1991)
Eve Beglarian

Illuminations
Music: *Les Illuminations for Tenor and Strings* (1939)
Benjamin Britten

I'm Old Fashioned
Music: *I'm Old-Fashioned*, based on a theme by Jerome Kern (1983)
Morton Gould

Images
Music: *"Gigues,"* from *Images* (1906–12); *"Nuages"* and *"Fêtes,"* from *Nocturnes* (1893–99)
Claude Debussy

In G Major
Music: *Piano Concerto in G Major* (1928–31)
Maurice Ravel

In Memory of . . .
Music: *Violin Concerto* (1935)
Alban Berg

Interplay
Music: *Interplay* (original title: *American Concertette*) (1945)
Morton Gould

In the Blue
Music: *Concerto in D Major for Violin and Orchestra, Op. 77* (1878)
Johannes Brahms

In the Night
Music: *Nocturnes, Op. 27, No. 1* (1835); *Op. 55, Nos. 1 and 2* (1843); *Op. 9, No. 2* (1830–31)
Frédéric Chopin

Into the Hopper
Music: *Orphée Sérénade* (1984)
William Bolcom

Introduction and Allegro for Harp
Music: *Introduction and Allegro for Harp, Flute, Clarinet and String Quartet* (1905)
Maurice Ravel

Introduction and Fugue from Suite No. 1
Music: *Suite No. 1 in D Major for Orchestra, Op. 43* (1879) (first movement—Introduction and Fugue)
Peter Ilyitch Tschaikovsky

Irish Fantasy
Music: Ballet music from *Henry VII* (1883)
Camille Saint-Saëns

Ives, Songs
Music: *The Children's Hour; Memories, Part A: Very Pleasant; Waltz; The Cage; The See'r; Two Little Flowers; At the River; Serenity; He Is There!; Tom Sails Away; White Gulls; Songs My Mother Taught Me; There Is a Lane; In Summer Fields; From the "Incantation"; Autumn; Like a Sick Eagle; Elégie*
Charles Ives

Ivesiana
Music: *Central Park in the Dark* (1906); *The Unanswered Question* (1906); *In the Inn* (1904–06?); *In the Night* (1906)
Charles Ives

Jazz (Six Syncopated Movements)
Music: *Jazz (Six Syncopated Movements)* (1993)
Wynton Marsalis

Jazz Concert
Please look under the individual titles of the ballets: *Creation of the World, Ragtime, Les Biches,* and *Ebony Concerto*

Jeu de Cartes
Music: *Jeu de Cartes* (1936)
Igor Stravinsky

Jeux
Music: *Jeux* (1912)
Claude Debussy

Jeux d'Enfants
Music: *Jeux d'Enfants, Nos. 2, 3, 6, 11 and 12* (1871)
Georges Bizet

Jewels
Music:
Emeralds: from *Pelléas et Mélisande* (1898) and *Shylock* (1889) by Gabriel Fauré
Rubies: *Capriccio for Piano and Orchestra* (1929) by Igor Stravinsky
Diamonds: *Symphony No. 3 in D Major, Op. 29* (1875) (second, third, fourth, and fifth movements) by Peter Ilyitch Tschaikovsky

Jinx
Music: *Variations on a Theme by Frank Bridge for String Orchestra* (1937)
Benjamin Britten

Jones Beach
Music: *Berkshire Symphonies (Symphony No. 1 for orchestra)* (1949)
Juriaan Andriessen

Jubilee!
Music: *Cakewalk* (1951)
Hershy Kay (after Louis Moreau Gottschalk)

Kaleidoscope
Music: *The Comedians* (1940)
Dmitri Kabalevsky

Kammermusik No. 2
Music: *Kammermusik No. 2* (1924)
Paul Hindemith

Kodály Dances
Music: *Marosszék Dances* (1930); *Dances of Galánta* (1933)
Zoltán Kodály

Lady of the Camellias
Music: Selections from *Nabucco* (1842), *Les vêpres siciliennes* (1855), *Macbeth* (1847), and *I Lombardi* (1843)
Giuseppe Verdi

L'Enfant et les Sortilèges
Music: *L'Enfant et les Sortilèges* (1920–25)
Maurice Ravel

Liebeslieder Walzer
Music: *Liebeslieder, Op. 52* (1869) and *Neue Liebeslieder, Op. 65* (1874)
Johannes Brahms

Lilac Garden
Music: *Poème for Violin and Orchestra, Op. 25* (1896)
Ernest Chausson

Lille Suite
Music: *Little Suite, Op. 1* (1888–89)
Carl Nielsen

The Magic Flute
Music: *The Magic Flute* (1893)
Riccardo Drigo

Ma Mère L'Oye (Fairy Tales for Dancers) (*later called* **Mother Goose**)
Music: *Ma Mère L'Oye Suite* (1908, orchestrated 1912)
Maurice Ravel

The Masquers
Music: *Sextet for Wind Instruments and Piano* (1930–32)
Francis Poulenc

A Mass (Missa Sicca)
Music: *Missa Sicca* (1990) (commissioned by Lincoln Kirstein)
Michael Torke

Mazurka from "A Life for the Tsar"
Music: *A Life for the Tsar* (1836)
Mikhail Glinka

Medea
Music: 13 piano pieces, including *Allegro Barbaro* (1911); and selections from *14 Bagatelles, Op. 6* (1908); *Mikrokosmos Suite: Op. 14* (1926, 1932–39); *4 Dirges* (1909–10)
Béla Bartók (orchestrated by Herbert Sandberg)

Meditation
Music: *Meditation, Op. 42, No. 1* from *Souvenir d'un Lieu Cher for Piano and Violin* (1878) (orchestrated by Alexander Glazounov)
Peter Ilyitch Tschaikovsky

Menuetto
Music: *Divertimento No. 17 in D Major, K.334 ("Menuetto")* (1779–80)
Wolfgang Amadeus Mozart

Mercury
Music: Excerpts from *Symphony No. 59 in A Major ("Five")* (1769); *Symphony No. 49 in F Minor ("La Passione") (1768);* and *Symphony No. 43 in E-flat Major ("Mercury")* (1772)
Music: Franz Joseph Haydn

Metamorphoses
Music: *Symphonic Metamorphoses on Themes of Carl Maria von Weber* (1943)
Paul Hindemith

Metastaseis & Pithoprakta
Music: *Metastaseis* (1953–54); *Pithoprakta* (1955–56)
Iannis Xenakis

A Midsummer Night's Dream
Music: Overture and incidental music to *Ein Sommernachtstraum, Opp. 21 and 61* (1826, 1842); Overture to *Athalie, Op. 74* (1845); Concert overture *Die schöne Melusine, Op. 32* (1833); excerpt from *Die erste Walpurgisnacht, Op. 60; Symphony No. 9 for Strings* [first three of four movements] (1823); Overture to *Die Heimkehr aus der Fremde, Op. 89* (1829)
Felix Mendelssohn

The Miraculous Mandarin
Music: *The Miraculous Mandarin, Op. 19* (1919)
Bela Bartók

Modern Jazz: Variants
Music: *Variants* for Orchestra and the Modern Jazz Quartet (1960) (commissioned by New York City Ballet)
Gunther Schuller

Monumentum Pro Gesualdo
Music: *Monumentum Pro Gesualdo* (1960)
Igor Stravinsky

Mother Goose Suite
Music: *Ma Mère L'Oye* (1911, orchestrated 1912)
Maurice Ravel

Movements for Piano and Orchestra
Music: *Movements for Piano and Orchestra* (1958–59)
Igor Stravinsky

Mozart Piano Concerto
Music: *Concerto No. 17 in G Major for Piano and Orchestra, K. 453* (1784)
Wolfgang Amadeus Mozart

Mozart Serenade
Music: *Serenades No. 4 and 5 in D Major, K. 203* (1774) and *204* (1779)
Wolfgang Amadeus Mozart

Mozartiana
Music: *Suite No. 4 in G Major for Orchestra, Op. 61 ("Mozartiana")* (1887)
Peter Ilyitch Tschaikovsky

A Musical Offering
Music: *A Musical Offering, BWV 1079* (1747)
Johann Sebastian Bach

Narkissos
Music: *Narkissos* (1966) (commissioned by New York City Ballet)
Robert Prince

Native Dancers
Music: *Symphony No. 5* (1945)
Vittorio Rieti

The New Blondes
Music: *Chaconne in D Minor, Chaconne in F Minor,* and *Hexachordum Apollinis*
Johann Pachelbel

The Newcomers
Music: *Rounds for String Orchestra* (1944)
David Diamond

Night Shadow (*from November 1960 called* La Sonnambula)
Music: Based on themes from operas by Vincenzo Bellini (1830–35, including *La Sonnambula, I Puritani, Norma,* and *I Capuletti ed i Montecchi*) (1946)
Vittorio Rieti

Noah and the Flood
Music: *The Flood* (1962)
Igor Stravinsky

Norwegian Moods
Music: *Four Norwegian Moods for Orchestra* (1942)
Igor Stravinsky

The Nutcracker
Music: *The Nutcracker* (1892)
Peter Ilyitch Tschaikovsky

Octandre
Music: *Octandre* (1924); *Intégrales* (1925)
Edgar Varèse

Octet
Music: *Octet for Wind Instruments* (1922–23)
Igor Stravinsky

Octuor
Music: *Octuor* for winds (1922–23)
Igor Stravinsky

Ode
Music: *Ode* (1943)
Igor Stravinsky

Ondine
Music: *The Four Seasons* (1725)
Antonio Vivaldi

Open Strings
Music: *Open Strings* (1996)
John King

Operetta Affezionata
Music: *Concerto No. 1 in F Minor for Piano and Orchestra, J. 114, Op. 73* (1811)
Carl Maria von Weber

Opus 19/The Dreamer
Music: *Concerto No. 1 in D Major for Violin and Orchestra, Op. 19* (1916–17)
Sergei Prokofiev

Opus 34
Music: *Accompaniment-Music for a Motion Picture, Op. 34* (1930)
Arnold Schoenberg

Orpheus
Music: *Orpheus* (1947)
Igor Stravinsky

Other Dances
Music: *Mazurkas, Op. 17, No. 4; Op. 41, No. 3; Waltz, Op. 64, No. 3; Mazurkas Op. 63, No. 2, Op. 33, No. 2*
Frédéric Chopin

PAMTGG
Music: *PAMTGG,* based on themes by Stan Applebaum and Sid Woloshin (1971) (commissioned by New York City Ballet)
Roger Kellaway

Panamerica
Music: by Latin American composers, edited by Carlos Chávez
Serenata concertante (second, third and fourth movements) (1954)
Juan Orrego Salas (Chile)
Preludios para percusión
Luis Escobar (Colombia)
Chôro No. 7 (1924)
Heitor Villa-Lobos (Brazil)
Sinfonía No. 5, for String Orchestra (1954)
Carlos Chávez (México)
Variaciones concertantes, Op. 23 (1953)
Alberto Ginastera (Argentina)
Ocho por Radio (1933)
Silvestre Revueltas (Mexico)
Sinfonía No. 2, for String Orchestra (Second movement) (1950)
Héctor Tosar (Uruguay)
Danzas sinfónicas (1955–56)
Julián Orbón (Cuba)

Papillons
Music: *Papillons for Piano, Op. 2* (1829–31)
Robert Schumann

Pas de Deux
Music: *Six Pieces for Orchestra, Op. 6* (1909)
Anton Webern

Pas de Deux and Divertissement
Music: Excerpts from *La Source [Naïla]* (1856) and *Sylvia, ou la Nymphe de Diane* (1876)
Léo Delibes

Pas de Deux Romantique
Music: *Concertino in E Flat for Clarinet and Orchestra, J. 109, Op. 26* (1811)
Carl Maria von Weber

Pas de Dix
Music: Excerpts from Act III of *Raymonda, Op. 57* (1896–97)
Alexander Glazounov

Pas de Trois
Music: Ballet music from *Russlan and Ludmilla* (Act II vision scene) (produced 1842)
Mikhail Glinka

Pas de Trois
Music: From *Paquita* (1881)
Léon Minkus

Pastoral Dances
Music:
"Dance of the Cow-Girl" from *The Mountain King* (1923)
Hugo Alfvén
Suite No. 3 for Violin, Viola and Strings, Op. 19, No. 1 ("Prelude" and *"Vision"* movements) (1917)
Kurt Atterberg
Pastoralsvit (Pastoral Suite), Op. 19 (Overture and Scherzo) (1938); *En Vintersaga (A Winter's Tale) for Violin and Orchestra, Op. 18* ("Siciliana," "Intermezzo," *Pastoral,"* and *"Epilogue"* movements*)* (1937–38)
Lars-Erik Larsson

Pastorale
Music: *Pastorale* (commissioned by Ballet Society) (1957)
Charles Turner

Pastorale
Music: *Pastorale* (1933)
Igor Stravinsky

Pavane
Music: *Pavane pour une infante défunte for piano* (1899; orchestral version, 1911)
Maurice Ravel

Perséphone
Music: *Mélodrame* in three scenes for tenor, narrator, mixed chorus, children's choir, and orchestra (1933)
Igor Stravinsky

Piano Pieces
Music: *Danse Caractéristique (Op. 72, No. 4), Le Paysan Prelude (Op. 39, No. 12); Chanson Populaire (Op. 39, No. 13); Polka (Op. 39, No. 14); Le Petit Cavalier (Op. 39, No. 3); Reverie (Op. 9, No. 1); La Sorciere (Op. 39, No. 20); November—Troika (Op. 37, No. 11); Natha Waltz (Op. 51, No. 4); Mazurka (Op. 39, No. 10); October—Chant d'Automne (Op. 37, No. 10); Polka de Salon (Op. 9, No. 2); June—Barcarolle (Op. 37, No. 6); Scherzo à la Russe (Op. 1, No. 1)*
Peter Ilyitch Tschaikovsky

Piano-Rag-Music
Music: *Piano-Rag-Music* for solo piano (1919)
Igor Stravinsky

Piccolo Balletto
Music: *Concerto in E-flat for Chamber Orchestra ("Dumbarton Oaks")* (1938)
Igor Stravinsky

Picnic at Tintagel
Music: *Garden of Fand* (1913–16)
Sir Arnold Bax

The Pied Piper
Music: *Concerto for Clarinet, Strings, Harp, and Piano* (1947–48)
Aaron Copland

Piège de Lumière (1952)
Music: *Piège de Lumière* (1952)
Jean-Michel Damase

Poulenc Sonata
Music: *Sonata for Two Pianos* (1953)
Francis Poulenc

Prague Symphony
Music: *Symphony No. 38 in D Major, K. 504 ("Prague")* (1786)
Wolfgang Amadeus Mozart

Prelude, Fugue and Riffs
Music: *Prelude, Fugue and Riffs* (1949)
Leonard Bernstein

Printemps
Music: *Printemps* (1887)
Claude Debussy

Prodigal Son
Music: *Le Fils Prodigue, Op. 46*
(1928–29)
Sergei Prokofiev

Prologue
Music: selected keyboard works,
arranged and orchestrated by
Robert Irving
William Byrd, Giles Farnaby, and
others

Pulcinella
Music: *Pulcinella* (1919–20; rev. 1949)
Igor Stravinsky

Punch and the Child
Music: *Punch and the Child, Op. 49*
(1947)
Richard Arnell

Quartet
Music: *String Quartet No. 2 in F
Major, Op. 92* (1941)
Sergei Prokofiev

Quatuor
Music: *String Quartet No. 1 in C
Major, Op. 49* (1935)
Dmitri Shostakovich

Quiet City
Music: *Quiet City* (1940)
Aaron Copland

Ragtime
Music: *Ragtime for Eleven Instruments*
(1918)
Igor Stravinsky

Rapsodie Espagnole
Music: *Rapsodie Espagnole* (1907)
Maurice Ravel

Raymonda Variations
Music: Excerpts from *Raymonda, Op.
57* (1896–97)
Alexander Glazounov

Red Angels
Music: *Maxwell's Demon* (1980)
Richard Einhorn

Refractions
Music: *Deep Flight* (1988) and *Before
Infrared* (1986)
Kamran Ince

Réjouissance
Music: *Bourrées No. 1 and 2; Menuets
No. 1 and 2*; and *Réjouissance* from
*Suite No. 4 in D Major for
Orchestra, BWV 1069* (ca. 1717–23)
Johann Sebastian Bach

Reliquary
Music: *A Reliquary for Igor Stravinsky*
(1975)
Charles Wuorinen

Requiem Canticles
In Memoriam: Martin Luther King
Jr. (1929–1968)
Music: *Requiem Canticles* (1965–66)
Igor Stravinsky

Reunions
Music: *Concerto Grosso No. 1 for
Strings with Piano Obligato*
(1924–25)
Ernest Bloch

Reveries (*from 1971, called* **Tschaikovsky
Suite No. 1**)
Music: *Suite No. 1 in D Major for
Orchestra, Op. 43* (1878–79)
Peter Ilyitch Tschaikovsky

Rhapsody in Blue
Music: *Rhapsody in Blue* (1924)
George Gershwin, arranged by Ferde
Grofé

**Robert Schumann's
"Davidsbündlertänze"**
Music: *Davidsbündlertänze, Op. 6*
(1837)
Robert Schumann

Roma
Music: *Roma Suite* (andante omitted)
(1861–68)
Georges Bizet

Romeo and Juliet
Music: *Romeo and Juliet* (Balcony
Scene) (1934–40)
Sergei Prokofiev

Rondo
Music: *Rondo in A Minor, K. 511*
(1787)
Wolfgang Amadeus Mozart

Rossini Quartets
Music: *Sonata No. 3 in C Major for
Strings* (ca. 1804); *Sonata No. 4 in
B-flat Major for Strings* (1804)
Gioacchino Rossini

Salome Dances for Peace
Music: *Salome Dances for Peace* (1989)
Terry Riley

Saltarelli
Music: *Concerto in D Minor;
Concerto Grosso in D Minor, Op. 3,
No. 11* (1711)
Antonio Vivaldi

Sarabande and Danse
Music: *Sarabande* (1901); *Danse*
(c. 1890)
Claude Debussy (orchestrated by
Maurice Ravel, 1923)

Scènes de Ballet
Music: *Scènes de Ballet* (1924)
Igor Stravinsky

Scherzo à la Russe
Music: *Scherzo à la Russe* (1925)
Igor Stravinsky

Scherzo Fantastique
Music: *Scherzo fantastique, Op. 3*
(1908)
Igor Stravinsky

Scherzo: Opus 42
Music: *Souvenir d'un lieu cher for
violin and piano, Op. 42* (1878)
Peter Ilyitch Tschaikovsky

Schoenberg/Wuorinen Variations
Music: *Variations for Orchestra,
Op. 31* (1928)
Arnold Schoenberg (arranged for two
pianos by Charles Wuorinen)

A Schubertiad
Music: *Fantasy in F Minor for Piano,
Four-Hands, D. 940, Op. 103*
(1828), *Impromptus for Piano,
D. 899, Op. 90, No. 3* (1827) and
D. 935, Op. 142, No. 4 (1827)
Franz Schubert (orchestrated by Paul
Schwartz)

A Schubert Sonata
Music: *Sonata in A Major, D. 574,
Op. 162 for Violin and Piano
("Duo")* (1817)
Franz Schubert

Scotch Symphony
Music: *Symphony No. 3, Op. 56*
(1842) (second, third, and fourth
movements)
Felix Mendelssohn

The Seasons
Music: *The Seasons* (1947) (commis-
sioned by Ballet Society)
John Cage

Serenade
Music: *Serenade in C for String
Orchestra, Op. 48* (1880)
Peter Ilyitch Tschaikovsky

Serenade en la
Music: *Serenade in A* (1925)
Igor Stravinsky

Serenade in A
Music: *Serenade in A* (1925)
Igor Stravinsky

Set of Seven
Music: *Contrasts* (1945); *Set of Five for
piano* (1952)
Mary Jeanne van Appledorn

Seven by Five (*later,* **Seven by Five Plus
Two**)
Music: *Septet in E-flat Major for
Piano, Trumpet, and String Quartet,
Op. 65* (1881)
Camille Saint-Saëns

The Seven Deadly Sins
Music: *Die sieben Todsünden* (1933)
Kurt Weill

Shadow'd Ground
Music: *Dance Panels* (1962)
Aaron Copland

Shadows
Music: *Petite symphonie concertante*
(1944–45)
Frank Martin

Shéhérazade
Music: *Shéhérazade: Ouverture de
Féerie* (1898)
Maurice Ravel

Sinfonia
Music: *Sinfonia* and *Danses suisses*
from *Le Baiser de la Fée* (1928, rev.
1950)
Igor Stravinsky

Sinfonia Mistica
Music: *Sinfonia Mistica* (1977)
Andrezej Panufnik

Sinfonietta
Music: *Sinfonietta in E* (1950)
Paul Hindemith

A Sketch Book
Music: *Water Music* (1717)
George Frideric Handel
La Battalia (1673)
Heinrich von Biber
*Fantasies for Unaccompanied Violin:
Largo Vivace, Grave* (1735)
Georg Philipp Telemann
Ballet music from *Les vêpres sicili-
ennes* (1855), and *Jérusalem* (1847)
Giuseppe Verdi
Spécimen de l'ancien régime (from
Péchés de vieillesse) (1857–68)
Gioacchino Rossini

Slaughter on Tenth Avenue
Music: *Slaughter on Tenth Avenue*
(1936)
Richard Rodgers (orchestrated by
Hershy Kay)

Slavonic Dances
Music: *Slavonic Dances, Op. 46*
(1878), *No. 2 in E Minor, No. 4 in F
Major, No. 7 in C Minor, No. 8 in
G Minor* (1878); and *Op. 72* (1886):
No. 2 in E Minor, No. 5 in B Major
Anton Dvorák

The Sleeping Beauty
Music: *The Sleeping Beauty, Op. 66*
(1888–90)
Peter Ilyitch Tschaikovsky

Sonata
Music: *Scherzo* from *Sonata in F
sharp Minor* (1903–04)
Igor Stravinsky

Sonatas and Interludes
Music: *Sonatas and Interludes for
Prepared Piano* (1946–48)
John Cage

Sonatine
Music: *Sonatine* (1903–05)
Maurice Ravel

The Song of the Nightingale
Music: *Le chant du Rossignol (Song of
the Nightingale)* (1917)
Igor Stravinsky

Songs of the Auvergne
Music: Thirteen French folk songs,
including: *Bailèro, Lou Coucut, La
Pastrouletta è Lou Chibaliè, Hé!
Beyla-z-y Dau Fé, N'ai pas Iéu de
Mio, Lo Calhé, Uno Jionto Postouro,
Malurous Qu'o Uno Fenno,
Brezairola, Chut, Chut, Lou Diziou
Bé, Pour l'Enfant, L'Aio dè Rotso,
Ound'onorèn Gorda?, Obal Din Lou
Limouzi*
Marie-Joseph Canteloube (orchestra-
tion and adaptation)

La Sonnambula
See *Night Shadow*

Sophisticated Lady
Music: *Sophisticated Lady* (1933);
Solitude (1934); *Don't Get Around
Much Anymore* (1942)
Duke Ellington (orchestrated by
André Kostelanetz)

La Source
Music: *La Source (Naila)* (1866)
(excerpts) and *Sylvia, ou la Nymphe
de Diane* (1876) (excerpts)
Léo Delibes

Souvenir de Florence
Music: *Souvenir de Florence, Op. 70*
(1890; rev. 1891–92))
Peter Ilyitch Tschaikovsky

Souvenirs
Music: *Souvenirs, Op. 28* (1952)
Samuel Barber

Space
Music: *The Four Sections for
Orchestra* (1987)
Steve Reich

Square Dance
Music: *Concertos for violins, strings,
and continuo, Op. 3 ("L'estro
armonico"): No. 10 in B Minor for
four violins; No. 2 in E Major for
one Violin*
Antonio Vivaldi
Sarabanda, Badinerie e Giga (arrangements for string orchestra of
movements from the sonatas for
violin and continuo, Op. 5, Nos. 7,
11, and 9, respectively) (*Sarabanda*
added in 1976)
Arcangelo Corelli

Stabat Mater
Music: *Stabat Mater* (1736)
Giovanni Battista Pergolesi

Stars and Stripes
Music: *Corcoran Cadets* (1890); *The
Thunderer* (1889); *Rifle Regiment*
(1886); *The Liberty Bell* (1893); *El
Capitan* (1896); *The Stars and
Stripes Forever* (1896)
John Philip Sousa (orchestrated by
Hershy Kay)

The Steadfast Tin Soldier
Music: *Jeux d'Enfants ("Petite Suite"),
Nos. 6, 3, 11, 12* (third, second,
fourth and fifth movements,
respectively) (1871)
Georges Bizet

Steel and Rain
Music: *String Quartet No. 4, Op. 91*
(1828)
Béla Bartók

The Still Point
Music: *String Quartet* (movements 1,
2, and 3) (1893)
Claude Debussy (orchestrated by
Frank Black)

La Stravaganza
Music:
*La stravaganza, Op. 4; "Dixit
Dominus"; Laudate pueri
Dominum, RV 601*
Antonio Vivaldi
Source of Uncertainty
Evelyn Ficarra
Éclats de voix
Robert Normandeau
Naïves
Serge Morand
Repulse
Ake Parmerud

Stravinsky: Symphony in C
Music: *Symphony in C* (1940)
Igor Stravinsky

Stravinsky Violin Concerto
Music: *Concerto in D for Violin and
Orchestra* (1931)
Igor Stravinsky

Suite from Histoire du Soldat
Music: Suite from "*L'Histoire du
Soldat*" (1917–18)
Igor Stravinsky

A Suite of Dances
Music: *Suites for Solo Cello* (ca. 1720)
Johann Sebastian Bach

**Suite of Dances (*from* The Dybbuk
Variations)**
Music: *The Dybbuk Variations* (1974)
(commissioned by New York City
Ballet)
Leonard Bernstein

Summerspace
Music: *Ixion* (1965)
Morton Feldman

Swan Lake
Music: Excerpts from *Swan Lake,
Op. 20* (1875–76)
Peter Ilyitch Tschaikovsky

Sylvia Pas de Deux
Music: *Sylvia, ou la Nymphe de Diane*
(produced 1876)
Léo Delibes

Symphonic Dances
Music: *Symphonic Dances, Op. 45*
(1940)
Sergei Rachmaninoff

Symphonie Concertante
Music: *Symphonie Concertante in E
flat Major for Violin, Viola and
Orchestra, K. 364* (1779)
Wolfgang Amadeus Mozart

Symphony in C
Music: *Symphony No. 1 in C Major*
(1855)
Georges Bizet

Symphony in E-Flat
Music: *Symphony in E-flat, Op. 1*
(1908)
Igor Stravinsky

Symphony in Three Movements
Music: *Symphony in Three Movements*
(1945)
Igor Stravinsky

Symphony No. 1
Music: *Symphony No. 1 in G Minor,
Op. 13 ("Winter Dreams,"* second,
third, and fourth movements)
(1868)
Peter Ilyitch Tschaikovsky

Tango
Music: *Tango* (piano version, 1940;
arranged for winds, 1953)
Igor Stravinsky

Tanzspiel
Music: *Tanzspiel* (1988) (commis-
sioned by New York City Ballet)
Ellen Taaffe Zwilich

Tarantella
Music: *Grand Tarantelle for Piano
and Orchestra, Op. 67* (ca. 1866)
Louis Moreau Gottschalk, recon-
structed and orchestrated by
Hershy Kay

Tea-Rose
Music: *Nocturne for Lily Pons* (1933); *Short Story* (1925); *Sleepless Night* (1936); *Sutton Place; Promenade ("Walking the Dog")* (1936)
George Gershwin (orchestrated by Michael Tilson Thomas, Larry Moore, and George Gershwin)

Tempo di Valse
1.
"Garland Dance" from The Sleeping Beauty, Act I
Music: "*Garland Dance*" from *The Sleeping Beauty, Act I* (1888–90)
Peter Ilyitch Tschaikovsky
2.
Valse-Scherzo
Music: *Valse-Scherzo in C Major for Violin and Orchestra, Op. 34* (1877)
Peter Ilyitch Tschaikovsky
3.
Waltz of the Flowers from The Nutcracker
Music: *Waltz of the Flowers* from *The Nutcracker* (1892)
Peter Ilyitch Tschaikovsky
4.
Valse à Cinq Temps
Music: *Valse à Cinq Temps, Op. 72, No. 16* (1873)
Peter Ilyitch Tschaikovsky
5.
Variation VI from Trio in A Minor
Music: *Variation VI from Trio in A Minor*
Peter Ilyitch Tschaikovsky
6.
Waltz from Eugen Onegin, Act I
Music: Waltz from *Eugen Onegin*, Act I
Peter Ilyitch Tschaikovsky

Theme and Variations
Music: *Suite No. 3 for Orchestra in G Major, Op. 55* (final movement) (1884)
Peter Ilyitch Tschaikovsky

Three Preludes
Music: *Three Preludes* (1926)
George Gershwin

Time Table
Music: *Music for the Theatre* (1925)
Aaron Copland

Le Tombeau de Couperin
Music: *Le Tombeau de Couperin* (1919, orchestrated 1920)
Maurice Ravel

Touch
Music: *Touch*
Richard Peaslee

Tricolore
Music: *Tricolore* (1978) (commissioned by New York City Ballet)
Georges Auric

The Triumph of Bacchus and Ariadne
Music: *The Triumph of Bacchus and Ariadne* (1947) (commissioned by Ballet Society)
Vittorio Rieti

Trois Valses Romantiques
Music: *Trois Valses Romantiques* (1883)
Emmanuel Chabrier (orchestrated by Felix Mottl)

Tschaikovsky Pas de Deux
Music: Excerpts from *Swan Lake, Op. 20, Act III* (1875–76)
Peter Ilyitch Tschaikovsky

Tschaikovsky Piano Concerto No. 2 (originally called *Ballet Imperial*)
Music: *Concerto No. 2 in G Major for Piano and Orchestra, Op. 44* (1879–80)
Peter Ilyitch Tschaikovsky

Tschaikovsky Pas de Quatre
Music: Excerpts from Acts I, III, and IV of *Swan Lake* (1875–76)
Peter Ilyitch Tschaikovsky

Tschaikovsky Suite (*later called Tschaikovsky Suite No. 2*)
Music: *Suite No. 2 in C Major for Orchestra, Op. 53* (1883)
Peter Ilyitch Tschaikovsky

Tschaikovsky Suite No. 3
Music: *Suite No. 3 in G Major for Orchestra, Op. 55* (1884)
Peter Ilyitch Tschaikovsky

Twilight
Music: *July for Saxophone Quartet* (1995)
Michael Torke

2 & 3 Part Inventions
Music: *Inventions & Sinfonias* (1720–23)
Johann Sebastian Bach

Two's Company
Music: *String Quartet in F Major, Op. 96 ("American")* (1st and 2nd movements) (1893)
Antonin Dvorák

Tyl Ulenspiegel
Music: *Till Eulenspiegels lustige Streiche, Op. 28* (1895)
Richard Strauss

Tzigane
Music: *Tzigane* (1924)
Maurice Ravel

The Unanswered Question
Music: *The Unanswered Question* (1906); *Calcium Light Night* (1907); *Fugue in Four Keys* (1897); *Mists* (1910); *The Housatonic at Stockbridge* from "*Three Places in New England*" (1913–14); *Sonata No. 2 for Violin and Piano* (second movement, "*In the Barn*") (1907–10); *Remembrance* (1921); and *An Old Song Deranged* (1903)
Charles Ives

The Unicorn, the Gorgon and the Manticore (or, The Three Sundays of a Poet)
Music: *The Unicorn, the Gorgon and the Manticore (or, The Three Sundays of a Poet)* (1956)
Gian Carlo Menotti

Union Jack
Music: Traditional British sources: "*Keel Row,*" "*Caledonian Hunt's Delight,*" "*Dance wi' My Daddy,*" "*Regimental Drum Variations,*" Scottish theme from *Water Music* by George Frideric Handel, "*Amazing Grace,*" "*A Hundred Pipers;*" music-hall songs, "*The Sunshine of Your Smile,*" "*The Night the Floor Fell In,*" "*Our Lodger's Such a Naice Young Man,*" "*Following in Father's Footsteps,*" "*A Tavern in the Town*" (ca. 1890–1914)
Adapted by Hershy Kay

Untitled
Music: Excerpt from *The Mission of Virgil* (1994)
Charles Wuorinen

Urban Dances
Music: *Urban Dances (Dance Suite in Five Movements)* (1997) (commissioned by New York City Ballet)
Richard Danielpour

La Valse
Music: *Valses Nobles et Sentimentales* (1911, orchestrated 1912), *La Valse* (1920)
Maurice Ravel

Valse Fantaisie
Music: *Valse Fantaisie in B Minor* (1839; orchestrated 1856)
Mikhail Glinka

Valse Triste
Music: Valse Triste (from *Kuolema, Op. 44* (1904)
Jean Sibelius

Variations for Orchestra
Music: *Variations: Aldous Huxley in Memoriam* (1963–64)
Igor Stravinsky

Variations on a Nursery Song
Music: *Variations on a Nursery Song for Piano and Orchestra, Op. 25* (1913)
Ernö Dohnányi

Variations Pour une Porte et un Soupir
Music: 14 out of 25 numbers from *Variations Pour une Porte et un Soupir* (first performed 1963)
Pierre Henry

Vienna Waltzes
Music: *Tales from the Vienna Woods, Op. 325* (1868), *Voices of Spring, Op. 410* (1885), *Explosions Polka, Op. 43* (1848)
Johann Strauss Jr.
Gold and Silver Waltz (1905)
Franz Lehár
first waltz sequence from *Der Rosenkavalier* (1909–10; arranged 1944)
Richard Strauss

Viola Alone . . . (with one exception)
Music: *Sonata for Viola Solo* (1937); *Sonata for Viola Solo Op. 25, No. 1* (1922); *Sonata for Viola and Piano, Op. 11, No. 4* (1919)
Paul Hindemith

Walpurgisnacht Ballet
Music: Ballet music from *Faust* (1859)
Charles Gounod

The Waltz Project
Music: "*A Waltz for Evelyn Hinrichsen*" by Lou Harrison; "*Valse*" by Peter Gena; "*Red Garnet Waltz*" by Joan Tower; "*Minute Waltz*" by Milton Babbit; "*Waltz*" by Robert Moran; "*Dejavalse*" by Tom Constanten; "*Waltz*" by Roger Sessions; "*Modern Love Waltz*" by Philip Glass; "*Valse Perpetuelle*" by Ivan Tcherepnin; "*Titles Waltz: After Max Steiner*" by Joseph Fennimore; "*Rag Waltz*" by Morton Gould

Waltz-Scherzo
Music: *Valse-Scherzo for Violin and Orchestra, Op. 34* (1877)
Peter Ilyitch Tschaikovsky

Waltz Trilogy
Music: *Invitation to the Dance, Op. 65* (1819)
Carl Maria von Weber, orchestrated by Hector Berlioz
Mephisto-Waltz (1858)
Franz Liszt
"Polonaise" and *"Waltz"* from *Eugen Onegin* (1879)
Peter Ilyitch Tschaikovsky

Watermill
Music: *Watermill* (1971)
Teiji Ito

West Side Story Suite
Music: excerpts from *West Side Story* (1957)
Leonard Bernstein

Western Symphony
Music: based on themes from *Red River Valley," "Old Taylor," "Rye Whiskey," "Lolly-Too-Dum," "Good Night Ladies," "Oh, Dem Golden Slippers," "The Girl I Left Behind Me"* (1954) (commissioned by New York City Ballet)
Hershy Kay

Who Cares?
Music: *Strike Up the Band* (1927); *Sweet and Low Down* (1925); *Somebody Loves Me* (1924); *Bidin' My Time* (1930); *'S Wonderful* (1927); *That Certain Feeling* (1925); *Do Do Do* (1926); *Lady Be Good* (1924); *The Man I Love* (1924); *I'll Build a Stairway to Paradise* (1922); *Embraceable You* (1930); *Fascinatin' Rhythm* (1924); *Who Cares?* (1931); *My One and Only* (1927); *Liza* (1929); *Clap Yo' Hands* (1926); *I Got Rhythm* (1930)
George Gershwin (orchestrated and adapted by Hershy Kay)

Will O'the Wisp
Music: selections from *Louisiana Story Suite* (1948) and *Acadian Songs and Dances (Louisiana Story Suite No. 2)* (1948)
Virgil Thomson

The Witch
Music: *Concerto in G Major for Piano and Orchestra* (1929–31)
Maurice Ravel

Woodland Sketches
Music: *Woodland Sketches* (1896)
Edward MacDowell (orchestrated by Camarata)

X-Ray
Music: *Violin Concerto*, third movement (1994) (commissioned by the Minnesota Orchestra, The London Symphony Orchestra, and New York City Ballet)
John Adams

Zakouski
Music: *Vocalise, Op. 34, No. 14* (1912; rev. 1915)
Sergei Rachmaninoff
Parasha's Song from the opera *Mavra* (1921–22) (arranged by the composer for violin and piano)
Igor Stravinsky
Cinq mélodies, No. 4 (1920)
Sergei Prokofiev
Valse-Scherzo, Op. 34 (1877)
Peter Ilyitch Tschaikovsky

Zenobia Pas de Deux
Music: *La Princesse Zenobia Ballet* (from the musical *On Your Toes*) (1936)
Richard Rodgers

New York City Ballet Videography

Accent on the Offbeat
Documentary and performance film
  of the Peter Martins and Wynton
  Marsalis collaboration on the ballet
  Jazz: Six Syncopated Movements
Ballet sequence directed by
  Peter Martins
Released by Sony Classical
1994

The Balanchine Celebration
Part One
Selections from *Apollo, Scherzo à la
  Russe* (complete), *Square Dance,
  Theme and Variations, Union Jack,
  Vienna Waltzes*, and *Walpurgisnacht
  Ballet*
Directed by Matthew Diamond
Choreography by George Balanchine
The Balanchine Library
Released by Nonesuch Records
1996

The Balanchine Celebration
Part Two
Selections from *Agon, Stars and
  Stripes, Western Symphony*, and *Who
  Cares?*
Directed by Matthew Diamond
Choreography by George Balanchine
The Balanchine Library
Released by Nonesuch Records
1996

Chaconne
Prodigal Son
Directed by Merrill Brockway
Choreography by George Balanchine
The Balanchine Library
Released by Nonesuch Records
1995

George Balanchine's *The Nutcracker*
Choreography by George Balanchine
Directed by Emile Ardolino
Released by Warner Bros. Family
  Entertainment
1993

Robert Schumann's
"Davidsbündlertänze"
Directed by Merrill Brockway
Choreography by George Balanchine
The Balanchine Library
Released by Nonesuch Records
1995

Selections from *Jewels,*
Stravinsky Violin Concerto
Directed by Merrill Brockway
Choreography by George Balanchine
The Balanchine Library
Released by Nonesuch Records
1996

Tzigane
Andante from Divertimento No. 15
The Four Temperaments
Directed by Merrill Brockway
Choreography by George Balanchine
The Balanchine Library
Released by Nonesuch Records
1995

Contributors

Armistead, Horace

Artist Horace Armistead designed some of the very first costumes and sets for Ballet Society, including *Punch and the Child* and *Lilac Garden*. For New York City Ballet, he created set designs for *Ondine, Scotch Symphony,* Balanchine's *The Nutcracker, Gounod Symphony,* and *Raymonda Variations*.

Auden, W. H. (1907–1973)

Wystan Hugh Auden, born in York, England, emigrated to the United States in 1939. He is the author of, among others, *Look, Stranger!, The Shield of Achilles, About the House, City Without Walls,* and *The Age of Anxiety,* which earned a Pulitzer Prize in 1948 and upon which Jerome Robbins's ballet is based. His critical essays are collected in the volumes *The Enchafed Flood, The Dyer's Hand,* and *Forewords and Afterwords*. With Christopher Isherwood he wrote plays, including *The Dog Beneath the Sun* and *On the Frontier*. Auden also collaborated on opera libretti, including Igor Stravinsky's *The Rake's Progress*. From 1956 to 1961 he held the poetry chair at Oxford.

Avedon, Richard (1923–)

Richard Avedon, born in New York, trained as a photographer in the U.S. Merchant Marine in World War II and began his career as a fashion photographer at *Harper's Bazaar* before going to *Vogue*. The author of *In the American West, Evidence,* and *An Autobiography,* Avedon's work has been exhibited around the world, including at the Whitney Museum of American Art.

Azoulay, Claude

Claude Azoulay was a *Paris Match* photographer in the 1960s.

Baraka, Amiri (1934–)

Born Leroi Jones in Newark, New Jersey, poet, dramatist, essayist, fiction writer, and political activist, Amiri

Baraka has written over fourteen volumes of poetry, including *Preface to a Twenty Volume Suicide Note, Transbluesency,* and *Funk Lore*. He has also produced over twenty plays, including *Dutchman,* which won an Obie Award in 1964. He is the author of an autobiographical novel, *The System of Dante's Hell*.

Baryshnikov, Mikhail (1948–)

Mikhail Baryshnikov has danced close to one hundred different works from the classical and neoclassical repertoire to modern dance. He has performed with most of the world's leading companies, and has been a member of the Kirov, American Ballet Theatre, and New York City Ballet. He was artistic director of American Ballet Theatre from 1980 until 1989, when he cofounded with Mark Morris the White Oak Dance Project, a group of modern dancers that he continues to commission works for and perform with. He has worked closely with the world's foremost choreographers, including George Balanchine, Frederick Ashton, Maurice Béjart, Martha Graham, Jerome Robbins, Kenneth MacMillan, Paul Taylor, Roland Petit, Antony Tudor, Alvin Ailey, Twyla Tharp, Eliot Feld, Mark Morris, Merce Cunningham, Dana Reitz, Trisha Brown, Lar Lubovitch, and many others.

Begley, Louis (1933–)

Born in Poland, Louis Begley is a New York lawyer and the author of *Wartime Lies, The Man Who Was Late, As Max Saw It,* and *About Schmidt*.

Berkow, Ira (1940–)

Ira Berkow is a sports columnist for the *New York Times*. He was a finalist for the Pulitzer Prize for Distinguished Commentary and is the author of over a dozen books, including *To the Hoop: The Seasons of a Basketball Life*.

Brubach, Holly (1953–)

Holly Brubach, born in Pittsburgh, is style editor of the *New York Times Magazine*. From 1988 to 1994, she wrote feature articles and the "In Fashion" column for *The New Yorker*. The author of *Choura: The Memoirs of Alexandra Danilova,* she has also been a staff writer at *The Atlantic* and *Vogue*.

Cadmus, Paul (1904–)

Paul Cadmus, born in New York, began painting professionally in 1931. Since then he has participated in thirty-seven exhibitions at the Whitney alone. Although attracted in general to scenes of the common masses at ease and at play, it was the subject of sailors on shore leave that particularly fascinated Cadmus, and he captures a homosexual undercurrent in these scenes, especially in his *Sailor Trilogy,* which was removed from an exhibition of WPA art.

Caras, Steven (1950–)

In 1969, when Steven Caras, who was born in Englewood, New Jersey, was a full-scholarship student at SAB, George Balanchine invited him to join the Company, where he stayed until 1983. When he retired from the stage, he began a second career in photography, and his photographs have appeared frequently in the *New York Times, Newsweek, Time, New York Magazine, Life, Vanity Fair,* and *Dance*. He is the author of *Peter Martins: Prince of the Dance*.

Carle, Eric (1929–)

Born in Syracuse, New York, but raised in Stuttgart, Germany, Eric Carle moved back to New York in 1952 and was a graphic designer at the *New York Times*. He is the author of more than seventy children's books, including *The Very Hungry Caterpillar,* which has been translated into over twenty-five languages, *Papa, Please Get the Moon for Me, The Grouchy Ladybug, The Very Quiet Cricket, The Very Lonely*

Firefly, From Head to Toe, and *Brown Bear, Brown Bear, What Do You See?* with Bill Martin Jr.

Caro, Robert A. (1936–)

New Yorker Robert A. Caro's *The Power Broker: Robert Moses and the Fall of New York* won both the Pulitzer Prize for Biography and the Francis Parkman Prize, awarded by the Society of American Historians to the book that "best exemplifies the union of the historian and the artist," in 1975. *The Path to Power,* the first volume of Caro's projected four-volume biography of Lyndon B. Johnson, received the National Book Critics Circle Award as the best non-fiction work of 1982. The second volume, *Means of Ascent,* won the National Book Critics Circle Award in 1990.

Cartier-Bresson, Henri (1908–)

Henri Cartier-Bresson, a Frenchman, studied under Cubist painter André Lhote. Influenced by the world of the marginal, the dispossessed, and the illicit, Cartier-Bresson embarked on a long career as a photographer and photojournalist, traveling through Europe, Africa, and Mexico. His photography has been exhibited in countless galleries and museums, including the Museum of Modern Art. In 1973 he gave up photography and returned to painting.

Chagall, Marc (1887–1985)

Recognized as one of the most significant painters of the twentieth century, Marc Chagall is noted for his distinctive use of color and form, which derived partly from Russian expressionism and most decisively from French Cubism. Born in Vitsyebsk, Russia (now Belarus), he studied art in St. Petersburg and in Paris, where he remained until 1914. He lived in Russia from 1915 to 1922, and in the United States from 1941 to 1948, but he considered France his home, where he lived and worked until his death in St. Paul de Vence.

Cheever, Susan (1943–)

New Yorker Susan Cheever is the author of five novels and three nonfiction books, *A Woman's Life, Treetops,* and *Home Before Dark.* A columnist, teacher, editor, and a frequent contributor to the *New York Times Book Review* and the *New York Times Magazine,* Cheever is a contributing writer at *Architectural Digest.*

Clemente, Francesco (1952–)

Francesco Clemente was born in Rome. In the 1970s he worked and traveled extensively in India before moving to New York City in 1981. Clemente's paintings, drawings, prints, and illustrated books have been exhibited at National Gallerie in Berlin, the Metropolitan Museum, the Museum of Modern Art, the Art Institute of Chicago, and the Fundacio Joan Miró in Barcelona. He was the only Italian represented in the Whitney Biennial.

Corman, Richard (1954–)

Richard Corman was born in New York and apprenticed with Richard Avedon in the 1980s. A portrait photographer, he has worked with people from Muhammad Ali to Madonna, and his photographs have been featured in *Vanity Fair, Rolling Stone, Sports Illustrated,* and *Vogue,* among others. His commercial clients include Nike, Reebok, IBM, Levi's, and New York City Ballet.

Cornell, Joseph (1903–1972)

American sculptor Joseph Cornell was a pioneer in the art of assemblage. Influenced by Max Ernst and surrealists such as Dali, Cornell took part in New York's first exhibition of surrealist art in 1922. Fascinated by the use of fragments of once-beautiful and precious objects, he became well known for his glass-fronted, 3-D collages: "boxes" that contained photographs, Victorian bric-a-brac, and other ephemera; intense desire and nostalgia are expressed in much of Cornell's work.

Costas (1937–)

Greek-born Costas is a photographer and the author with Ellen Switzer of the children's books *Mozart, The Magic Flute, and the Salzburg Marionettes,* and *Greek Myths.* His photographs have appeared in many books, including *Balanchine's Complete Stories of the Great Ballets* and *Peter Martins: Far from Denmark.* He and writer Nancy Reynolds collaborate each year on the Balanchine calendar.

Craft, Robert

Robert Craft, an American music critic, conductor, and commentator on culture, is the author of more than a dozen books, including *Stravinsky: Chronicle of a Friendship, Stravinsky: Glimpses of a Life, Present Perspectives, Prejudices in Disguise,* and *Current Convictions.*

de Mille, Agnes (1905–1993)

A pioneer in American dance and a charter member of American Ballet Theatre, Agnes de Mille was the first female American choreographer to achieve mass appeal. Two of her ballets, *Rodeo* and *Fall River Legend,* became instant classics. By combining ballet, folk, and her own inimitable touch, she extended her talents to Broadway musicals, including *Oklahoma!, Carousel,* and *Brigadoon.*

Denby, Edwin (1903–1983)

Born in China to American parents, Edwin Denby was a dancer, poet, and essayist who studied both ballet and modern dance in Europe. He wrote a regular dance column for *Modern Music* and was dance critic for the New York *Herald Tribune.* The recipient of a Guggenheim grant to study ballet in Europe, his dance essays and reviews are collected in *Dance Writings: Edwin Denby* and his poetry in *The Complete Poems.*

Didion, Joan (1934–)

Joan Didion is the author of, among others, *The White Album, Slouching Towards Bethlehem, Play It As It Lays, Democracy, Salvador, Miami, After Henry,* and *The Last Thing He Wanted.*

Eisenstaedt, Alfred (1898–1995)

A preeminent photojournalist of his time, Alfred Eisenstaedt emigrated in 1935 from Prussia to the United States, where Henry Luce hired him for the start-up magazine "Project X," which one year later debuted as *Life,* where Eisenstaedt's work regularly appeared. From the American Depression to World War II and the Korean War, and from subjects such as Ernest Hemingway and countless others, he captured the annals of American life.

Erté (1892–1990)

Russian-born, Paris-based Erté (Romain de Tirtoff) is best known for his fashion and theater designs of the 1910s and 1920s. From 1915 to 1936, Erté was associated with *Harper's Bazaar,* furnishing readers with fashion designs, cover art, and word-pictures of the European fashion scene.

Evans, Walker (1903–1975)

Born 1903 in St. Louis, Missouri, Walker Evans was part of Roy Stryker's Farm Security Administration as a staff photographer in the Southern United States from 1935 to 1937. A three-time Guggenheim Fellow and an associate editor at *Fortune* from 1945 to 1965, Evans's work has been exhibited at the Museum of Modern Art, the Art Institute of Chicago, the National Gallery, the Victoria and Albert in London, and at Lenbachhaus in Munich.

Fehl, Fred (1906–1995)

A Vienna native, Fred Fehl photographed over sixty ballet and dance companies, nearly a thousand Broadway and off-Broadway productions, and the New York City Opera. His interest in the performing arts was borne of a childhood infatuation with ballet and theater and led him to New York City Ballet at City Center, where his specialty was photographing dancers in action rather than in posed studio shots. He is the author of *Stars of the Ballet and Dance.*

Francés, Esteban (1913–1976)

Catalán artist Esteban Francés began painting in Barcelona, where he met surrealist artists Paul Eluard, Oscar Dominguez, and Remedios Varo. After the Spanish Civil War, he left for Paris, where he was a contemporary of Pablo Picasso, Joan Miró, and Alexander Calder. The psychological world and the conceptualization of dreams were the predominant themes of his work. In 1945, he moved to New York and began his long association with Ballet Society and later New York City Ballet, designing sets and costumes for ballets, including *Zodiac* (1947), *Till Eulenspiegel* (1951), *Jeux d'Enfants* (1955), *The Figure in the Carpet* (1960), *Don Quixote* (1965), and others.

Freedman, Danielle (1969–)

Danielle Freedman is a former dancer who studied at the School of American Ballet after graduating from St. Paul's School. She performed briefly with Pacific Northwest Ballet and Ballet Chicago before entering Columbia University, where she received a B.A. in psychology in 1995. She is a press associate at New York City Ballet.

Freud, Lucian (1922–)

Berlin-born painter Lucian Freud moved to England with his parents in 1931. His artistic career began when the Merchant Navy rejected him in 1942. Best known for his portraits and nudes, he has sometimes been described as a "realist" and even a "super-realist," but the subjectivity and intensity of his work have set him apart from the sober tradition characteristic of most British figurative art since World War II.

Giovanni, Nikki (1943–)

Born in Knoxville, Tennessee, Giovanni emerged from the Black Arts Movement in the late 1960s and is the author of over fourteen volumes of poetry, including *Love Poems, Selected Poems, Black Feeling Black Talk/Black Judgement,* and *My House.* Her children's books include *The Genie in the Jar, Grand Mothers, Shimmy Shimmy Shimmy Like My Sister Kate,* and *The Sun Is So Quiet.* In 1998 she added an NAACP Image Award to her long list of honors. She is a professor of English at Virginia Polytechnic.

George, Carolyn (1927–)

Born in Dallas, Carolyn George came to New York in 1946 to study at the School of American Ballet, but her money ran out and she took up dancing on Broadway, appearing in *Bloomer Girl* and *Oklahoma!* After a stint with the San Francisco Ballet from 1949 to 1951, she appeared in Jerome Robbins's *Call Me Madam* on Broadway. In 1974 she began taking photographs of the Company—including many performances with her husband, Jacques d'Amboise.

Gorey, Edward (1925–)

Originally from Chicago, Illinois, Edward Gorey is well known for his drawings, illustrations, and ballet sets and costumes for, among others, *Swan Lake, Giselle, Le Bal,* and *Dracula,* which garnered two Tony nominations. The author of such books as *Amphigorey, The Gilded Bat, The Lavender Leotard* (inspired by NYCB), *The Gashlycrumb Tinies,* and *The Bug Book,* he began attending performances of New York City Ballet in 1957 and created the "Five Positions" poster along with many other designs for City Ballet.

Graham, Martha (1894–1991)

Born in Pittsburgh, Martha Graham joined the Denishawn School in Los Angeles in 1916, where she danced several important roles, including Ted Shawn's *Xochitl.* In 1927 she opened the Martha Graham School of Contemporary Dance in New York. Pieces from that period, such as *Immigrant, Vision of Apocalypse, Lamentation,* and *Revolt,* deal with social problems. In 1939, Merce Cunningham and Erick Hawkins, whom she later married, joined her company, and in the 1940s she created *El Penitente, Letter to the World,* and *Appalachian Spring,* her first collaboration with Isamu Noguchi. In 1973 she created *Lucifer* and *The Scarlet Letter* for Margot Fonteyn and Rudolf Nureyev, who, in 1984, invited her company to the Paris Opera. That same year the French government awarded Graham the Legion d'Honneur.

Guare, John (1938–)

John Guare's *Six Degrees of Separation* won the 1991 New York Drama Critics Circle Award for best play, the Hull Warriner Award, and an Obie. Guare's *The House of Blue Leaves* won the New York Drama Critics Circle Award for best play in 1971 and received four Tony awards in its revival at Lincoln Center in 1986. Mr. Guare, born in New York, is a longtime member of the Dramatists Guild and was elected in 1989 to the American Academy of Arts and Letters.

Haas, Ernst (1921–1986)

Vienna-born Ernst Haas's photographs appeared in *Life* in the 1950s. A pioneer of color photography, Haas was interested in the emotional content of his images. In 1962, the Museum of Modern Art gave Haas a major exhibit of color photography. He published many color photography books, most notably *The Creation.*

Haring, Keith (1958–1990)

Keith Haring was preeminent among young artists whose work responded to the street culture of the 1980s. He set out to reach a wide audience with early drawings in New York's subways and quickly gained recognition in the Downtown art world. Despite his early death, from AIDS, Haring's imagery has become a universally recognized visual language of the twentieth century.

Hays, David (1930–)

David Hays has designed nearly a hundred sets for Broadway productions, New York City Ballet, and the Metropolitan Opera. The recipient of several Tony nominations, a Fulbright scholarship, and a Ford Foundation Grant, he has been a lecturer at Harvard College and an adjunct professor at Connecticut College. In 1967, Hays founded the National Theatre of the Deaf and remains its artistic director.

Hirschfeld, Al (1903–)

Born in St. Louis, Al Hirschfeld moved to New York at age eleven to study at the Art Students League. He has since become legendary for his lithographs, etchings, and drawings, primarily of theater, film, and other personalities, which appear regularly on the front page of the Arts & Leisure section of the Sunday *New York Times.* His work is included in the permanent collections of the Smithsonian Institution, the Metropolitan Museum of Art, the Museum of Modern Art, and other museums and galleries around the world.

Indiana, Robert (1928–)

Born in New Castle, Indiana, as Robert Clark, Indiana studied at the Chicago Art Institute School, the Edinburgh College of Art, and London University. His early works were inspired by traffic signs, automatic amusement machines, and commercial stencils. In the early 1960s he developed his style of vivid color surfaces involving letters, words, and numbers. He is best known for silk screen prints, posters, and sculptures that take the word *love* as their theme.

James, Jon (1971–)

Jon James was born in Hartford, Connecticut. After graduating from Cornell University with degrees in painting and photography, he was invited to paint with art critic and historian Clement Greenberg. A New York City artist, he has had solo exhibits at Alternative Space and Prism Gallery and his work is part of Exxon, Bear Stearns, and Lehman Brothers' corporate collections, among others.

Johns, Jasper (1930–)

Born in Augusta, Georgia, Jasper Johns was discovered and encouraged in the 1940s by New York gallery owner Leo Castelli. Ingeniously uniting new representational motifs with long-abandoned painterly techniques, Johns helped usher in a new era in American art—pop art—

and created works such as American flags that now stand as some of the most recognizable icons of late-twentieth-century America.

Johnson, Philip (1906–)

Educated at the Harvard School of Architecture, Philip Johnson was the founder and director (1930 to 1936 and 1946 to 1954) of the Museum of Modern Art's department of architecture. He designed New York State Theater, which opened in 1964. His many awards include the American Institute of Architects' Gold Medal, The Pritzker Prize, and the Lifetime Achievement Award from the New York Society of Architects. In 1993 he was named a fellow of the American Institute of Arts and Letters.

Karinska (1886–1983)

Barbara Karinska, well known for the design and creation of countless costumes for New York City Ballet, had ateliers in Paris, Monte Carlo, London, and Hollywood. In 1949, George Balanchine asked her to make and design the costumes for *Bourrée Fantasque,* and thus began her long association with New York City Ballet. Born in the Ukraine, she worked with many renowned choreographers, producers, and designers, including Frederick Ashton, Agnes de Mille, Victor Fleming, and George Cukor. Her detailed costume work also ran the gamut of theatrical genres from the Folies Bergère to film to Broadway. She won an Academy Award for her costumes in the 1948 Ingrid Bergman film *Joan of Arc.*

Kelly, Ellsworth (1923–)

Since 1948 Ellsworth Kelly's work has focused on an exploration of pure abstraction. He defines his process by a distillation of color and shape, which has culminated in his most well-known monochromatic single- and multi-panel paintings. Kelly has been the subject of major exhibitions around the world, including at the

Museum of Modern Art, the Whitney Museum of American Art, the Stedelijk Museum, Amsterdam, The Musée Nationale d'art Moderne, Centre Pompidou, and the National Gallery of Art. In 1996 the Solomon R. Guggenheim Museum organized a major retrospective of Kelly's paintings, drawings, and sculpture, which traveled to the Museum of Contemporary Art, Los Angeles, The Tate Gallery, London, and the Haus der Kunst, Munich.

Koch, Kenneth (1925–)

Kenneth Koch has published several volumes of poetry, including *Straits, On the Great Atlantic Railway/Selected Poems 1950–1988*, and *One Train*, for which he was awarded the Bollingen Prize for Poetry. He is the author of *Making Your Own Days/The Pleasures of Reading and Writing Poetry* and *The Gold Standard, a Book of Plays. The Banquet*, an opera for which he wrote the libretto (with music by Marcello Panni), was presented in Bremen in June 1998. Koch teaches poetry and writing at Columbia University.

Kolnik, Paul (1950–)

Paul Kolnik, a native of Chicago, moved to New York in 1975 and worked with Martha Swope, then the photographer for New York City Ballet. His intimate affiliation with the Company over the past three decades has produced thousands of photographs, and his work appears regularly in the *New York Times*. He has worked with many major dance companies, including American Ballet Theatre, The Pennsylvania Ballet, San Francisco Ballet, Paul Taylor Dance Company, and with Martha Graham and Twyla Tharp. His work has been exhibited across the country, most notably a one-man retrospective at the National Museum of Dance in Saratoga, New York.

Kotlowitz, Robert (1924–)

Robert Kotlowitz is the author of *Before Their Time*, a memoir about World War II. Kotlowitz is a program consultant for Channel 13, New York's public television station and his writings over the years about the New York City Ballet have appeared in *Harper's, Show, Holiday*, and other publications.

Lachaise, Gaston (1882–1935)

Now recognized as one of the most important figures in the history of modern American sculpture, Paris-born Gaston Lachaise was championed by Lincoln Kirstein throughout the artist's career, culminating in the Lachaise retrospective at the Museum of Modern Art in 1935, which Kirstein helped organize. This was the first exhibition accorded to a living American artist by the Museum of Modern Art, and Kirstein wrote the catalog essay.

Tanaquil Le Clercq (1929–)

Dancer, teacher, and photographer Tanaquil Le Clercq was born in Paris and began her ballet career with Ballet Society in 1946. She was quickly promoted to soloist, and when the company became New York City Ballet in 1948, Le Clercq was immediately made a principal. George Balanchine created roles for her in such ballets as *The Four Temperaments, Symphonie Concertante, Symphony in C, Orpheus, Bourrée Fantasque, La Valse, Divertimento No. 15, Metamorphoses, Apollo*, and many others. Jerome Robbins created roles for her in *The Age of Anxiety, The Pied Piper, Afternoon of a Faun*, and *The Concert*. Le Clercq also appeared in ballets by Frederick Ashton, Antony Tudor, John Taras, Ruthanna Boris, and Merce Cunningham. She taught at the Dance Theatre of Harlem school and is the author of *Mourka: The Autobiography of a Cat* and *The Ballet Cookbook*.

Leibovitz, Annie (1949–)

Connecticut-born Annie Leibovitz was named *Vanity Fair*'s first contributing photographer and had her first solo exhibition in 1983. In 1991, the International Center of Photography and the National Portrait Gallery held the exhibition "Photographs Annie Leibovitz 1970–1990." Her books include *Olympians, Dancers*, and *Photographs Annie Leibovitz 1970–1990*.

L'Engle, Madeleine (1918–)

Madeleine L'Engle's *A Wrinkle in Time* won the Newbury Award in 1963. She is also the author of over fifteen books, including *A Swiftly Tilting Planet, The Young Unicorns*, and *A Circle of Quiet: The Crosswicks Journal*, her autobiography. She is the librarian at the Cathedral of St. John the Divine in New York.

Lichtenstein, Roy (1923–1997)

One of America's leading pop artists, New York–born Roy Lichtenstein reproduced the BenDay dots of comic strips by laying a metal screen over his canvas, spreading paint with a roller, and rubbing it in with a toothbrush. His work, first shown at the Leo Castelli Gallery, was shown in 1993 for a major retrospective at the Guggenheim.

Lowell, Robert (1917–1977)

Born in Boston, Robert Lowell won Pulitzer Prizes for *Land of Unlikeness* in 1946 and for *Dolphins* in 1973. He also received the National Book Award in 1959 for *Life Studies* and the National Book Critics Circle Award in 1977 for *Day by Day*. His other major works include *Lord Weary's Castle, The Mills of the Kavanaughs, Life Studies, Imitations* (poetry translations), *For the Union Dead, Near the Ocean*, and *For Lizzie and Harriet*.

Lynes, George Platt (1907–1955)

George Platt Lynes is recognized as one of the great portrait photographers—especially those of male nudes and dancers. In 1934, he began collaborating with George Balanchine on a series of studio photographs, which served as a chronicle of New York City Ballet repertory and its dancers. Through his understanding of the human body and his great experience photographing it, Lynes managed to capture, as few others have, the essence of this ephemeral art.

Marden, Brice (1938–)

Brice Marden was born in Bronxville, New York. His work is in the collections of the Museum of Modern Art, the Tate Gallery, the Baltimore Museum of Art, the Hirschhorn Museum and Sculpture Garden, the San Francisco Museum of Modern Art, and the Pompidou. Marden has studios in New York City, Eaglesmere, Pennsylvania, and Hydra, Greece.

Meredith, William (1919–)

Born in New York City, William Meredith wrote his first volume of poetry, *Love Letter from an Impossible Land*, during his World War II tour with the navy. It won the Yale Series of Younger Poets competition. His collection *Partial Accounts* won the Pulitzer Prize in 1988, and *Effort at Speech* won the National Book Award in 1997.

Merrill, James (1926–1995)

James Merrill is the author of twelve books of poems, among them the Pulizer Prize–winning *The Changing Light at Sandover* and *Late Settings*. "Final Performance" appeared in *The Inner Room*, for which he won the first Bobbit National Prize for Poetry from the Library of Congress. Born in New York, he also wrote novels, *The Diblos Notebook* and *The Seraglio*, two plays, *The Immortal Husband* and *The Bait*, essays, and a memoir, *A Different Person. A Scattering of Salts* was published just before his death.

Moore, Marianne (1887–1972)

Born in Missouri, Marianne Moore began writing poetry as a student at Bryn Mawr College and was first published in the May 1915 issue of *Poetry*. In 1924 her collection *Observations* won the Dial Award, and in 1952 her *Collected Poems* captured the National Book Award, the Bollingen Prize, and the Pulitzer Prize. T. S. Eliot said of her: "She has written part of the body of durable poetry written in our time."

Muhlstein, Anka (1935–)

Anka Muhlstein was born and educated in Paris. In 1974, she married Louis Begley and came to live in New York. She is the author of many biographies, including *LaSalle: Explorer of the North American Frontier*, and historical essays. Her latest book, *Astolphe de Custine*, was published by Grasset, Paris, in 1996.

Noguchi, Isamu (1904–1988)

Sculptor and creator of landscapes, Isamu Noguchi was an artist whose career took him from an apprenticeship in Paris to long periods of carving stone in Italy and Japan. In addition to his sculptures of stone, wood, and metal, Noguchi is well known for the sets he created for choreographer Martha Graham, and for his many furniture designs, including the paper and bamboo lamps that he called Akari. Believing that the experience of art is intimately connected to the quality of space it occupies, Noguchi designed a museum to house his works, across the street from his former studio in Long Island City.

O'Hara, Frank (1926–1966)

Frank O'Hara was born in Baltimore in 1926 and lived in New York from 1951 until his death. A critic for *Art News* and associate curator at the Museum of Modern Art, his published works include *Second Avenue, Meditations in an Emergency, Lunch Poems*, and *The Collected Poems of Frank O'Hara*, which won the 1970 National Book Award for Poetry.

Owen, Walter (1896–)

Walter Owen was a dance photographer who photographed the Company in the late 1940s and early 1950s.

Padgett, Ron (1942–)

Ron Padgett, born in Tulsa, Oklahoma, is the author of *Great Balls of Fire, Triangles in the Afternoon, The Big Something*, and *New & Selected Poems*, a translation of *The Complete Poems of Blaise Cendrars*, and *Creative Reading: What It Is, How to Do It, and Why*. The editor of *The Complete Poems of Edwin Denby*, Padgett serves as publications director at Teachers & Writers Collaborative in New York and teaches imaginative writing at Columbia University.

Paschen, Elise (1959–)

Elise Paschen's collection of poems, *Infidelities* (Story Line, 1996), received the Nicholas Roerich Poetry Prize. Her poems have appeared in *The New Yorker*, the *New Republic, Poetry*, and in many anthologies. A Harvard University graduate, she received her M.Phil. and D.Phil. degrees from Oxford University. She is the executive director of the Poetry Society of America and coeditor of *Poetry in Motion*.

Penn, Irving (1917–)

Born in Plainfield, New Jersey, Irving Penn began his photography career at *Vogue*, where Alexander Liberman, who was then the art director, encouraged him to take his first color photograph, which appeared on the magazine's cover in October 1943. Penn's work is in the permanent collections of museums in America and abroad, including the Metropolitan Museum of Art, Moderna Museet in Stockholm, and the Museum of Modern Art.

Plimpton, George (1927–)

George Plimpton, born in New York, was the originator of "participatory journalism" and is the editor of the *Paris Review*. His books include *Paper Lion, Out of My League, The Bogey Man, Open Net, The Curious Case of Sid Finch, The X-Factor*, and *Truman Capote*.

Prose, Francine (1947–)

Francine Prose is the author of nine novels, including *Primitive People* and *Hunters and Gatherers*, two story collections, and a collection of novellas, *Guided Tours of Hell*. Her stories and essays have appeared in *The New Yorker*, the *New York Times, Antaeus*, and other publications. The winner of Guggenheim and Fulbright fellowships, two NEA grants, and a PEN translation prize, she has taught at the Iowa

Writers' Workshop, and the Bread Loaf and the Sewanee Writers' Conferences.

Rauschenberg, Robert (1925–)

Robert Rauschenberg was born in Port Arthur, Texas. He participated in John Cage's Theatre Piece #1, which has been acknowledged as the first "happening." In 1949 he moved to New York City, and his first solo show was held at the Betty Parsons Gallery. In 1998 the Museum of Fine Arts, Houston, organized a retrospective of his work. He has designed sets and costumes for Merce Cunningham, Paul Taylor, Viola Farber, Steve Paxton, Trisha Brown, and others since the 1950s.

Rosenquist, James (1933–)

One of the preeminent American pop artists, James Rosenquist was born in Grand Forks, North Dakota, and trained at the University of Minnesota from 1953 to 1954. While at the Art Students League in New York, he supported himself as a billboard painter. He is best known for his use of imagery from advertising and print media, cutting, enlarging, and juxtaposing many visual elements to create his multifaceted, multilayered works.

Rouault, Georges (1871–1958)

Georges Rouault's introduction to art began in 1885 with apprenticeships to a stained-glass maker while attending the École des Arts Decoratifs. His early work reflects a preoccupation with social issues and religious questions, although he is predominantly associated with the arresting colors and wild strokes of the Fauves. Rouault ultimately developed a somber, heavy style that gave his subjects a humane and spiritual quality, and for which he is best remembered today.

Solomon, Andrew (1963–)

Andrew Solomon, a graduate of Yale and Cambridge Universities, is a contributing writer for the *New York Times Magazine* and a regular contributor to *The New Yorker*. He is the author of *The Irony Tower: Soviet Artists in a Time of Glasnost* and *A Stone Boat*, a novel.

Sontag, Susan (1933–)

New Yorker Susan Sontag is a novelist, essayist, and playwright. She is the author of *The Volcano Lover, Illness as Metaphor and AIDS and Its Metaphors, On Photography*, and the play *Alice in Bed*, among many other works.

Steinberg, Saul (1914–)

Saul Steinberg, Romanian-born, began publishing artwork in *The New Yorker* and *PM* magazine in 1941. In 1943 he had his first solo exhibition at the Wakefield Gallery in New York, and since then he has had exhibitions at the Pace Gallery, the Whitney Museum of American Art, the Guild Hall Museum in East Hampton, and elsewhere around the world. He has been artist-in-residence at the Smithsonian Institution and has also published several books of drawings. Steinberg is a member of the American Academy and Institute of Arts and Letters.

Stern, Bert (1929–)

Bert Stern was born in New York. His earliest professional assignment for Smirnoff vodka became one of the legendary advertising campaigns of the 1960s. Stern ushered in a new era of commercial photography by juxtaposing a single martini glass against the Pyramid of Giza, and he quickly became a photographer of Olympian proportions, taking on assignments that included work for such publications as *Vogue* and *Life*.

Stravinsky, Igor (1882–1971)

Trained as a lawyer, Russian-born Igor Stravinsky was mentored by composer Nikolai Rimsky-Korsakov. In 1909 Diaghilev, leader of the Ballets Russes, commissioned Stravinsky to write his first ballet score, *The Firebird*, which premiered at the Paris Opera and made him an instant celebrity. The creator of hundreds of scores, including those for opera, Stravinsky was known for his command of rhythm and exotic tonalities. Later in life, Stravinsky's music was influenced by forces as diverse as Baroque counterpuntal techniques and jazz.

Swope, Martha

Texan Martha Swope studied at the School of American Ballet. She photographed the Company through the Balanchine era and was known as the "dean" of theatrical and dance photography. She photographed such Broadway productions as *Evita* and *Cats*, the Martha Graham Dance Company and American Ballet Theatre, and made movie history with her now-legendary photograph of John Travolta in *Saturday Night Fever*. Swope's collection is at Time Inc.

Taper, Bernard (1918–)

Professor emeritus of journalism at the University of California at Berkeley, Bernard Taper was born in London and from 1956 to 1995 was a staff writer for *The New Yorker*, where he produced three profiles of George Balanchine. He is the author of four books, including *Balanchine: A Biography*.

Taylor, Paul (1930–)

Born in Allegheny, Pennsylvania, Taylor was a soloist with the Martha Graham Dance Company from 1955 to 1962 while at the same time presenting his own work in the United States and Europe. In addition to his Paul Taylor Dance Company, Mr. Taylor formed Taylor 2 in 1993, a company of young dancers. He is the author of *Private Domain*, an autobiography.

Tchelitchev, Pavel (1898–1957)

Born in Kaluga (outside Moscow), Pavel Tchelitchev's work was bought by museums and collectors worldwide, and his portraits were commissioned in France, England, and the United States. He was recognized as an innovator in theater design by Diaghilev in the late 1920s and by Balanchine, Massine, and Louis Jouvet in the 1930s. His work has been exhibited at the Museum of Modern Art, the Museum of Fine Arts, Boston, and the Fogg Art Museum at Harvard, among other places.

Ter-Arutunian, Rouben (1920–1992)

Originally from Tblisi in the former Soviet Union, Rouben Ter-Arutunian created costume and stage designs for opera, ballet, theater, and television both in Europe and America. His work for New York City Ballet extended from Balanchine's *The Nutcracker* to *Variations Pour une Porte et un Soupir* to *Union Jack* to *Vienna Waltzes*. He created designs for virtually every major choreographer in America over a span of thirty years, among them Glen Tetley, John Butler, Jerome Robbins, Martha Graham, Paul Taylor, Robert Joffrey, and Alvin Ailey. His operatic productions included sets for the Hamburg State Opera, where he first worked with Balanchine, the Spoleta Festival, the Paris Opera, La Fenice, La Scala, New York City Opera, and Santa Fe Opera. His Broadway credits include Edward Albee's *All Over,* Bob Fosse's *New Girl in Town,* as well as plays by Williams, Chekov, and Ionesco. His European design credits include Anouilh's *Medea* with Anna Magnani in Rome, as well as works for the Hamburg Schauspielhaus and the Vienna Akademie Theater.

Thompson, Jerry L. (1945–)

Jerry L. Thompson is a photographer who specializes in portraits and photographs of art objects. He works regularly with contemporary artists as well as museums, and he collaborated with Lincoln Kirstein on several books, including *Quarry* and *Memorial to a Marriage*. He is the author of *The Last Years of Walker Evans.*

Vaës, Alain (1952–1992)

Frenchman Alain Vaës has designed sets and costumes for New York City Ballet, including George Balanchine's *La Sonnambula* and *Swan Lake,* Peter Martins's *Songs of the Auvergne, The Waltz Project, Les Gentilhommes, A Mass,* and *Stabat Mater,* and Richard Tanner's *Variations on a Nursery Song.* He has also written and illustrated the children's books *The Porcelain Pepper Pot, The Wild Hamster, and 29 Bump Street,* and he illustrated an edition of *The Steadfast Tin Soldier* by Hans Christian Andersen and *Puss in Boots* (retold by Lincoln Kirstein). Vaës has the rare distinction of being one of only two living artists (with Maurice Sendak) to have exhibited at the Pierpont Morgan Library.

Vasillov, William (1914–1961)

After serving during World War II in the U.S. Army corps of engineers, Pennsylvania-born Wasil William Vasillov joined Vogue Studios in New York, where he worked with Horst B. Horst, Irving Penn, and George Platt Lynes. Vasillov's photographs are in the collections of the Metropolitan Museum of Art and Museum of Modern Art.

Volkov, Solomon (1944–)

Solomon Volkov is a musician, cultural critic, and author. Since emigrating to the United States in 1976, he has published a series of books on Russian artists, including *St. Petersburg: A Cultural History* and *Balanchine's Tschaikovsky: Conversations with Balanchine on His Life, Ballet, and Music.* He is also the author of *Conversations with Joseph Brodsky.*

Wasserstein, Wendy (1950–)

New Yorker Wendy Wasserstein was educated at Mount Holyoke College and the Yale School of Drama. Her plays include *Uncommon Women and Others, Isn't It Romantic,* and *The Heidi Chronicles,* which won the Tony award for Best Play and the Pulitzer Prize for Drama in 1989. She is also the author of *Bachelor Girls.*

Weisgall, Deborah (1947–)

Deborah Weisgall, an American, was born in Prague and has contributed to the *New York Times,* the *Atlantic, Esquire,* and *Fortune.* She has written extensively about music, dance, and the visual arts for the *New York Times Magazine,* including several articles on New York City Ballet. She has published poems in *Poetry* and the *Atlantic,* and has written several libretti, including one in verse for a Boston Symphony Orchestra production of the Mozart opera *The Impresario.* She is the author of *Still Point,* a novel.

Wiest, Dianne (1948–)

Dianne Wiest, born in Kansas City, Missouri, began her acting career touring with the American Shakespeare Company. She has appeared in five Woody Allen films, including *The Purple Rose of Cairo, September, Radio Days, Hannah and Her Sisters*, and *Bullets over Broadway.* She earned Academy Awards for Best Supporting Actress for *Hannah and her Sisters* and *Bullets over Broadway.*

Wuorinen, Charles (1938–)

New Yorker Charles Wuorinen's many honors include a MacArthur Foundation Fellowship and the Pulitzer Prize; he is the youngest composer to receive that award. His compositions include works for orchestra, chamber ensemble, soloists, ballet, and stage. Wuorinen is a member of the American Academy of Arts and Letters and the American Academy of Arts and Sciences.

Permissions

Acknowledgments

This book would not have been possible without the dedication of many exceptional artists and writers, each of whom shared their talents and perspectives to describe the broader aesthetic of New York City Ballet.

Special thanks to Doris Cooper our editor at William Morrow, Kristina Cordero and Lydia Harmsen at New York City Ballet, and Susan Evans and Brian Sisco of Sisco & Evans, each of whom brought skill, commitment, and passion in abundance to this project.

Sincere thanks also go to the following friends of the Company for their own significant contributions:

Bill Adler	Lynne Foster	Ron Protas
Richard Aquan	Jim Frawley	Charles Perrier
Lorie Barber	Gina Guy	Sharyn Rosenblum
Jamie Bennett	Janet Jackson	Linda Sadoff
Frank Bidart	Nicholas Jenkins	Thomas Schoff
Edward Bigelow	Judith Johnson	Perry Silvey
Jean-Pierre Bonnefoux	Howard Kaplan	Ellen Sorrin
Andreas Brown	Peter Kayafas	Jean Stein
Wolf Buchner	Betty Kelly	Bill Stockland
Peter Caleb	Deborah Koolish	Myron Switzer
Randal R. Craft, Jr.	Carol Landers	Serapio Walton
William Crawford	Tommy Lemanski	Harry H. Weintraub
Julio Cruz	Mark Mongold	Ana Zapata
Rob Daniels	Michael Murphy	
Ruth Ann Devitt	Thomas Nau	
Paul Fedorko	Joshua Nefsky	
Zoe Fitzgerald	Madeleine Nichols	
Kacey Foster	Brooks Parsons	
	Debra Pemstein	

New York City Ballet extends its profound gratitude and appreciation to the extraordinary group of individuals who contributed the editorial counsel for Tributes.

New York City Ballet 50th Anniversary Editorial Advisory Committee

Anne H. Bass
Agnes Gund and Daniel Shapiro
Halley Harrisburg
Barbara Horgan
Robert Kotlowitz
Nancy Norman Lassalle
Shelley Wanger
Mr. and Mrs. Andrew Saul